DECOLONIZING

RESEARCH

IN

CROSS-CULTURAL

CONTEXTS

Decolonizing Research in Cross-Cultural Contexts

Critical Personal Narratives

Edited by

Kagendo Mutua

Beth Blue Swadener

STATE UNIVERSITY OF NEW YORK PRESS

Published by
State University of New York Press, Albany

For information, contact State University of New York Press
www.sunypress.edu

Production, Laurie Searl
Marketing, Anne. M. Valentine

Library of Congress Cataloging-in-Publication Data

Decolonizing research in cross-cultural contexts : critical personal narratives / edited by Kagendo Mutua, Beth Blue Swadener.
    p. cm.
Includes bibliographical references and index.
ISBN 978-0-7914-5979-9 (hbk. alk. paper) 978-0-7914-5980-5 (pbk.)
    1. Cross-cultural studies—Research.   2. Cross-cultural orientation—Research.   3. Decolonization—Research.   4. Hybridity (Social sciences)—Research.   I. Mutua, Kagendo, 1966–   II. Swadener, Beth Blue.

GN345.7 .D43   2004
306—dc22

2003064727

10 9 8 7 6 5 4 3 2 1

Contents

Foreword: Decolonizing Research in Cross-Cultural Contexts: Issues of Voice and Power

LOURDES DIAZ SOTO

The interrelations among voice and power for the scholars in this volume represent a journey for the voices often represented as 'the other' in a dialogue with colleagues and allies. Leela Gandhi's (2000) description is apt for how the 'othering' of third world (in our case women of color and our allies) can ultimately signify that "we become someone's private zoo" (p. 85). The conception of a private zoo is powerful in helping to explicate the realities of voice and power within the complexities of cross-cultural research. How can we chart a liberating path leading toward a decolonizing space for research in cross-cultural contexts? This is the challenge posed in Kagendo Mutua and Beth Blue Swadener's volume.

These two scholars themselves have forged an extraordinary friendship that speaks of alliances, struggle, healing, voice, and power. Their work begins to model how the dialogic and dialectic relations among student/teacher and teacher/student can move beyond existing mentoring paradigms. I have with my own eyes seen how these two women have traveled in altruistic dream spaces.

For most scholars of color and their allies we are the 'colonized,' feeling the consequences of the eurocentric, scientifically driven epistemologies in which issues of power and voice are drowned by the powerful 'majority' players reflecting the 'master's' ideology. For us, *there is no postcolonial*, as we live our daily realities in suffocating spaces forbidding our perspectives, our creativity, and our wisdom. Reaching for a postformal lens, we can see how "riddled with ethnocentric and class-biased conceptions . . . make(s) no allowance for the ravages of poverty, racism and other forms of disadvantage in many children's lives" (Kincheloe and Steinberg, 1999, p. 45)

Our feelings are depicted by the poet's words that become an integral part of our innermost feelings of oppression. "*Deslenguadas*" is the term Anzaldua (1999) uses to describe linguistic terrorism: "Because we speak with tongues of fire we are culturally crucified" (p. 80). In our attempts to pursue ethical research that decolonizes prevailing research models we experience crucification because we do not fit neatly into the anticipated established norms.

Linda T. Smith's (1999) portrayal of colonized scholarship is extremely valuable in describing our colonized existence in the academy; as are Belensky, Clinchy, Goldberger, and Tarule's (1986) accounts of 'silence' from both Western and non-Western perspectives. Quoting Adrienne Rich they state,

> Where language and naming are power,
> silence is oppression,
> is violence. (p. 24)

The multiplicity and complexities of othering are an integral part of our daily lived realities and experiences. Our friendships as colleagues is as valued as a the sweet songs and words of wisdom from our ancestors. This is a true gift that we can strive for in our scholarship and the academy since it is a gift of love.

The notion of agape love demonstrated by altruistic bilingual children (Soto, 2002) is one we can pursue as we decolonize scholarship and our lives.

Thich Nhat Hanh (1992) reminds us,

> seeing with the eyes of compassion and understanding,
> we can offer the next century
> a beautiful garden and a clear path. (p. 134)

Much discussion has evolved from Gayatri Spivak's (1995) question, "Can the subaltern speak?" Her inquiry has helped us to claim or disclaim our reality that we have little or emerging voice and power. How to address the complexities inherent in these issues? What avenues can we pursue? These scholars provide the optimistic possibility that the journey has begun and that we are indeed reaching our space for healing and our dreamspace of social justice and equity.

REFERENCES

Anzaldua, G. (1999). *Borderlands: La Frontera. The new Mestiza.* 2d ed. San Francisco: Aunt Lute Books.

Belensky, M., B. Clinchy, N. Goldberger, and J. Tarule. (1997). *Women's ways of knowing.* New York: Basic Books.

Gandhi, L. (1998). *Postcolonial theory.* New York: Columbia University Press.

Hahn, T. N. (1992). *Peace is every step.* New York: Bantam Books.

Kincheloe, J. (1999). Trouble ahead, trouble behind: Grounding the post-formal critique of educational psychology. In J. Kincheloe, S. Steinberg, and P. Hinchey (Eds.), *The post-formal reader.* New York: Falmer Press.

Kincheloe, J. and S. Steinberg. (1999). A tentative description of post-formal thinking: The critical confrontation with cognitive theory. In J. Kincheloe, S. Steinberg, and P. Hinchey (Eds.), *The post-formal reader.* New York: Falmer Press.

Smith, L. T. (1999). *Decolonizing methodologies: Research and indigenous peoples.* London: Zed Books.

Soto, L. D. (2002). *Making a difference in the lives of bilingual/bicultural children.* New York: Peter Lang.

Spivak, G. (1995). Can the subaltern speak? In B. Ashroft, G. Griffiths, and H. Tiffin (Eds.), *The post-colonial studies reader.* New York: Routledge.

Acknowledgments

We have benefited enormously from the work of Linda Tuhiwai Smith, which has inspired and influenced our thinking about issues of decolonizing research within cross-cultural contexts. We are also grateful to the contributors to this volume for sharing their personal narratives, dilemmas, and insights about the possibilities for decolonizing research and for their timely response to our editorial feedback and questions. Completing any book is a challenge, and this one involved collaborating with researchers on five continents.

We would like to thank our families, specifically our spouses Carlton McHargh and Daniel Swadener and daughter Rachel Blue Swadener for their patience and enthusiastic support of our work, and our parents, whose belief and support of us has always been unconditional and unwavering.

Finally, we would like to thank our colleagues at SUNY Press, including Priscilla Ross, Laurie Searl, and Anne M. Valentine, for their guidance, from offering useful editorial suggestions to production and marketing.

We dedicate this book to Makena Bell McHargh. May her triple heritage enrich her life and the lives of those around her. We also dedicate this work to Mary Smith Arnold, sister–friend and mentor, whose life was committed to social justice and ending oppression.

Introduction

KAGENDO MUTUA, BETH BLUE SWADENER

Colonialism's . . . most important area of domination was the mental uni-
verse of the colonised, the control, through culture, of how people perceived
themselves and their relationship to the world.

Ngugi wa Thiong'o (1986, p. 16)

This volume represents the work of scholars who are attempting to decolonize their work and deconstruct their personal/professional experiences
in the context of various framings of cross-cultural research. The chapters
in this book represent the authors' struggles and attempts to deal with the
im/possibilities engendered by and inherent in carrying out decolonizing
work. These works stand at the center of the "beginning of the presencing" (Bhabha, 1994) of a disharmonious, restive, unharnessable (hence,
unessentializable) knowledge that is produced at the ex-centric site of
neo/post/colonial resistance, "which can never allow the national (*read:*
colonial/Western) history to look itself narcissistically in the eye" (Bhabha,
1994, p. 168).[1] These authors are among the transgressive authorizing
agents whose position at once marginalizes and singularizes the totalizing
meta-texts of colonial knowledge. Their works shift the terrains of knowledge, relocating and reinscribing, redrawing with new radical cartogra-
phies spaces for decolonizing knowledge and re/claiming discursive
territories for hybridity, neonomadism, postcoloniality, and migrancy.

Research itself has been described as a colonizing construct, with a
legacy that Linda Tuhiwai Smith (1999, p. 80) summarized as "they
came, they saw, they named, they claimed." Smith (1999, p. 1) further
states that "from the vantage point of the colonized, a position from

1

which I write and choose to privilege, the term 'research' is inextricably linked to European imperialism and colonialism. The word itself, 'research,' is probably one of the dirtiest words in the indigenous world's vocabulary" (p. 1).

Decolonizing Research in Cross-Cultural Contexts represents the culmination of many years of conversations and experiences that happened in the context of our multifaceted relationships as colleagues, friends, researchers, and travelers in colonial/post/neocolonial spaces and as interlopers in each other's cultures and national contexts. It was immediately after the second author's return from living and doing research in Kenya, the first author's home country, and at the beginning of the first author's doctoral work in the United States when the coauthors first met. This ongoing collaborative project and collection of critical personal narratives also stands at the center of a number of interesting intersections of lives and relationships. Therefore, this work reflects complex relations, journeys, and conversations in which we have engaged over a period of several years in multiple shared spaces, including research conferences (e.g., Reconceptualizing Early Childhood Theory, Practice, and Policy; American Educational Research Association; Society for Disability Studies, and Council on Anthropology and Education) and while developing and preparing manuscripts for collaborative publications (e.g., Swadener and Mutua, 1996, 2000, and 2001).

One role our work has played in these professional meetings and other venues is that of raising questions. At an American Educational Research Association (AERA) symposium (Swadener and Mutua, 2001, April) regarding the dynamics, complexities, and contradictory nature of "decolonizing research," we joined other panel members, several of whom have chapters in this book, in lively discussion of a range of issues and challenges. Questions raised for discussion included, but were not limited to, the following:

- Whose agenda is decolonizing research?
- Why might problematizing postcolonial theory be critical to decolonizing research?
- Who has the power to name, and how does naming reify existing power relations?
- Who defines and legitimizes what counts as "scholarship"?
- Where are some of the current "data plantations" in educational research?
- Is experience, particularly "indigenous insiders' experience," a necessary precursor for asking the right questions in pursuit of culturally legitimate scholarship—or can the privileging of "insider" experience be problematic?

- Are the tools for decolonization available only to indigenous researchers or can this be a shared process?
- In what ways are reductive, binary categories (e.g., "developed" versus "developing," "first world" versus "third world," "Western" versus "non-Western") dangerous dichotomies that polarize discourses and reinscribe patterns of exploitation and privilege?
- How might hybridity theory inform the struggle to decolonize research—not serve as a "resolution," but complicate it in critical ways?
- What are some of the subtle dynamics of third world intellectuals working within the first world academy?
- What are contradictions of finding power at the margins or being marginal at the so-called center? What are limitations of persistent core/periphery binary categories?
- What are contributions and contradictions of feminism[s] to decolonizing research/perpetuating colonial power relations?
- What role do funders of research play in attempts to decolonize it?
- What are some of the dynamics, tensions, and possibilities of cross-cultural alliances?
- What happens when researchers find themselves "outside" when doing "insider" research?
- How has the discourse on decolonizing research been colonized or appropriated?

Many of these questions, and related dilemmas, are addressed by the contributors to this volume.

Over the years, our conversations have changed considerably, as we have actively engaged/grappled with decolonizing our work and our research. We have moved away from the initial proclivity of our earlier collaborative work, when we tended to create and reproduce forced binaries that placed us immovably on opposite poles as expressing/embodying emic and etic perspectives, respectively. However, we now acknowledge and recognize the impossibility of such forced polarities that might appear to suggest that indigenous scholars engaging in research within their own native spaces are always positioned as "insiders" while foreign scholars are always constructed as "outsiders." Rather, we are now more acutely aware of the possible multiplicity of the subject positions that we occupy, which often locate us fluidly in ever-shifting positions and assign us changing roles that are neither always emic nor always etic. For example, in chapter 10, John Pryor and Joseph Ampiah explore these changing researched/researcher roles, relationships, and positions. Similarly, in chapter 5, Dudu Jankie describes the complexities of returning home from doctoral work in the United States to do "insider ethnography" only to discover ways in which she was viewed as an "outsider" to teachers in Botswana. Indeed, in her work, Smith (1999) troubles the roles and position of the 'native intellectuals' in postcolonial contexts in ways that offer critical insight into the nature of their contested/resisted subject positions.

> Currently the role of the 'native' intellectual has been reformulated not in relation to nationalist or liberationary discourses but in relation to the 'post-colonial' intellectual. Many intellectuals who position themselves as 'post-colonial' move across the boundaries of indigenous and metropolitan, institution and community, politics and scholarship. Their place in the academy is still highly problematic. (p. 71)

The location of research (i.e., the academy as the locus of scholarship) and attempts to "decolonize" it have also been increasingly contested. Calling for a reframing of the field, Rogers and Swadener reposition the field at the center for defining and initiating research agendas, as well as functioning in a dialectical relationship with the Western academy. Therefore, within the framework that Rogers and Swadener (1999) suggest in advocating a reframing of the field, researchers actively decenter the Western academy as the exclusive locus of authorizing power that defines research agenda. Working within this sort of reframed field, the researcher, whether foreign or indigenous, can never be permanently located at either the emic or etic pole. Such a deconstruction of the Western academy and the validity of its role in defining research and scholarship reconstitutes, redistributes, and reauthors the power of the margins (hooks, 1989; McCarthy, 1998).

This redefined field is rife with new, possible researcher identities for both the indigenous and foreign researcher as the "allied other," a point that Julie Kaomea explores in chapter 1. Rogers and Swadener (1999) describe an "allied other," drawing in part from an anti-oppressive, feminist alliance model (Swadener, 1998). Framed broadly, none of us carries only "one" colonized/colonizer subjectivity/identity, as Lisa Cary demonstrates in chapter 4. Rather, we often reflect hybrid subject positions and identities in our lives and our scholarship, as Susan Matoba Adler (chapter 6) and Miryam Espinosa-Dulanto (chapter 2) illustrate.

JOURNEYING INTO DECOLONIZING RESEARCH

In the following sections, each of us discusses our journeys as researchers and how we came to work with decolonizing discourse and collaborative methodologies.

KAGENDO'S NARRATIVE: ROOTS TO ROUTES—
MY IDENTITY 'IN-BETWEEN'

Reflecting on the road that led me to this moment causes me to ponder the slippages between the terms that articulate my identity: post(-)colonial, diaspora, or migrant. Despite the unmonitored or "unmoniterable" differ-ànce (Derrida, 1976) engendered in my identity, all its facets are under-girded by a "deeper sense of historical displacement . . . the 'halfway between not being defined. . . .' But it is precisely in these banalities that the unhomely stirs, as the racialized society falls most enduringly on the details of life: where you can sit, or not; how you can live, or not; what you can learn, or not; who you can love, or not, *who you can be, or not, what you can write, or not*" (Bhabha, 1994, p.13, 15).[2]

What I choose to reflect on here is one such banality: my "educa-tional" experiences starting as a first-year African/international graduate student in predominantly white institutions in the United States to today. I recall participating in numerous formal and informal "educational" fo-rums where I was asked (and continue to be asked) to reflect on my expe-riences as a female African student in Kenya. I often found (and still do) such sessions (whether formal or informal) less tolerable and increasingly oppressive and essentializing, and therefore harder to participate in ways that were synchronous with oppressive colonizing representations of what was or is supposed to be my experience as an African woman. Frequently, I would be confronted with a question that required that I either validate, negate, or counter what I saw as oppressive colonizing "scientific" or tech-nical reports in which descriptions of third world women were and still are classified by objective criteria of their physical well-being including their fertility rates, health, nutrition, il/literacy, education, not to forget HIV/AIDS infection (Mohanty, 1991). Like other African women, the objectification of the African woman sealed our foreclosure (Spivak, 1999) as authorizing agents of their experiences (in colonizing donor research).

Within those oppressive, colonizing discourses, the impossibility of the construction of the African women as intelligent thinking feeling beings is clearly self-evident. Further, the production of Africa as a static, frozen-in-time monolithic culture and people provide a credible alibi legitimating her foreclosure (Spivak, 1999) in Western/colonizing discourses, thereby rendering silent her people who, within this oppressive colonial discursive, cannot possess the authorizing power of agency. As I grew less and less pa-tient with representations that framed me as a singularized, totalized monolithic African who bore no-to-little resemblance to any recognizable space or people in Africa, I realized then that my impatience stemmed from my resistance to mindfully contribute to my own discursive and material oppression. I longed for transgression, to subvert those accounts and to reauthor my experience in my own words and in my own way. For me, this work represents that transgressive act of self-definition and self-re/construction and re/constitution.

BETH'S NARRATIVE: ALLY INTENTIONS,
TROUBLING ASSUMPTIONS

As a European-American woman benefiting from an array of unearned privileges, I have actively interrogated ways in which my work may be re-producing colonial, exploitive, or oppressive patterns and relationships. This current work has been strengthened by my participation in "unlearn-ing oppression" and multiracial alliances since the early 1980s, as well as by my activism in social justice movements from the early 1970s through the present. I have been doing research in sub-Saharan Africa since the mid-1980s, and have worked in high poverty, urban school settings in the United States for the past thirteen years.

Prior to using the language of decolonization, I spoke (and wrote) about "authentic collaboration" or "partnership research," and attempted, in my collaborative work with classroom teachers and African colleagues, to foreground the voice and worldviews of such collaborators. I have also raised concerns about urban schools serving as "data plantations" that serve the researcher and exploit those in urban communities and schools, without sustained relationships being built or reciprocal possibilities explored.

Similarly, doing cross-cultural or cross-national work in neocolonial settings presents many ethical and methodological dilemmas, particularly when there is a conscious attempt to decolonize the research (Gandhi, 1998; Smith, 1999). I had been deeply influenced in the early 1990s by reading Harrison's (1991) *Decolonizing Anthropology*, although I often saw irony and troubling contradictions in postcolonial theory. When I first began to write about decolonizing research in the mid-1990s, I still em-phasized authentic collaboration in which colleagues in the setting of study are as fully involved as possible, functional, and desirable to them—framed in relationship to the still-centered "visiting researcher." At that time, Kenyan colleagues and I generated the following guidelines for decoloniz-ing research involving "insider" and "outsider" partners, which we as-serted involved (at minimum) the following (Swadener, Kabiru, and Njenga, 2000):

- Collaboration on all phases of the study (development of research questions, design, development of protocols, collection and analy-

sis of data—particularly cultural interpretation of findings, and write-up and dissemination)
- Sustained time in a cultural context—either through repeated visits or longer time in setting (recognizing the time limits in our professional lives!)
- Studying the language(s) and cultures to the degree possible and developing the ability to code-switch and understand indigenous "ways of knowing" and communicating
- Coauthorship of all papers and publications resulting from the collaborative work
- Compensation of local collaborators, translators, and research partners for their time (may be in-kind for school partners, including graduate credit, field-based masters)
- As an outsider, assuming that "I do not know" and listening, including reading "signs" and making meaning as collaborative endeavors
- Making findings available in relevant ways to local shareholders, including finding funding to distribute publications in home country of local community
- Participating in the community in ongoing [nonmissionary!] ways . . . volunteer, mobilize awareness after leaving the country/setting, follow the issues and support organizations doing "decolonized" work [versus charities that maintain dependency]
- Interrogating privilege and the "myths of meritocracy," while strengthening alliances

In more recent years, I have been interrogating and "troubling" my comfortable, rule-governed formulas for decolonizing research across differentiated power relationships, wherever they may be found. I have confronted the likelihood that decolonizing research is a messy, complex, and perhaps impossible endeavor. Yet, I have affirmed that attempting to decolonize one's work is a project worth pursuing in solidarity with local colleagues and movements. My sense is that decolonization transcends individual action and requires working with alliances that concern themselves with decolonizing projects. I will admit that in my most self-critical moments, I have considered (as John Pryor writes about in chapter 10), focusing only on anti-racist social justice scholarship in my local community. This distancing from international projects/collaborations has never lasted long. I return nearly every year to Kenya, and now my visits are more about relationships and community volunteer projects than about my research agenda.

Co-editing this book has also served as a catalyst for reengagement with the possibility that decolonizing methodologies might be discernable and that, if they are, it will be in large part through a decentering of privileging Western academic/globalized/anglicized assumptions about research and through a process of listening deeply and humbly to indigenous colleagues and friends.

POSTCOLONIAL AND DECOLONIZING RESEARCH:
THEORIES, CONTRADICTIONS, AND [IM]POSSIBILITIES

Postcolonial literature has grown into a reckonable genre of critical theory. However, several scholars including Leela Gandhi (1998) argue that "postcolonial studies have come to represent a confusing and often unpleasant babel of subaltern voices" (p. 3). Despite its imprecise definition, postcolonial studies have taken on an interdisciplinary character ranging, within the humanities, from education, history, cultural studies, to literary criticism. Although it is nearly impossible, given the contested issues it embodies, to articulate what postcoloniality *is*, what seems more possible is the articulation of what it is *not*. Yet, even in doing this, one does not easily escape the lure to semantically anatomize it in terms of whether or not the term is or should be post(-)coloniality (see Appiah, 1991). With or without the hyphen in postcoloniality, it is not possible to monitor all the differance in the term postcoloniality with the more obvious slippages in meaning occurring when postcoloniality is situated geographically, historically, and institutionally. For instance, echoing "postmodernity," "postcoloniality" can be taken to be the indexical marker of a "contemporary state, situation, condition, or epoch" (Shohat, 1992, p. 101). The use of postcoloniality, employed this way, implies a supercession, a linearity that is not entirely what postcoloniality is.

Even more dangerous is the unmonitored differance that results when the postcolonial formulations collapse national-racial formations that are very different as being equally postcolonial. Paraphrasing Shohat's (1992) argument, for example, situating the United States and Kenya in relation to an imperial "center," simply because they were both colonies, masks the unequal relations of the colonized white settlers (of the United States) to the Europeans at the "center" with that of the colonized indigenous (Kenyans) to the European colonizers. As Shohat (1992) argues, the critical slippage in meaning occurs when the suffice "post" is applied to two very different experiences of colonization—namely, colonization as experienced by indigenous people (e.g., of Africa, South America, Australia, New Zealand, the United States) and Europe's domination of the European elites in the colonies (e.g., of the United States, Canada, or Australia.) This differance is further simultaneously aided and complicated by the spatiotemporality ambiguity inherent in the term postcoloniality that allows for the masking of material histories of violence that indigenous people faced under colonization and still continue to face under neocolonization. Critics of postcoloniality (e.g., Shohat, 1992) argue that this undifferentiated use of postcoloniality has diminished its political agency.

Discursively speaking, postcoloniality, when aligned with other terms that utilize the prefix the same way, including post-Marxism, poststructuralism, and postmodernism, imply a movement beyond, thereby postcoloniality becomes the discursive marker of the beginning of presencing (Bhabha, 1994). However, exactly what postcoloniality indexicalizes at the beginning of its presencing is a highly contested issue. At this site, new identifies emerge, most of them bearing marks of oppression that a discursive reading of postcoloniality does not acknowledge. A materialist reading of postcoloniality "sees" and acknowledges the minorities/marginalized people that colonization creates. It also acknowledges the historical and continuing brutalities that serve to construct those minorities. One the other hand, a discursive reading of postcoloniality does not trouble the façade of equality that postcoloniality pawns as a common experience of all ex-colonials.

Some scholars have argued that the term postcolonial is ambiguously positioned historically and politically and that it has lost, or perhaps never possessed any, political agency (Shohat, 1992). Shohat argues that "since the 'post' in the 'postcolonial' suggests 'after' the demise of colonialism, it is imbued, quite apart from its users intentions, with an ambiguous spatio-temporality" (p. 102). Within this reading, postcoloniality simultaneously indexicalizes actual geopolitical spaces (specifically third world countries) that became independent after World War II, thereby periodicizing postcolonialism (McLeod, 2000) and at the same time postcoloniality "refers to the Third World diasporic circumstances of the last four decades—from forced exiles to 'voluntary' immigration—within First World metropolises" (Shohat, 1992, p. 102), or, as McLeod (2000) reads it, postcolonism in this sense refers to the discursively dissimilar forms of representations, practices, and values.

On the other hand, Gandhi (1998) traces the ambiguity of postcoloniality to its lack of an "originary moment" as well as a concise methodology. In her reading of the field of postcolonial studies, Gandhi identifies both a materialist postcoloniality in the literature, which looks to materialist philosophies such as Marxism, and a discursive postcoloniality, which draws from poststructural critiques of Western knowledge and its privileged ways of knowing. Utilizing this distinction, Gandhi draws out two distinct strands of postcolonial work: (1) postcolonial politics, which connects postcoloniality through a materialist function, and (2) postcolonial theory, which locates postcoloniality through a discursive function.

Although scholars like Gandhi and Shohat might initially appear to be in disagreement about what postcoloniality is/is not, it is clear from their arguments that certain strands of postcolonial studies possess a materialist underpinning, while others have a discursive underpinning. Therefore, the current polarization of the field of postcolonial studies has positioned postcoloniality on either the discursive or the materialist pole/binary. Within this logic, therefore, proponents of postcolonial theory see the Western academy as the site for the discursive production of the oppression of non-Western knowledge forms, specifically indigenous epistemologies. On the other hand, those on the postcolonial politics pole see a materialist side to postcoloniality. In other words, they argue that several historical, cultural, political, and economic factors intricately intersect at the site of the production of the postcolonial condition.

Connecting postcoloniality with decolonizing/decolonization, we argue for both a materialist and discursive connection. In our engagement with possibilities for decolonizing research, we argue that the materialist and the discursive function in decolonization are merely two ends of the same pole. A complete project of decolonization has to chip away at colonization that is discursively located and colonization that serves a materialist function.

Given the diverse needs and the dispersion in the fields from which calls for decolonization are currently being heard, the necessity to discursively and materially decolonize the "field"[3] is both evident and critical. For example, as Maori scholar Linda Tuhiwai Smith (1999) points out, there remains a very real ambivalence in indigenous communities toward the role of Western education and those who have been educated in Western universities. Smith's point resonates with a materialist reading of the decolonization project. This point is clearly brought to bear by Julie Komea in chapter 1, Dudu Junkie in chapter 5, and Kathryn Manuelito in chapter 14.

Locating the work of decolonization discursively, Spivak (1999) notes the very real ambivalence in Western universities about the legitimacy of indigenous knowledge and the role of indigenous intellectuals in the academy. The need to decolonize the Western academy that privileges Western knowledges over indigenous epistemologies is a clearly needed function of the decolonizing project. Several chapters further unpack this matter, including Miryam Espinosa-Dulanto in chapter 2, Geeta Verma in chapter 3, and Dudu Jankie in chapter 5.

Similar to the interdisciplinary nature of postcolonial studies, calls for the decolonization have been sounded by voices from fields ranging from education, women's studies, linguistics, literature, to filmmaking. Given the diversity of the voices calling for decolonization within their own fields, then it is clear from the outset the lack of a clear definition of what decolonization is. However, by tracing the contours of the materialist and discursive morphologies of decolonization from this wide variety of fields, one emerges with a sense of what decolonizing work looks like.

Writing from a materialist feminist perspective, Donaldson (1992) calls for decolonizing feminism in order to produce a counternarrative that does not reify and privilege the singularized hermeneutic truths that feminism's imperialism has tended to articulate. Writing in other fields, other scholars take on the decolonization project in literature (Okonkwo, 1999; Stead, Lessing, and Gordimer, 1998), literary criticism (Lawrence, 1992), and filmmaking (Foster, 1999). What is common among these very diverse texts is their collective attempt to reauthor experiences that have historically been excluded in the master texts and redirect the Foucouldian gaze and to rearticulate fresh and flexible diasporic modes of subjectivity and decolonize the centered and decentric "field" discursively and materially.

The chapters in this volume represent the researchers' struggle to dis-encrypt discourses underpinned by investigatory research that has sustained colonial oppression, discursively and materially. Further, these researchers attempt to inscribe instead a new language of research that valorizes their experiences, thereby positioning them squarely and actively at the center and at the apex of discourses that produce/define them. The works of the researchers and scholars presented in this volume are synchronous with the call Michael Oliver (1999) makes to disability researchers (another marginalized discourse that has traditionally produced disabled people as silent and voiceless) where he points out that

> . . . as researchers we labour to produce ourselves and our worlds. We do not investigate something out there, we do not merely deconstruct and reconstruct discourses about our world. Research as production requires us to engage with the world, not distance ourselves from it, for ultimately we are responsible for the product of our labours and as such we must produce a world in which we can live as truly human beings. (p. 189)

When we were thinking about how to construct the context of this work and how we wanted our work to be read, we realized that in speaking about decolonizing research, there is the tendency to create forced binaries where colonization is either spatially defined, thereby placing it securely in the past, or is defined in temporal terms that therefore situates it in the present only within those countries/geographic spaces where colonial rule is ongoing. Within this definition, therefore, decolonization becomes an act that is possible or available only to those people who were previously colonized and not those undergoing colonization or those having never historically experienced colonization. We argue that this view of coloniality/decolonizing is reductionist and that it fails to recognize the existence of colonizing tendencies of particular practices, individuals, and/or institutions within post/neo/non/colonial contexts, with the latter referring to contexts in which the historical experience of colonization has never occurred, or at least never been openly acknowledged.

Within this volume, therefore, we recognize the colonizing tendency of the act of research itself as a practice particularly when it is carried out in contexts in which the individuals have been stripped off their power for self-definition and self-expression by being cast in the role of the marginalized Other. It bears mentioning the strong correlation between the world's most powerless people and the historical experience of colonization. Therefore, when speaking about decolonizing research, we are necessarily focusing a great deal on research conducted in third world countries, former/ex-colonies, and the third worlds within the first world, which often and coincidentally are populated largely by people of color.

RESISTING ESSENTIALIZING BORDERS AND BINARIES

The culturally unmarked term of a binary opposition—such male *as opposed to female,* white *as opposed to nonwhite, or* modern *as opposed to primitive—always occupies the grammatical position of* him, *never* I *or* you, *and always operates as if not dependent on rhetoric to maintain its position. That is, it aligns rhetoric with non-truth, and maintains itself as essentially restrained, neutral, transparent, beige.*

MacCannell (1992, p. 131)

We realized that our work had to go beyond the binary oppositional categories of these essentializing discourses of liminality that might attempt to delimit the work of decolonizing research spatially or temporally vis-à-vis colonization. Such liminal boundaries minimize the scope of decolonization by defining coloniality solely as a historical experience that is spatially and temporally defined. This task of decolonizing research therefore is not an easy one in that current research methodologies are mostly investigatory in nature and often utilize oppressive colonizing language developed within a colonizing oppressive research tradition. Attempting to conduct and write research that is decolonizing is therefore complicated by both these facts of lack of decolonized research methodologies and lack of research language to represent it. Linda Smith's (1999) work offers strategies for decolonizing research, in part through highlighting twenty-five research projects currently being carried out by indigenous peoples. In providing a contextual overview of this scholarship Smith states,

The projects are not claimed to be entirely indigenous or to have been created by indigenous researchers. Some approaches have arisen out of social science methodologies, which in turn have arisen out of methodological issues raised by research with various oppressed groups. Some project invite multidisciplinary research approaches. Others have arisen more directly out of indigenous practices. . . . Indigenous methodologies are often a mix of existing methodological approaches and indigenous practices. The mix reflects the training of indigenous research which continues to be within the academy, and the parameters and common sense understanding of research which govern how indigenous communities and researchers define their activities. (pp. 142–143)

In describing the twenty-five highlighted indigenous research projects, Smith (1999, pp. 143–161) uses words like claiming, testimonies, storytelling, celebrating survival, indigenizing, intervening, revitalizing, connecting, reading, writing, representing, gendering, envisioning, reframing, restoring, returning, democratizing, networking, naming, protecting, creating, negotiating, discovering, and sharing to describes them.

Within this book, we have consciously selected a mode of representation that extends our attempts and commitment to decolonize research by encouraging contributors to present their work in ways that best meet the need of the message of their contribution. For instance, Lisa Cary (chapter 4) uses poetry, while Miryam Espinoza (chapter 2) uses several story vignettes to illustrate the "placelessness" of the "Little" hybrid within a society that has not come to terms with its own cultural diversity in her discussion of the *Mestiza* and her own Muchik heritage. Ellen Demas and Cinthya Saavedra also draw from *Mestiza* scholarship and consciousness in framing their deconstruction of bilingual education and language advocacy in chapter 13. These chapters exemplify our steps toward developing decolonized language/modes of representing/decolonizing research.

This volume on decolonizing research, therefore, is not a book only about researching former (and persistent) colonies, but also it documents the struggles and efforts of indigenous scholars/researchers and their allies, both individually and collectively, to produce themselves in ways that are emancipatory and committed to producing empowering discourses and knowledges. Hegemonic colonial/colonizing research about the Other has often cast the Other into roles of victims, needy, helpless, thereby effectively disempowering and silencing the voices such as those represented in this volume. Having said that, however, we hasten to add that this is not a volume about "giving voice." Rather, the chapters presented in this volume are about ways in which the individual contributors understand, enact, and engage with the act of decolonizing research and ways in which they have encountered and challenged the oppressive structures that colonizing research paradigms construct that have produced them as marginalized silenced subjects.

Additionally, the chapters presented in this volume illustrate that decolonizing research requires that we consider the ways in which oppressive structures are produced and iterated in research by investigating the actions of the oppressors. The end product of this kind of research is the production of methodologies and knowledge that is useful to the oppressed/colonized peoples as they struggle to emancipate themselves individually and collectively in both discursive and material ways. This type of research, therefore, neither parasites on the oppression experienced as everyday life by colonized/oppressed people nor does it extrematize/exoticize those experiences or minimize their lives of oppression as most "giving-voice/colonizing" research has often tended to do.

LANGUAGE AND COLONIZATION: NAMING LINGUICIDE

If it was the gun which made possible the mining of this gold and which effected the political captivity of their owners, it was the language which held captive their cultures, their values, and hence their minds.
Ngugi wa Thiong'o (1993, p. 31)

A chord that joins the chapters in this volume, regardless of the author or whether the author has focused on the notion of coloniality that centers around the territorial enterprise of subaltern imperialism, or has defined coloniality more broadly to include tendencies of institutionalized practices such as research that creates and subsequently silences the Other, language as a vehicle of colonization has been extensively discussed. A growing body of scholarship has asserted that language is playing an increasingly important role as a means of control and domination (e.g., Oda, 2000; Macedo, Dendrinos, and Panayiota, 2003; Phillipson, 2000; Skutnabb-Kangas, 2000). Skutnabb-Kangas coined the term "linguicide" and has referred to English as a "killer language," given its growing global hegemony and power to further marginalize indigenous languages. Her work, and that of other language rights advocates, has also made provocative connections between the loss of local languages and the loss of biodiversity. For example, the Preamble of the *Code of Ethics of the International Society of Ethnobiology* (adopted November 28, 1998) states that "culture and language are intrinsically connected to land and territory, and cultural and linguistic diversity are inextricably linked to biological diversity."

As discussed by Ellen Demas and Cinthya Saavedra in chapter 13, the language rights or multilingual right movement is global and is composed

of human rights lawyers, politicians, linguists, sociolinguists, and philosophers to name a few (Skutnabb-Kangas, 2000). According to this group,
safeguarding language diversity is key to maintaining the physical and cultural diversity of the world (Phillips, 2000; Skutnabb-Kangas, 2000).
Demas and Saavedra, however, go on to argue that some of the language
rights activists "deify linguists and their Western concepts of language"
and that "their vision of multilingualism is a utopia."

Dudu Jankie, in chapter 5, reminds us of the privileged commodity
status of English in Botswana and the normalizing roles it performs in that
education system:

> My discursively constituted hybridized identities stem partially
> from my language or linguistic experiences. Language is a means
> of identity as much as it is a tool of empowerment and represen-
> tation. Not only is language central to how knowledge is con-
> structed, authorized and the purposes it fulfills, it is essential in
> "working the hyphens" (Fine, 1994, p. 72) that separates and at
> the same time shapes the relationships, experiences and interac-
> tions of the colonizers and the colonized. (Fine,1994; Thiong'o,
> 1986, 1993)

Several other authors in this volume discuss the loss of indigenous language, and therefore culture, in their own lives or those of children in their
natal home. These include Miryam Espinosa-Dulanto's reflection on the
loss of (her ancestral tongue) Muchik (chapter 2), Bekisizwe Ndimande's
discussion of the loss of IsiZulu and other African languages in post-
apartheid South African curriculum (chapter 12), Leodinito Cañete's discussion (chapter 8) of language issues in conducting research among
Philippine communities in Greece, Kathryn Manuelito's discussion of the
importance of maintaining Navajo language and literacy, or Haoua
Hamza's concern about what gets lost when data are collected in four languages, then research translated entirely into English (chapter 7). Aware of
the profound meanings carried as nuances in many indigenous languages,
Susan Matoba Adler (chapter 6), although not being fluent in Japanese,
frames her findings in traditional Japanese phrases to bring out the often
subtle issues of doing research in Japanese-American communities, while
Denise Proud draws from her (aboriginal) Murri language and culture in
collaboration with coauthor Cynthia à Beckett to create a model for their
view of education (chapter 9). Similarly, Julie Kaomea (chapter 1) uses indigenous Hawaiian concepts in framing her research and attempts to decolonize her work, and Kathryn Manuelito draws on Navajo language and
culture to deconstruct multiple meanings of "self-determination." Finally,
Ellen Demas and Cinthya Saavedra use code-switching from English to

Spanish as a powerful device that serves, in part, to decenter English and foreground *Mestiza* culture.

Against the backdrop of a growing English-only movement in the United States and the globalizing impacts of English as the official language of instruction in many nations, the hegemony of dominant language and loss of mother tongue is indeed an issue that is central to any discussion of decolonizing education or cross-cultural research. As more students prefer to learn in English, in part due to the power of corporate globalization, the persistence of language as a tool of colonization seems obvious.

CRITICAL PERSONAL NARRATIVE, AUTO/ETHNOGRAPHY AND DECOLONIZING METHODOLOGIES

Burdell and Swadener (1999) discuss a rapidly growing genre in education literature, termed critical personal narrative and auto/ethnography. This genre tends to draw from poststructural and postcolonial themes, is often multivocal, and "question[s] previous assumptions of empirical authority, while also interrogating the construction of subjectivity" (p. 21). Although such texts often use poststructural forms, their content typically draws from critical theories, "in that they embody a critique of prevailing structures and relationships of power and inequity in a relational context" (ibid., p. 21). In other words, either implicitly or explicitly, writing in this genre typically assumes materialist social forms or discursive structures that serve particular social interests. Hence, the addition of the marker "critical" to personal narrative "to signify this explicitly political project" (ibid., p. 21).

After reading and editing all the chapters, we decided to change the subtitle of the book to reflect our view that all the work reflected the spirit of this genre of critical personal narrative. Though chapters vary in their critical perspectives and liberatory projects, we urged authors to explore the complexities, contradictions, and [im]possibilities of decolonizing research in essays or personal narratives.

Another, related genre that is reflected in many of the chapters within this volume is autho/ethnography, defined by Reed-Danahay (1997) as a form of self-narrative that places the self within a social context, serving as both a method and a text (Reed-Danahay, 1997, p. 9). She further describes auto/ethnography as exploring intersections of gender and voice, border crossing, dual consciousness, multiple identities, and selfhood, and situates it within the context of the changing field of anthropology, while noting the "changing nature of field work in a post-colonial and post-modern world" (Reed-Danahay, 1997, p. 1). Importantly, for this book, is Reed-Danahay's assertion that the auto/ethnography movement "has sought to transcend the binary split between the self and the social through genres of writing that provide collective representations" (p. 10).

Chapters that might be viewed enacting an auto/ethnographic project more explicitly include those by Geeta Verma (chapter 3), Lisa Cary (chapter 4), Susan Matoba Adler (chapter 6), Cynthia a Beckett and Denise Proud (chapter 9), John Pryor and Joseph Ghartey Ampiah (chapter 10), and Vilma Seeberg and Haiyan Qiang (chapter 11). Several authors also address the issue of dual consciousness, and the complexities of insider/outsider dualities when indigenous researchers return home and find themselves constructed at times as outsider in some contexts. Dudu Jankie (chapter 5), echoes Narayan's (1993) question of "how native is a 'native' anthropologist?' in poignant ways. In Junkie's (chapter 5) words, drawing from Narayan, Junkie finds that:

> Narayan's analysis of "native" anthropologist helps understanding the relation between knowledge-and-power, researchers and researched in colonial and postcolonial contexts. Narayan indicates that researchers use their own sense of identity and image as "insiders" as well as "outsiders" to construct themselves and the researched. In this sense, all the researchers-including the "natives" of a culture-bring to the field acquired knowledge and experiences which shapes the researcher-researched relationship, the specific roles each one assume, the knowledge obtained, how it is interpreted and used.

This passage reflects a theme that cuts across many of the chapters in this collection of critical personal narratives. Although Spivak (1999) and others have been critical of hybridity theory, we feel that it can be a useful lens for reading the pervasive subtexts of this volume. We would join Narayan (1993) in arguing "for the *enactment of hybridity* in our texts; that is, writing that depicts authors as minimally bicultural in terms of belonging simultaneously to the world of engaged scholarship and the world of everyday life" (p. 672).

The notion of hybridity and the theme of resisting binary categories are further reflected in the following quote, found in Lisa Cary's essay in this volume (chapter 4):

> What is theoretically innovative, and politically crucial, is the need to think beyond narratives of originary and initial subjectivities and to focus on those moments or processes that are produced in the articulation of cultural differences. These 'in-between' spaces provide the terrain for elaborating strategies of selfhood - singular or communal - that initiate new signs of identity, and innovative

sites of collaboration, and contestation, in the act of defining the idea of society itself. (Bhabha, 1994, p. 2)

Yet another related genre that has influenced several of the chapters in this book and could arguably be described as a form of decolonizing writing-as-methodology is the Latin American *testimonio*, or bearing witness, an autobiographic form of radical narrative originating in the 1960s and also widely used in refugee politics in the United States (Chamberlain and Thompson, 1998). They further describe this genre as follows: "Its key feature, as the name *testimonio* indicates, is as a secular spiritual testimony, telling a life as a left-wing moral with the overt intention of raising consciousness" (Chamberlain and Thompson, p. 6). Chapters that embody the *testimonio* tradition include those by Espinosa-Dulanto (chapter 2), Ellen Demas and Cinthya Saavedra (chapter 13), Leodinito Cañete (chapter 8), and Bekisizwe Ndimande (chapter 12).

While we do not intend to unnecessarily deconstruct the contributions to this volume or overdetermine them in terms of forms of emerging education research genres, we do want to emphasize the linkages of decolonizing methodologies to critical personal narrative, auto/ethnography, and *testimonio*.

ORGANIZATION OF THE BOOK

If chapters defy categorization in many ways, this was reflected in our challenging task of grouping them thematically into three broad and often overlapping sections of the book. We have attempted to provide side-by-side narratives (Burdell and Swadener, 1999) in ways that at least partially replicate the years of dialogue in various conferences, on e-mail, and in other contexts in which this book was first conceived.

Part I, Engaging/Performing Theories of Decolonizing Research, extends the discussion of our Introduction, as authors draw on an array of theories to complicate assumptions about postcolonial theory, decolonizing research, and crossing borders layered with identity politics, cultural contradictions, and power relations. Given the dynamic, personal, and critical nature of these chapters, we framed this opening section in terms of engaging/performing theories of decolonizing research. The first two chapters in this section draw from indigenous genres including storytelling and *testimonio* (bearing witness). Julie Kaomea (chapter 1) draws on the native Hawaiian practice of storytelling, combined with Marxist poststructuralist theory to problematize her role as an indigenous native Hawaiian academic working in indigenous schools and communities. In chapter 2, Miryam Espinoza-Dulante utilizes fictionalized narration in her questioning of the indigenous-outsider binary. Geeta Verma, in chapter 3, reminds readers of the problematic role that colonial science has played in the mystification of colonial knowledge while noticing the persistence of the colonizing tendencies of science within the U.S science standards movement. Lisa Cary (chapter 4) uses original autobiographical poetry to deconstruct her journeys as a white curriculum Australian scholar, complicating and questioning her multiple subjectivies in colonial/postcolonial settings.

Part II, Critical Personal Narratives on Decolonizing Research Methodologies, reflects the subtitle of the book, which is also a bridging theme for many of the chapters in the book. Chapters in this section draw from work with a rich array of cultures and transnational experiences, and address issues and tensions of "homecoming." This section could have been titled "border crossings," given the diverse settings, issues, and cultural groups described. In particular, authors in this section grapple with their insider/outsider subjectivities and related linguistic issues. Dudu Junkie (chapter 5) and Haoua Hamza (chapter 7) describe their experiences as indigenous African scholars returning home from the United States for dissertation data collection and grappling with complex insider/outsider and linguistic issues. Susan Matoba Adler (chapter 6) reflects on her research with Asian-American families, including work with three generations of Japanese-American families, and on the ethnic socialization of Japanese, Chinese, Korean, Filipino, and Hmong children in the United States. Leodinito Cañete (chapter 8) reflects on methodological issues of his research on basic education issues, including home-school relations and language patterns, in Philippine communities in Greece. Although the chapters in this section often raise more questions than they answer, such questions are critical and indeed central to the decolonizing project.

Chapters in Part III, Cross-Cultural Collaboration and Decolonizing Research, explore the dynamics and insights of sustained, international/intercultural collaboration as an approach to decolonizing research. They also address methodological and theoretical issues, often framed in personal ways. Moving from the highly personal intertwined narratives of coauthors Cynthia à Beckett and Denise Proud (chapter 9), to the methodologically complex work of collaborators John Pryor and Joseph Ghartey Ampiah (chapter 10), to a case study that contradicts the "brain-drain" model of higher education by longtime collaborators Vilma Seeberg and Hiayan Qiang in chapter 11, these chapters raise an array of issues and offer ways to frame cross-cultural collaboration with the challenging context of decolonizing research.

The final chapters, constituting Part IV, Complicating Decolonizing Education and Research: Challenges and [Im]possibilities, further investigate issues in decolonizing education and research. Bekisizwe Ndimande (chapter 12) provides a provocative and at times personal analysis of curriculum in post-apartheid South Africa, particularly as it relates to language policy, and forms what he terms "[re]-anglicization" and recolonization. In chapter 13, Ellen Demas and Cinthya Saavedra reconceptualize language advocacy and bilingual education, serving as an example of ways in which a well-known field, its literature, and its commonsense assumptions may be viewed through a critical decolonizing lens. This chapter engages with code-switching and draws heavily from *Mestizaje* consciousness. The final chapter, written by Kathryn Manuelito, examines how one American Indian tribal group, the Ramah Band of the Navajo Tribe, defines and practices self-determination, including the contrasting meanings of this popular neoliberal term between the colonizing discourse of dominant white culture and indigenous meanings and enactments.

CONCLUDING REFLECTIONS

We invite readers to engage with the many critical narratives included in this book, and join Soto and Swadener (2002) in asking how we might continue to explore ways to decolonize research and create spaces of liberatory praxis:

> Our experimental and newly emerging orientations will mean that we are traveling creative paths, as architects, as builders, as wisdom keepers, as healers discovering, building, and charting newly liberating spaces of hope and possibility. Only when we collaboratively envision research that is built on a theory of cultural democracy and acknowledges the issues of power and the political nature of the field can we begin to reconfigure policy and practice in a discourse of "hope." Only then will we find ourselves in our roles as cultural workers invested in healing.

We would argue, with Dimitriadis and McCarthy (2001, p. 119), that a "strategy of alliance might allow us to produce new anti-discriminatory pedagogies that will respond to this fraught and exceedingly fragile moment of globalized, postcolonial life." We are indebtedly conscious that the intellectual space that this book occupies grows from the works of many scholars, particularly Linda Tuhiwai Smith, whose ideas on decolonizing research methodologies have influenced our personal thinking and praxis. Indeed, many of the themes in Smith's (1999) book, *Decolonizing Methodologies*, are affirmed in the chapters of this book. To quote Smith (1999),

Indigenous people across the world have other stories to tell which not only question the assumed nature of those [common sense/taken for granted western academic] ideas and the practices they generate, but also serve to tell an alternative story: the history of Western research through the eyes of the colonized. These counter-stories are powerful forms of resistance, which are repeated and shared across diverse indigenous communities. (p. 2)

We welcome readers to decenter pervasive Western/modernist/epistemology and engage with the narratives and chapters that follow. They offer contrasting counterstories and shared resistance to the frequently colonizing masterscripts of cross-cultural research.

NOTES

1. Italicized parenthetical statement added.
2. Italicized statement added.
3. For our reading of "the field," see Rogers and Swadener, 1999.

REFERENCES

Appiah, K. A. (1991). Is the post- in postmodernism the post- in postcolonial? *Critical Inquiry*, Winter, 17.

Bhabha, H. K. (1994). *The location of culture*. London: Routledge.

Burdell, P. and B. B. Swadener. (1999). Critical personal narrative and autoethnography in education: An emerging genre. *Educational Researcher*, 28(6), 21–26.

Chamberlain, M. and P. Thompson. (Eds.). (1998). *Narrative and genre*. New York: Routledge.

Derrida, J. (1976). *Of grammatology*. Baltimore: Johns Hopkins University Press.

Dimitriadis, G. and C. McCarthy. (2001). *Reading and teaching the postcolonial: From Baldwin to Basquiat and beyond*. New York: Teachers College Press.

Donaldson, L. E. (1992). *Decolonizing feminisms race, gender, and empire-building*. Chapel Hill: University of North Carolina Press.

Fine, M. (1994). Working the hyphens. In N. K. Denzin and Y. S. Lincoln (Eds.). *Handbook of Qualitative Research*. Thousand Oaks, CA: Sage.

Foster, A. G., (1998). *Women filmmakers of the African diaspora and Asian diaspora: Decolonizing the gaze, locating subjectivity*. Carbondale: Southern Illinois University Press.

Gandhi, L. (1998). *Postcolonial theory: A critical introduction.* New York: Columbia University Press.

Harrison, F. V. (Ed.). (1991). *Decolonizing anthropology: Moving further toward an anthropology for liberation.* Washington, DC: Association for Black Anthropologists, American Anthropological Association.

hooks, bell. (1989). *Talking back: Thinking feminist, thinking black.* Boston: South End Press.

Lawrence, K. R. (1992). *Decolonizing tradition: New views of the twentieth-century "British" literary canons.* Urbana: University of Illinois Press.

MacCannell, D. (1992). *Empty meeting grounds: The tourist papers.* London: Routledge.

McCarthy, C. (1998). *The uses of culture: Education and the limits of ethnic affiliation.* New York: Routledge.

Macedo, D., Dendrinos, B., and Panayiota, G. (2003). *The hegemony of English.* Boulder, CO: Paradigm Publishers.

McLeod, J. (2000). *Beginning postcolonialism.* Manchester: Manchester University Press.

Mohanty, T. C. (1991). Under western eyes: Feminist scholarships and colonial discourses. In C. T. Mohanty, A. Russo, and L. Torres, *Third world women and politics of feminism.* Bloomington: Indiana University Press.

Ngugi wa Thiong'o. (1986). *Decolonising the mind: The politics of language in African literature.* London: James Currey

Ngugi wa Thiong'o. (1993). *Moving the center: The struggle for cultural freedom.* Nairobi: East African Educational Press.

Oda, M. (2000). Linguicism in action: Language and power in academic institutions. In R. Phillipson (Ed.), *Rights to language: Equity, power, and education.* Mahwah, NJ: Lawrence Erlbaum.

Okonkwo, C. (1999). *Decolonization agonistics in postcolonial fiction.* New York: St. Martin's Press.

Oliver, M. (1999). Final accounts and the parasite people. In M. Corker and S. French (Eds.), *Disability discourse.* Philadelphia: Open University Press.

Phillipson, R. (Ed.). (2000). *Rights to language: Equity, power, and education.* Mahwah, NJ: Lawrence Erlbaum.

Reed-Danahay, D. (Ed.), (1997). *Auto/ethnography: Rewriting the self and the social.* New York: Berg.

Rogers, L. J. and B. B. Swadener. (1999). Reflections on the future work of anthropology and education: Reframing the field. *Anthropology and Education Quarterly*, 30 (4), 436–440.

Shohat, E. (1992). Notes on the "post-colonial." *Social Text*, 31/32, 99–112.

Skutnabb-Kangas, T. (2000). *Linguistic genocide in education—or worldwide diversity and human rights?* Mahwah, NJ: Lawrence Erlbaum.

Smith, L. T. (1999). *Decolonizing methodologies: Research and indigenous peoples.* London: Zed Books.

Soto, L. D. and B. B. Swadener. (2002). Toward liberatory early childhood theory, research and praxis: Decolonizing a field. *Contemporary Issues in Early Childhood*, 3(1), 38–66.

Spivak, G. C. (1999). *A critique of postcolonial reason: Toward a history of the vanishing present.* Cambridge: Harvard University Press.

Stead, C., D. Lessing, and N. Gordimer. (1998). *From the margins of the empire.* Ithaca: Cornell Univeristy Press.

Swadener, B. B., Kabiru, M., and Njenga, A. (2000). *Does the village still raise the child? A collaborative study of changing child rearing in Kenya.* Albany: State University of New York Press.

Swadener, B.B. and K. N. Mutua. (1996, November). *"Multi-culturalism" and education in Kenya: Emic, etic and collaborative perspectives.* Paper presented at the Annual Meeting of the American Anthropological Association, San Francisco, Cal.

Swadener, B. B. and K. Mutua. (2001). Mapping terrains of homelessness in postcolonial Kenya. In V. Polakow and C. Gulliean (Eds.). *Homelessness in international context: Contributions in sociology* (263–287). Wesport: Greenwood Press.

Swadener, B. and K. Mutua. (2001, April). *Problematizing "decolonizing research" in cross cultural contexts: Complexities, contradictions and [im]possibilities.* Annual Meeting of the American Educational Research Association, Seattle, Wash.

PART I

Engaging/Performing Theories of Decolonizing Research

CHAPTER ONE

Dilemmas of an Indigenous Academic: A Native Hawaiian Story

JULIE KAOMEA

For the past several years I have been studying Native Hawaiian educational initiatives and the representation of Native Hawaiians in elementary and early childhood curricula in (post)colonial Hawai'i. While I have since completed that initial study, my relationship with the Hawaiian community where I first conducted my research continues. In fact, it seems that with each successive year, my work and research in this setting become more entangled, more complicated, and more politically sensitive. While I assumed that over time I would grow more comfortable with my role as an indigenous academic, to this day I continue to struggle with "unhomely" (Bhabha, 1994, p. 9) feelings of "disconnection" (Smith, 1999, p. 5) as I proceed uneasily, partially as insider and partially as outsider within both the academy and my native community.

The unhomely[1] disconnection felt by indigenous academics who return to work in our native communities is not a new phenomenon. The problematic position of western-educated, indigenous intellectuals has been addressed by Franz Fanon (1963), Edward Said (1993), Gayatri Spivak (1990), and more recently by Maori scholar Linda Tuhiwai Smith (1999). As Smith (1999) points out, there remains a very real ambivalence in indigenous communities toward the role of western education and those who have been educated in western universities. Likewise, there is a very real ambivalence in western universities about the legitimacy of indigenous knowledge and the role of indigenous intellectuals in the academy (Spivak, 1990).

Consequently, indigenous academics who attempt to work and research in our native communities assume a difficult position as we struggle to meet the sometimes competing expectations of the academy and our home communities. For instance, in my experience I have found that while the academy expects that its members will speak from theory, Native Hawaiian communities expect that their members will speak from experience. While the academy expects that research relationships will be detached and objective, Native Hawaiian communities expect that these relationships will be intimate and enduring. While the academy expects that its members will contribute to the scholarly community through rigorous intellectualism, Native Hawaiian communities expect that their members will contribute through vigorous activism.

This chapter chronicles my attempts to reconcile the conflicting expectations placed on me as a Native Hawaiian intellectual through the development of a hybrid[2] Hawaiian/Western research methodology that draws from and speaks to both indigenous and western ways of knowing and being. In the Hawaiian tradition of *haʻi moʻolelo* or storytelling, I have chosen to write this chapter as a personal narrative. While I acknowledge the limitations of such a small-scale, personal story, it is my hope that its familiar themes and characters will invoke in my readers a set of shared understandings and meanings, and that in the process it will bring the abstract theoretical conversations surrounding indigenous research to an accessible level by generating discussions of what indigenous research methodologies might look like in practice.

HYBRIDITY AND METHODOLOGICAL PURITY

Consistent with the logic of postcolonialism and its declining emphasis on grand theories and narratives, my hybrid methodology, and thus my story, is intentionally eclectic, mingling, combining, and synthesizing theories and techniques from disparate disciplines and paradigms. Writing as a Native Hawaiian in the middle of the Pacific, far removed from the academic center of the metropolis, I do not attach myself to any one theoretical perspective, but instead draw widely from an assortment of structuralist and poststructuralist theorists, moving within and between sometimes competing or seemingly incompatible interpretive perspectives and paradigms. Consequently, you will find that my study has both a deconstructive playfulness as well as a Marxist sincerity. It engages with Michel Foucault's critique of the pervasive power of discourse as well as Karl Marx's concern with material effects. And, all the while, it consciously and unapologetically privileges Native Hawaiian values and concerns.

While some may liken my attempt to combine Marxist, poststructuralist, and Native Hawaiian insights and theories to trying to ride two (or, in this case, three) horses at one time (O'Hanlon and Washbrook,

1992), I believe that postcolonial studies demand such theoretical innova-tion and flexibility. In this (post)colonial era, where methodological purity can only be achieved by "sweeping marginalised narratives and perspectives once again under the carpet of class and capitalism" (Loomba, 1998, p. 253), I suggest we heed the words of Gyan Prakash who urges postcolo-nial intellectuals to "hang on to two horses, inconstantly" (1992, p. 184). Although I do not deny the possible contradictions between these various theoretical perspectives, I believe that if we are to meet the demands of postcolonial studies for both a revision of the past and an analysis of our ever-changing present, we cannot work within closed paradigms.

THE INITIAL STUDY: CURRICULAR REPRESENTATION AND EARLY CHILDHOOD EDUCATION

The curricular representation of historically marginalized peoples and cul-tures is an important concern at all levels of education, particularly in the early years of schooling when children are first forming their conceptions of themselves and "others." Thus, in 1996, I began my research by studying young children's written comments and drawings about various races and ethnicities in the State of Hawai'i. When studying the children's written comments, I was particularly disturbed by their misinformed or stereotypical remarks about Native Hawaiians. For instance, one part-Hawaiian child por-trayed Native Hawaiians as living in grass huts and subsisting on a traditional diet of *lau lau, lomi* salmon, and *poi*. Others described us as "old people who know how to survie [*sic*] in the wild" or "tanned, tall, biult [*sic*] people" who "ware [*sic*] different comtumuse [costumes] and play nice music."

While I was initially surprised that these children would describe Hawaiians in such distanced and stereotypical terms, after further study I determined that their comments were actually not as surprising as they may at first seem. Following the work of Michel Foucault (1970, 1972, 1979), I used a method of genealogical discourse analysis to demonstrate how these children's surprising and stereotypical remarks draw from age-old colonial discourses about Hawaiians and other indigenous people. These discourses continue to hold sway over contemporary society and permeate our children's textbooks, encyclopedias, world atlases, and vari-ous other aspects of our school curricula.

When I shared these concerns with classroom teachers in the local Hawaiian community, they smiled knowingly and assured me that there was already a state curriculum in place to address just this sort of problem. They were referring to the State of Hawai'i's Hawaiian studies curriculum, which mandates instruction in Hawaiian culture, history, and language at all public elementary schools throughout the state. The Hawaiian studies curriculum was developed in the late 1970s in response to Native Hawaiian demands for increased visibility of our native people in our state schools and colleges. During this period, curricula from kindergarten to college nationwide were undergoing revision to reflect non-European and nonwhite contributions to history and culture. The Hawai'i state curriculum was no exception.

After speaking with these teachers about the Hawaiian studies curriculum, I was optimistic and relieved. I immediately dived into the program's instructional materials, expecting to find them full of positive images of Native Hawaiians that would serve to overturn the students' misinformed stereotypes. But after doing a close reading of the elementary Hawaiian studies textbooks and curricular guides, I began to get the sense that there was both more and less going on with this curriculum than appears on the surface.

A CRITICAL CLUE

My concern about the textbooks began with what Slavoj Zizek (1991) would refer to as a critical clue. It's something "odd," "queer," or "fishy," "that *in itself* is quite insignificant . . . but which nonetheless . . . denatures the scene of the crime and . . . renders the whole picture strange" (p. 53). In this case the critical clue came to my attention when I was inquiring into popular Hawaiian studies textbooks used by teachers in the early elementary grades. One of the titles that was referred to several times was *Hawaii the Aloha State*. After hearing the title from a number of different teachers I decided to borrow a copy of the book from our state library. But when I looked up the title in the computer catalog, I found that there were at least a dozen other books with exactly the same name. There was the classroom textbook (Bauer, 1982), and then several other similarly titled Hawaiian tour books. For instance, sitting side by side on the library shelf was the classroom textbook, a 1974 Hawaiian travel guidebook with the same name (*Hawaii the Aloha State*, 1974), and a 1985 tour book namesake (Seiden, 1985).

This critical clue spurred me to investigate the comparison further. As I did, the similarities between the Hawaiian studies textbooks and Hawaiian tour books became glaringly apparent. Building on Foucault's (1970, 1972, 1979) work in discourse genealogy, I incorporated the new historicism's (Greenblatt, 1989) technique of reading a text alongside an unlikely partner from another genre in order to identify historical discourses that the two have in common. Through this analysis, I discovered that the stereotypical images of Hawai'i and Hawaiians represented in these Western-authored textbooks are strikingly similar to the exoticized perceptions that were first projected on our people by early colonial voyagers and have since been perpetuated through Hawai'i's visitor industry.

By juxtaposing the Hawaiian studies classroom texts with Hawaiian tour guide books and documents used for the training of tourist industry workers, I explored how the material interests of the tourist industry are expressed in this "Hawaiian" curriculum. With example after example, I found that these Western-authored Hawaiian studies textbooks subtly and not so subtly promote a distorted notion of the Hawaiian culture as an exotic commodity to be consumed by visiting foreigners, while simultaneously recruiting young Hawaiian students as its frontline peddlers.

CRITICAL THEORY AND INDIGENOUS RESEARCH

I began to feel at this point that my research was bordering on dangerous territory. As a native Hawaiian I understand the distrust in Hawaiian communities toward academic research on Hawaiian educational initiatives. While I believed that my particular study would ultimately serve positive ends, I knew full well that if I chose to continue with my critique of this Hawaiian-initiated program, there would likely be many Hawaiians who had been involved in the original design and implementation of the curriculum and numerous others who are strong supporters of the program whom I might unintentionally offend.

In her discussion of the special difficulties facing indigenous researchers conducting insider research, Smith (1999) suggests that one of the most difficult risks indigenous researchers can take is to pursue a critical study that challenges taken-for-granted views or practices of their native community. Such studies can unsettle beliefs, values, and relationships within the community with consequences that the researchers, their families, and the community will have to live with on a daily basis. At the same time, however, if these critical studies are conducted in a reflexive, ethical, and respectful manner, they have the potential for ultimately strengthening the community by giving voice to previously silenced perspectives and questioning the basis of taken-for-granted assumptions. A good example of this is the recent development of Maori women's studies that critically question taken-for-granted patriarchal accounts of Maori society that have previously been provided by Westerners and Maori men (Te Awekotuku, 1992).

As I struggled with my own conflicted feelings about the relative costs and benefits of continuing with my own critical study, I turned to Hawaiian tradition and protocol for guidance on how I should proceed. In Hawaiian tradition, when one finds oneself in a position where one is about to commit a wrong that is unavoidable or somehow necessary for the larger good, one is expected to ask for forgiveness in advance. Before you picked a plant, you would pray and say, "Please forgive me for taking this plant. I need it to cure grandmother who is sick." Or, if it was necessary to walk on volcanic land, "Forgive me, *Pele* (Goddess of fire), for walking on your domain" (Pukui, Haertig, and Lee, 1972, p. 246).

At this point in my research I made my own apology or *mihi* and asked our larger Hawaiian community for *kala* (forgiveness) for the *hala* (wrong) I was about to commit. While I, from the vantage point of hindsight, critically questioned the current efficacy of the Hawaiian studies curriculum and pondered its suitability to the present Hawaiian state of affairs, in doing so I meant no disrespect to our wise elders or *kūpuna* who had the foresight to initiate this program or those who since have worked long and hard to contribute to its current success.

The process of decolonization requires our continual efforts toward questioning and revealing hidden colonial influences in past and current beliefs and practices, those of the *haole* (or foreigner) as well as those of our own *kānaka maoli* (indigenous people), including our *kūpuna* (elders), our ancestors, and ourselves. Through my *mihi* I asked for the Hawaiian community's understanding that my humble critique, however irreverent, was my small attempt to help our Hawaiian people move one step further along the path toward decolonization. Our *kūpuna* have taken us this far—now we must do the rest.

SHARING KNOWLEDGE AND REPORTING BACK

With this apology, I humbly continued. When I concluded my study of the Hawaiian studies textbooks, I immediately took my findings back to the Hawaiian community. Through a series of formal and informal presentations, I shared my newfound knowledge with a wide range of audiences, including native Hawaiian university students, Hawaiian immersion classroom teachers, native Hawaiian elders, and Hawaiian sovereignty activists. During this process of "sharing knowledge," I learned to talk about my research in a culturally appropriate manner and in a language appropriate for each particular audience. In the conversations that ensued I learned that what I was reporting was consistent with the experiences of many others in the Hawaiian community and resonated with what they had known and felt intuitively.

Following Smith (1999), when I speak of "sharing knowledge" with the community, I use the term deliberately. For beyond just sharing the surface "information" or the "in a nutshell" findings of my research, I was diligent about sharing with the Hawaiian community the critical theories and analyses that informed my study. In doing so, I aimed to demystify the way in which academic knowledge is constructed and represented. Through this process, I was able to introduce members of the Hawaiian community who may have had little formal schooling to a wider world, a world that includes other indigenous people who have experienced similar oppressions, share in similar struggles, and voice their concerns in similar ways.

COMMUNITY ACTIVISM AND GIVING BACK

Whenever and wherever I shared my findings in the Hawaiian community, I was careful to make it explicitly clear that my concern was not with the Hawaiian studies curriculum per se, but with the overwhelming influence of western-authored textbooks that intentionally or unintentionally serve ends inimical to our own. I was very clear about my belief that this Hawaiian curriculum should be under Hawaiian control and offered several suggestions for ways to ensure this.

Although my presentations and suggestions were clearly appreciated by the Hawaiian community, it soon became apparent that, as far as the community was concerned, my work on this project had just begun. For along with the rights and privileges that I enjoyed as a member of this community came accompanying *kuleana* or community obligations and responsibilities. Unlike an outsider researcher who might conduct a study in an indigenous setting and then simply present his or her findings through a written report or academic presentation, with no further responsibility to the community, indigenous academics who live and work in their home communities are inevitably implicated in a set of insider dynamics that make it impossible to simply present one's findings and walk away.

When I presented my critique of the elementary Hawaiian studies curriculum to my fellow Hawaiians in various community settings, the questions that followed weren't abstract, academic questions concerning sample size or methodology. They were pressing, action-oriented questions of "What are we going to do to remedy this?" or "What should we do next?" (It is interesting to note that the Hawaiian language has two different forms of the word "we"—*mākou*, or we exclusive of the listener, and *kākou*, or we, all of us, the listener included. The latter, inclusive, form of the word was the form used here.)

As a contributing member of the Hawaiian community, it was my *kuleana* to follow my research with action by assuming an active role in community efforts toward remedying the problems I uncovered. So when my informal presentations and conversations inspired a group of Hawaiian language immersion teachers to band together to write a new Hawaiian studies textbook from the long silent Native Hawaiian perspective, I gladly offered my assistance. The teachers and I wrote the text collaboratively and gave formal and informal presentations about our textbook and its unique approach at local education workshops for Hawaiian studies teachers and Native Hawaiian classroom elders. We also traveled together to the American Southwest where we shared our Native curriculum project with other indigenous educators at the international Stabilizing Indigenous Languages Conference and the Pueblo of Zuni, New Mexico.

Similarly, when another group asked if I might also take a look at the Hawaiian elder component of the Hawaiian studies curriculum, I once again obliged. The proponents of the Hawaiian elder program assured me that while the Hawaiian studies textbooks may leave much to be desired, it needn't be such a major concern. They explained that the "real" instruction in elementary Hawaiian studies comes from weekly classroom visits from Native Hawaiian *kūpuna* or elders who are hired as part-time teachers to assist the (typically non-Hawaiian) classroom teachers with the implementation of the curriculum.

According to teachers and principals who speak highly of the program, the *kūpuna* are "invaluable resources" in the teaching of the Hawaiian culture and language, and they also bring a special feeling of "warmth and aloha" to the elementary school classrooms. The *kūpuna* epitomize Hawaiian cultural values and the aloha spirit and provide positive intergenerational exchanges for those children who do not have grandparents of their own (Afaga and Lai, 1994). The *kūpuna*, everyone seemed to agree, are the backbone of the Hawaiian studies program, the keepers of the Hawaiian traditions. So I optimistically set out to pay these classroom elders a visit.

DECONSTRUCTING THE HAWAIIAN ELDER PROGRAM

On my first few visits, just to see the stir that these *kūpuna* create when they arrive on campus—the warm greeting they receive from youngsters who run clear across the playground to shower them with hugs, and the way the older students rise from their seats when the *kūpuna* arrive at their classroom door—seeing all of this for the first time was heartwarming. However, as I stayed on and talked with the *kūpuna* and followed them through their days, I began to realize that there was once again more and less going on with the *kūpuna* program than initially meets the eye.

To delve below the surface appearance, I observed and interviewed *kūpuna*, students, and teachers in eight elementary schools across the state. I also studied students' drawings and end-of-the-year written reflections on what they remembered about their *kūpuna*'s visits. I then employed various deconstructive techniques, including Derrida's (1976) concept of *sous rature*,[3] to look beyond the manifest text, and instead examine the subtext, or that which was put under erasure.

For instance, take a look at the student drawing featured in Figure 1.1. If we strictly read the surface of this image, we see a cheerful drawing of a

Figure 1.1. A surface look at the *kūpuna* program.

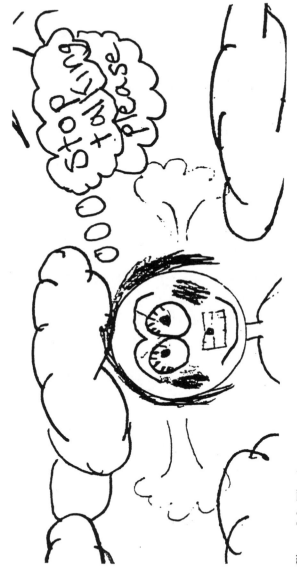

Figure 1.2. The *kūpuna* program up close.

smiling *kūpuna* teaching outdoors on a sunny day surrounded by thick grass, fluffy white clouds, and beautiful flowers. On the surface, the image seems to epitomize what the *kūpuna* program purportedly is all about: Hawaiian elders from the community coming to our Western-dominated schools to instruct Hawaii's youngsters in native Hawaiian ways of life—an indigenous form of education that may best be taught outside the four walls of the institutionalized classroom. But let's now take a second look at this picture. (See Figure 1.2.) This time instead of focusing on the surface picture, let's pay closer attention to what was rubbed out from the picture, literally put under erasure. If we study the child's illustration with the same care that an art historian would give an artistic palimpsest,[4] we discover that beneath the image of the smiling *kūpuna* lies another hidden picture, a first text that has been rubbed out and covered by the second.

Like a psychoanalyst interpreting a verbal slip, we find that a former, repressed text can be glimpsed through the gaps in the latter. Beneath the *kūpuna*'s bright, round eyes, cheerful smile, and rosy cheeks, we find a face flushed with anger, with gritting teeth, cutting eyes, and pent-up steam bursting from both ears. When we inspect the *kūpuna*'s accompanying dialogue we see that it too readily comes undone. The two-tiered configuration of the dialogue bubble suggests that our *kūpuna*'s calm request that her students "Stop talking please," originally stood as the abrupt command of a *kūpuna* short on patience ("Stop talking!"), and was later softened with the subsequent addition of the word "please." Try as they might, however, these and other subsequent smoothing modifications, such as the fluffy white clouds and cheerful flowers that have been superimposed over the earlier scene, can never fully disguise the underlying angry picture.

After months of visitations and candid conversations it became clear to me that beneath the surface of this heartwarming *kūpuna* program, many of these gracious Hawaiian elders were justifiably angry and impatient. They had little authority in the classroom, little control over their curriculum, and they were invariably overwhelmed and overextended.

HUMILITY AND KNOWING ONE'S PLACE

At this point, I once again found myself, a native Hawaiian academic, in an awkward situation. Like many native Hawaiians, I have been taught since birth to honor our Hawaiian *kūpuna*, the wise ones who have paved the way before us, the keepers of our ancient traditions. Knowing that the *kūpuna* may not come across entirely favorably in my study, I seriously considered stopping my research short rather than exposing the *kūpuna* program's many weaknesses.

When outlining the particular difficulties of indigenous insider research, Smith (1999) suggests that insider research needs to be as ethical and respectful, as reflexive and critical, as outsider research, but it also needs to be humble. It needs to be humble because as an active member of the indigenous community, the insider researcher is entwined in a complex set of roles and relationships that often serve to negate the "expert" status typically enjoyed by academics in other communities. Indeed, regardless of my academic degrees, within the Native Hawaiian community that privileges elders and the holders of traditional Hawaiian knowledge, I am merely a young, thirty-three-year-old woman with little life experience to draw from. It is therefore essential that I remember my place in the Hawaiian community and always act with humility.

I had already earned myself a reputation in the Hawaiian community as an incorrigible academic. While most tolerated my critique of the western-authored textbooks, they surely would not be as forgiving if it seemed that I was now turning my sights on the respected and defenseless *kūpuna*. Many of these *kūpuna* are retired tour guides and Waikīkī musicians who rely on these part-time positions for much-needed income. Perhaps, I thought, my critique of this *kūpuna* program, which already struggles for funding from year to year, may be one study best left unfinished.

However, after much soul searching and introspection, I decided that this seeming irreverence was once again necessary to achieve a larger good. After all, my intent was never to lay blame on the *kūpuna*, but instead to use the interpretive methods at my disposal to uncover the structural problems that are contributing to their difficult position. I never intended to fault them for their underlying angry dispositions, but instead aimed to find and remedy the source of their anger. I never meant to be disrespectful, but instead aimed to restore to these *kūpuna* the dignity and respect that they deserve.

With this understanding in mind, I once again made my *mihi* (apology) and humbly continued on, this time attending to the deep structures that lay below the surface. As I continued my studies I found that beneath the veneer of a respectful Hawaiian studies program based on the Hawaiian value of reverence for elders, our expert *kūpuna* are poorly treated, alienated from their work, and, as the erasures in the following student drawings suggest, they are virtually disembodied.

THE DISEMBODIED KŪPUNA

In Figure 1.3 we see a drawing of students rehearsing a song-and-dance performance for their school's annual May Day celebration. The boys in the picture are making a parody of their featured song "Pearly Shells" by

I remember from last year
when [Kūpuna] told us a song
called perly shells and me larry
and Dave all ways make fun of
it like curly fries from Mcdonolds
something like that then we all
got basted.

Figure 1.3. The *kūpuna* erased.

I remember when we made the ltea leaf lei and we did the may day dance (e-pele e-pele) out on the courtfield without our shirts and it was real fun dancing our may day dance in front of everyone.

Figure 1.4. The disembodied *kūpuna*.

changing the words. That's interesting in itself. But what I find most interesting is what has been rubbed out or erased from the picture—that is, the *kūpuna* who was directing the rehearsal. The *kūpuna* was initially drawn in from a back view, with legs astride and arms crossed. But then she was curiously erased, with only her *ipu* or gourd instrument remaining to mark her place.

Similarly, in Figure 1.4, a drawing depicting an actual May Day performance, all we see of the *kūpuna* is her hand grasping the neck of a large *ipu*. The rest of her body is cropped or cut off from the picture, leaving us to imagine it outside the frame. In these and several other student reflections on the *kūpuna*'s visits, the *kūpuna* are literally disembodied—cropped, left out altogether, or erased.

KŪPUNA AS HIRED HANDS

In his discussion of the disfiguring, dehumanizing effects of capitalism and the division of labor, Karl Marx (1867/1977) describes how the capitalist laborer is severed from his productive knowledge, judgment, and will, and becomes "a mere fragment of his own body" (p. 482)—a hand, watched, corrected, and controlled by a distant brain. Under capitalism, the labor process is dissociated from the skill and knowledge of the worker, and there is a sharp division between those who conceptualize and plan for others (the "head labor"), and those who execute the work (the "hand labor"). As management controls and dictates each step of the labor process, people are dehumanized and alienated from the right to that which is essential to their nature—the right to be in control of their own activities.

Such is the fate of these *kūpuna* who are hired under the guise of Hawaiian studies experts but on entering our schools are treated as little more than hired hands. Virtually homeless in our schools, with no classroom or even office space to speak of, these itinerant seniors scurry back and forth through the halls on an efficiency-maximizing teaching schedule that has them running from room to room at a hectic and even dizzying pace.

Once in the classroom these expert *kūpuna* are expected to execute a song-and-dance curriculum or a series of prescripted "*kūpuna*-proof" lessons, all under the watchful supervision of the ever-present classroom teacher. Subject to an oppressive program with rigid work schedules, uncompromising curricular demands, and closely regulated teaching situations, our expert *kūpuna* is dehumanized and disembodied—a hand controlled by a distant brain.

Within the factory system of our schools, these *kūpuna* are low-paid laborers whose ultimate function is to reproduce the existing capitalist relations of exploitation. Limited to a restrictive performance-based curriculum and substandard, alienating working conditions, these retired Hawaiian tour guides, musicians, and Waikīkī performers unwittingly ensure the survival of Hawai'i's visitor industry as they participate in their own reproduction through the interpellation of a new generation of compliant Hawaiian tourist industry workers.

EMBODYING OUR KŪPUNA

While this is where my story ends, my work continues. Since completing this study I have once again shared my findings with various groups in the Hawaiian community. Together we are working to embody our *kūpuna* through larger, structural changes in school policies. By lobbying for classroom and office space for our *kūpuna*, full-time hiring, reasonable teaching schedules, and a greater degree of curricular independence, we aim to emancipate our *kūpuna* from the alienating conditions of our schools. In the process we hope to enable our Hawaiian youngsters to learn from these experts in a dignified setting that gives both our Hawaiian elders and our Hawaiian culture the respect they truly deserve.

PANI (CONCLUSION)

This is the story of my personal journey, a chronicle of my attempts to come to terms with my "unhomely" position as a Native Hawaiian academic working and researching in a Hawaiian educational community. It is a tale full of twists and turns, with many crises of confidence, and a good deal of introspection and soul searching. Its one recurring theme is the progressive development of a hybrid Hawaiian/Western research methodology that attempts to bridge the knowledge of the western world with the traditional wisdom of my native community in an effort to reconcile these disconnected aspects of my being.

In offering this *mo'olelo* to you, I ask that you think on the *kaona* (underlying messages and meanings) of the story—the questions raised, the protocol followed, the responsibilities expected and fulfilled. Although mine is just one small story, it is my hope that in the oral tradition of *ha'i mo'olelo* (Hawaiian storytelling) this story will inspire others to tell stories of their own. As others begin to relate the tales of their efforts and dilemmas in indigenous research, and more voices and perspectives are added to the mix, we can begin to build a knowledge base of ideas for reconnecting indigenous researchers with our home communities through the development of indigenous research protocols and methodologies that are ethical, respectful, and empowering. For above all else, indigenous research should be about healing and empowerment. It should involve the return of dignity and the restoration of sovereignty, and it should ultimately bring formerly colonized communities one step further along the path to self-determination. We should think on these factors as they apply to our own research, and if and when we decide to proceed, we should do so humbly, in an effort to serve.

NOTES

This is reprinted with permission of *Contemporary Issues in Early Childhood*, in which an earlier version was published in Volume 2, Number 1, 2001.

1. For a discussion of the "unhomeliness" engendered by the colonial encounter and its disruption of familiar meanings and identities, see Homi Bhaba (1994).

2. While I am aware of the controversy surrounding the postcolonial concept of "hybridity" and the term's racist, imperial roots, following Homi Bhaba (1994) and Robert Young (1995) I use the term deliberately in an effort to reclaim the concept for liberatory ends.

3. *Sous rature*, a term usually translated as "under erasure," is one of the central concepts in the work of deconstructionist Jacques Derrida (1976). To put a term *sous rature* is to write a word, cross it out, and then print both word and deletion. Because the word is inaccurate, or rather inadequate, it is crossed out; because the word is necessary, it remains legible.

4. The term palimpsest, from the Greek *palimpsçstos* "rubbed again," refers to writing material, such as a parchment or tablet, that has been written on or inscribed several times after the earlier writing has been rubbed or papered over, but never completely erased.

REFERENCES

Afaga, L. B. and M. K. Lai. (1994). *Evaluation of the State of Hawaii Department of Education's Hawaiian studies program.* Honolulu: Curriculum Research and Development Group.

Bauer, H. (1982). *Hawaii the Aloha State.* 2d ed. Honolulu: Bess Press.

Bhabha, H. K. (1994). *The location of culture.* London: Routledge.

Derrida, J. (1976). *Of grammatology.* Baltimore: Johns Hopkins University Press.

Fanon, F. (1963). *The wretched of the earth.* New York: Grove Press.

Foucault, M. (1970). *The order of things: An archaeology of the human sciences.* Trans. A. Sheridan. New York: Pantheon.

Foucault, M. (1972). *The archaeology of knowledge*. Trans. A. M. Sheridan Smith. New York: Pantheon.

Foucault, M. (1979). *Discipline and punish: The birth of the prison*. Trans. A. Sheridan. New York: Vintage.

Greenblatt, S. (1989). Towards a poetics of culture. In H. A. Veeser (Ed.), *The new historicism* (pp. 1–14). New York: Routledge.

Hawaii the Aloha State. (1974). Honolulu: W.W. Distributors.

Loomba, A. (1998). *Colonialism/postcolonialism*. London: Routledge.

Marx, K. (1977). *Capital: A critique of political economy* (Vol. I). Trans. B. Fowkes. New York: Vintage. (Original work published 1867).

O'Hanlon, R. and D. Washbrook. (1992). After Orientalism: Culture, society, and politics in the Third World. *Comparative Studies in Society and History, 34*(1), 141–167.

Prakash, G. (1992). Can the "subaltern" ride? A reply to O'Hanlon and Washbrook. *Comparative Studies in Society and History, 34*(1), 168–184.

Pukui, M. K., E. W. Haertig, and C. A. Lee. (1972). Nānā i ke Kumu *(Look to the source)*. Vol. II. Honolulu: Hui Hanai.

Said, E. (1993). *Culture and imperialism*. London: Chatto and Windus.

Seiden, A. (1985). *Hawaii the Aloha State*. Honolulu: Island Heritage.

Smith, L. T. (1999). *Decolonizing methodologies: Research and indigenous peoples*. London: Zed Books.

Spivak, G. (1990). Questions of multiculturalism. In S. Harayasam (Ed.), *The postcolonial critic: Interviews, strategies, dialogues* (pp. 59–60). New York: Routledge.

Te Awekotuku, N. (1992). *He whiriwhiri wahine*: Framing women's studies for Aotearoa. *Te Pua* 1, 46–58.

Young, R. J. C. (1995). *Colonial desire: Hybridity in theory, culture and race*. London: Routledge.

Zizek, S. (1991). *Looking awry: An introduction to Jacques Lacan through popular culture*. Cambridge: MIT Press.

CHAPTER TWO

Silent Screams: Deconstructing (Academia) the Insider/Outsider Indigenous Researcher Positionalities

MIRYAM ESPINOSA-DULANTO

There are three goals for this chapter. First is to present different stages of the discussion on who gets to be a native/indigenous versus a foreigner/outsider. Following that is a brief reflection on the issues of power and paradoxical situations presented when using hegemony for understanding the native/outsider unit. The last goal is to work with fiction as an alternative tool to illustrate historical changes and border crossings.

TELLERVO

Once upon a time, there was a tall, luscious, full-of-ripe-fruit tree, her name was Tellervo. Her only purpose was to stand upright protecting us, the children of Pinky-Times. Under her shadow, boys and girls came to have their morning snack, their afternoon nap, and their all-day laugh. Tellervo grew taller, powerful, pushing her roots deep inside Mother Earth for her daily nourishment, the town sounds of peace and happiness. For Pinky-Timers, nothing was more beautiful, peaceful, and powerful than Tellervo, the tall, luscious, full-of-ripe fruit tree. She was a safe haven from earthquakes, floods, droughts, sadness, and loneliness. One just needed to come closer to feel the goodness coming from the tree. Tellervo gave out protection and peace.

One day, a group of people, the Progress-and-Changers, came to town with many strange, loud things called digging machines. They were fast-pacers, eagerly digging the soil, stopping only when a geyser of dark, heavy liquid came from the Earth's insiders. The Progress-and-Changers were so thrilled with their achievement that they invited more people to join them. Amazingly, their pace got faster and faster, building and digging, digging and building. They put together large homes with many more rooms than people living in them. In exchange for our land, little green papers with old men's pictures and numbers on them. Money, they called it.

Pinky-Times became a lot more noisy, more populated, adding one more geyser of dark and heavy liquid every so often, but still, there was enough space for everyone. Suddenly, Tellervo began to curl up all over, losing her leaves and shining greenness. That was different! We didn't know what to do. So, we sat around her. Tellervo couldn't get her nourishment, her roots were debili-tated from the dark, heavy geysers that were surrounding her. Use your money! the Progress-and-Change people told us. So, we put all the green papers around the tree and waited for the money to work, to give Tellervo back. Tellervo was the only thing we wanted, so we waited. And, waited. And, waited more. She became a small, dark, coil, millenarian reliquia, a re-minder of our rosy times. A hundred years have passed and in Pinky-Times, we still are waiting. How much longer do we need to wait? What else do we have to do to get Tellervo back? (Adapted from M. Espinosa-Dulanto, 1999)

The *Tellervo* story is a fictionalized narration that could be applied to a variety of cultural encounters. It explains the intrinsic ties between cul-tural traditions, social agency, and social awareness. There is also the real-ization that encounters between civilizations transform individuals and societies in so many levels that life as it was understood becomes no longer valid. This is the case of the Americas. In the 1400s, consequent waves of foreign *invaders* arrived to these lands with diverse purposes but under the same ideological umbrella; colonizers declared themselves saviors of the "discovered new" land and its peoples. With the same arrogance that granted the foreigners the savior's title, they classified the native people ei-ther as fauna and flora, or ultra-barbarians or pure savages. These invaders profited both from the *naiveté* as well as from domestic political struggles among the indigenous peoples of the Americas. Thus, rather expeditiously the *invaders* got established, became powerful as they controlled basic re-sources while inscribing newer, different sets of rules that became widely imposed and rendered by all—natives and foreigners—inhabitants of the land (Lockhart, 1983; Pagden, 1990).

In an ideal democratic society as the one pictured in Tellervo, both groups—the Progress-and-Changers and the Pinky-Timers—shared the land and learned to recover, recreate, and reinvent their living environ-ments. Nevertheless, the Americas—as well as the current globalization process—differ remarkably from the idealized society pictured in Tellervo (Abu-lughood, 1990; Rosaldo, 1986). Indeed, the Americas received waves of foreigners but no equal sharing happened; instead the foreigners became its conquerors, its colonizers, and imposed their ways—called religion and civilization—through war and death (Trujillo, 2001). Since the 1400s, any cultural difference from, first the European cannon, now the homogeneous globalized world, was not respected but treated as major disability and needed to be either corrected or eradicated (Escobar, 1984). One dramatic irony (of many) is that the colonizers officially transformed natives into their *protégées*, based on the imposed laws. As such, foreigners were entitled to make decisions over the indigenous peoples' lives, their wealth, and their future. It didn't take long before the colonizers were able to take control over everything they considered of value (Lockhart, 1983; Pagden, 1990).

The following years . . . Big-machine, a tall red-haired Progress-and-Changers newcomer, got pretty sick. His big appetite made him swallow oil-contaminated food. He loved to eat no matter what, so he did it. After a while, Big-machine's only activity was to run to the septic hole and, soon enough, he was covered by his own inmundicia because he couldn't run fast enough. He gobbled blue, red, gold, and transparent pills but nothing gave him any relief.

Margarita-flor was there all the time. She knew Big-machine from the time when all Progress-and-Changers arrived in town. Margarita-flor was not Big-machine's partner but she did everything at his home except for shar-ing his oil-money or his oil-food. Margarita-flor did everything as having two children by him, a boy—Little-Big-machine, and a girl—Little-Margarita-flor. They were part of the Littles. The ones who had no personal names because there were no names for their kind, these children were neither Pinky-timers nor Progress-and-Changers. There were many more Littles wondering around town. Who may they be with? No one knew how to act, what to teach, or what to do with their Littles. Sometimes, they look and act as any Pinky-Timer but other times they were soooooooooo different. Big-machine need not worry; he died in his smelly bed leaving Margarita-flor with the little ones inside his huge, almost empty house (Espinosa-Dulanto, 2002).

Thus, the traditional discussion of what is "indigenous"—as the only truthful inhabitants of the land, who are the colonized—versus what is ex-ogenous—including outsiders, invaders, Western ravagers, who are the colonizers—gets more complicated when adding into the discussion an-other group, the mixed breed—the *Mestizos*, the offspring of intergroup unions who are both, insiders/outsiders as well as a group on their own. As a *Mestiza* myself, I ask: Where should *Mestizos/as* be placed in this dis-cussion and controversy? Are we considered indigenous, colonized? Or exogenous, colonizers? Or, as in our breed, should we be considered both and maybe be supported and recognized in our heterogeneity and agency?

Furthermore, in this often problematic debate, indigenous—truthful inhabitants vs. exogenous—dominant Westerners gets even more entangled when taking into consideration issues of power within and outside the groups' borders. Currently, with the worldwide flow of information, capital, people, and goods, it may seem that a homogeneous global culture is arising—as presented by the transnational industries' eagerness to develop a global market for their products, (i.e., Coke, McDonalds, Disney, Nike). Imagining a "global culture" implies a wiping out of diversity, local traditions, cultures, and identities, as well as eliminating the differentiation between what is indigenous and exogenous (Inda and Rosaldo, 2002). Then, the world becomes one with homogeneous access and capability to buy internationally marketed goods.(Gwynne and Christobal, 1999).

The absurdity of this proposal, however, is shown daily when the global homogenization tendency points increasingly to a differentiation and reconstitution of "the" local (Castillo and Nigh, 1998). In the Americas, a multitude of traditions, cultures, and identities—that is, Mayans, Machiguengas, Quechuas, Kayapos, and Mestizos/as—are recreating, reacquiring, and transforming their local spaces where people become both, engaged and released by the global economy through the worldwide flow of information, capital, people, goods, and exogenous/Western cultural values.

I follow Gramsci's (1971) position on hegemony to understand the roles played by the diverse groups—colonizers/colonized and/or indigenous/exogenous—"to explain how and why subordinate groups accept as legitimate the power of the dominant, so that coercion is coupled with consent" (Gal 1989). Hegemony is not only inflected by the dominant group but also requires the subordinate groups' consent, which dialectically produces counterhegemony and social agency. All these forces are in constant struggle to change the hegemonic patterns and constantly build on each other. It is the local, as social agent, with its unplanned, displaced traditions and differences that would derange the order of the homogeneous-hegemonic plan (Lears,1985; Mouffe,1979).

As a way to conclude this section, I want to bring back the voice of a non-pure indigenous, a *Mestiza* rejected and discriminated against by all sides regardless of the fact that, as a mixed breed, a *Mestiza* shares the same mind, flesh, and feelings that the multiple "pure" groups he or she comes from (Anzaldúa, 1987; Behar, 1993). Similar to the "Littles" of Pinky-Times, the *Mestiza* is one who mirrors the contradictory times we live. The individual never feels complete not because she or he lacks an identity but because she or he has a multiplicity of sometimes contradictory identities—or, as in my own case, not because I have several languages but because I cannot comprehend the traditional sounds of my Muchik heritage.

MECHERRAE CHAEMA (LADY CHAEMA)

There is so much pain while writing in a language that is not one native's tongue, but that pain can't be compared to the unbearable fact of not having the option to write in one's native tongue because it was banned by each of the hegemonic forces in turn. Then, its sounds and teachings were denied and, over time, the language of the ancestors, the language in which Muchik traditions were immersed, was lost and has not been spoken at large.

Mecherrae Chaema's answers are silent screams. A response to the hegemonic powers that were responsible for taking her sounds away even before her grandparents grandparents were born, even before her heritage-line was begun. Here it comes. It is *Mecherrae Chaema*'s silent scream— the sound of the words she can feel but was not allowed to learn.

For *Chaema* growing up was a beautiful task with no conscience of how much that beauty weighted in other people. *Chaema* was lucky; she was surrounded by caretakers who showed her nothing but the comfortable side of life. She learned that Western meant modern and likeable but with one set of rules and traditions, the "good" ones. She lived among them looking/acting like a Westerner while receiving loving care from brown women. Having her weeks spent in the all-girls Catholic boarding school and her summers and weekends submerged in brown sand and life. That is how *Chaema* grew up to be a *Mestiza*, a woman from the borderlands. A woman of mixed blood and heritages who was denied the language of her Muchik ancestors and was taught only Spanish together with Western ways and "civilized" rules brought by the European colonial powers through her grandparent grandparents.

This *Mestiza*, *Mecherrae Chaema*, spoke only Spanish but understood the feelings, the sounds, and the smells of the native ocean-desert from which she learned the significance of love in the Muchik sense. How can anyone forget the traditions that came in beautiful dreams with unknown beings? Or the senses exuded by Nin-eng on her disputes to protect *Mecherrae Chaema* from the other elements? Or the desert with its intrinsic life hidden to neophyte eyes? How could anyone deny that behind *Chaema*'s light skin and Western "civilized" modes were the Muchik powers taking care of her life?

She cannot speak Muchik, but Chaema is not quiet! She has the power of her voice, she has reclaimed her story and tells it louder and louder . . . this time the powers are obligated to hear. Mecherrae Chaema masters the colonizers' languages and her story is told in Quechua first, Castellano later, and English now (Espinosa-Dulanto, 2002).

Who is this *Mestiza*? Who is this *Mecherrae Chaema*? A woman who was born and grew up in one of the driest desert areas of the world, the northern coast of Peru, a *costeña*, a *norteña*. *Mecherrae Chaema* is also a

Latina, sometimes Hispanic, always a wetback foreigner in the United States, and occasionally a professor in charge of a teaching program in a major U.S. research university. What is in *Mecherrae Chaema*'s heart? The pain of being a nonspoken Muchik, with diluted blood, because in Western terms she is a mixture of many races, ethnicities, worldviews—in which the powerful colonizers are included. That is the inheritance of a *Mestiza*, full of contradictions, guilt, and pride (Anzaldúa, 1987).

In this section, I elaborated on adding layers into the traditional discussion on who gets to be a native/indigenous versus a foreigner/outsider. As an outcome of using hegemony, counterhegemony, and social agency as analysis tools I presented a brief reflection on power issues within and outside groups' borders. Through the section, I work with fiction as an alternative tool to better illustrate historical changes and border crossings. In short, I hope for this section to be a celebration of difference, social agency, and multiplicity represented by the mixed breed, the *Mestiza*, the *Mecherrae Chaema*, and the *Littles* of the world—a celebration of *Mestiza* identity/ies in which contradictions and confusion are not problems but requirements to survive.

REFERENCES

Abu-lughood, L. (1990). The romance of resistance: Tracing transformations of power through Bedouin women. *American Ethnologist, 17*(1) 41–55.

Anzaldúa, Gloria (1987). *Borderlands: La Frontera. The new Mestiza.* San Francisco: Aunt Lute Books.

Behar, R. (1993). *Translated woman. Crossing the border with Esperanza's story.* Boston: Beacon Press.

Castillo, H., R. High and R. Nigh. (1998). Global processes and local identity among Mayan coffee growers in Chiapas, Mexico. *American Anthropologist* 100(1), 136–147.

Escobar, A. (1984). Discourse and power in development: Foucault and the relevance of his work to the Third World. *Alternatives,* 10(3) 377–400.

Espinosa-Dulanto, M. (1999). *The social complexity hidden under the Hispanic/Latino label: Mestiza genres as a proposal for teaching.* Unpublished dissertation, University of Wisconsin–Madison.

Gal, S. (1989). Language and political economy. *Annual Review of Anthropology, 18,* 345–367.

Gramsci, A. (1971). *Selections from the prison notebooks.* New York: International Publishers.

Gwynne, R. and K. Cristobal. (1999). *Latin America transformed: Globalization and modernity.* New York: Oxford University Press.

Inda, J. and R. Rosaldo. (2002). *The anthropology of globalization*. Malden, MA: Blackwell Publishers.

Lears, J. (1985). The concept of cultural hegemony: Problems and possibilities. *American Historical Review*, 90(3), 567–593.

Lockhart, J. (1983). *Early Latin America: A short history of colonial Spanish America and Brazil*. New York: Cambridge University Press.

Mouffe, C. (1979). Hegemony and ideology in Gramsci. In C. Mouffe (Ed.), *Gramsci and Marxist theory* pp. 168–204. London: Routledge.

Pagden, A. (1990). *Spanish imperialism and the political imagination: Studies in European and Spanish-American social and political theory, 1513–1830*. New Haven: Yale University Press.

Rosaldo, R. (1986). When natives talk back: Chicano anthropology since the late sixties. In *Renato Rosaldo. Lecture Series Monograph*, Vol 2, Series 1984–1985:3–20. Tucson: Univiversity of Arizona.

Trujillo, C. (2001). *By the sword and the cross: The historical evolution of the Catholic world monarchy in Spain and the New World*. Westport: Greenwood Press.

CHAPTER THREE

Performing Colonial and Postcolonial Science in India: Reenacting and Replaying Themes in the United States

GEETA VERMA

In the process of writing this chapter, I have come to recognize that my writing is becoming one of the many forms of therapeutic expression of my experiences. Here, I speak with two voices. The first is that of an immigrant intellectual placed in the center of the technological and industrial world. In pursing the two themes of hybridity and duality (postcolonial subject, woman, and science educator), I have tried to make sense of the conflicted biography of being born and educated in the periphery and coming into academic practice as an immigrant intellectual beginning to operate in the imperial center—the United States.

The second voice is that of an academic whose formal education was in a former British colony, India. I was born in India and at the age of fifteen was 'guided' by my parents, teachers, and other stakeholders interested in my future to opt for the science track in high school. At that time, it appeared to be a rational decision because I was a student in excellent academic standing. However, I did not realize that being a woman and a person of color would have strong implications for my successes, failures, or alienation in the perceived "inherently neutral nature of science" (Abraham, 1998). Historically and traditionally, science has kept marginalized groups, including women, people of color, and slaves at the periphery. At any cost, there was no turning back for me after that decision. I became a student of science and received my initial training to be a scientist.

During my formal and informal cultural life in education and society, I started noticing various missing pieces of a puzzle. I suppose that these pieces reveal the connections that are a part of everyday existence of a post-colonial subject. Education was one of the many sites for the transaction of competing needs, desires, and interests of the metropole and the indigene (McCarthy, 1998). Most of the curriculum content in science, many school rituals, and most end-of-the-year examinations pointed to a "black hole" that was not a part of my "being." Yet my whole educational and professional career was more or less driven and controlled by the results of my performance on the criteria housed in this black hole. The black hole to me represented the "eye of the power" (Bhabha, 1994) and I was one of the postcolonial subjects who still had to deal with the remnants of this power as a result of the long history of British colonialism in India. It was a long and tedious journey, but it gave me an opportunity to visit many places of wonder and amazement. Thus, I feel confident to speak of matters of cultural hybridity firsthand.

This chapter begins with a brief historical background of precolonial, colonial, and postcolonial science in India, weaving themes around science and science education in these periods/times. The second part of the chapter is an exploration of the interconnecting themes between science in colonial and postcolonial India and a strong yet feasible argument that similar themes are now being replayed and reenacted in science education in the United States through various current reform movements such as Science for All Americans. My argument is based on observations by other scholars (e.g., McCarthy, 1998) that it is a result of blurring of boundaries between the metropolis and the past colonies through the two-way traffic between the metropolis and the colonial subjects (e.g., for scientists and educators). Unlike the colonial phase, the traffic has increased more from the direction of the colonial subjects to the metropolis and relatively more postcolonial voices are now present and audible on the post postcolonial horizon.

SCIENCE IN PRECOLONIAL INDIA

For those familiar with the ancient and medieval history of India, it will be easy to understand that it is extremely difficult and an almost impossible task to present a coherent picture of the long history of science that was prevalent in precolonial times in a brief section of a book chapter. First of all, "science and technology" did not constituent an analytically different domain, but instead were woven with the other institutions of society (Baber, 1995). A few examples may illustrate the deep-rooted existence of science and technology in precolonial India.

One of the most interesting of the early accounts of medical practice is a detailed description of the indigenous method of inoculation against smallpox in eighteenth-century India. British observers noted that the practice of inoculation known by the people of India as *tikah* was in existence for about one hundred fifty years before the arrival of British in the eighteenth century. The process included rubbing and creating a shallow wound in the skin of a person caused by dry friction and thereby swabbing it with a linen rag charged with "varioulous matter" (Baber, 1995). British observers further noted that the medical practitioners were aware of the causative principles underlying smallpox and the practice of inoculation, thus it is safe to conclude that it must have been originally founded on the basis of rational principles and experiments.[1]

The production of Indian steel or "Wootz" provides an example in the field of mining and metallurgy. British observers found that method of producing crucible-cast steel was discovered and perfected in India. They further noted, "It appears to admit of a harder temper than any thing we are acquainted" (Baber, 1995, p. 65). It was concluded that although the method of steel production was not based on any explicit knowledge of modern theoretical chemistry, the method of roasting iron was perfected based on years of experimentation, improvisation, and the accumulation of empirical knowledge.

Other fields in science, technology, and mathematics that include a list of Indian contributions would include: trigonometry, the concept of sines, the concept of zero and the modern numeral system, the concept of power technology, the cotton gin, the "parallel worm" rolling mill, the toe stirrup, the drill plough, and crucible-cast steel (Baber, 1995). In summary, one can confidently say that precolonial India was hardly a tabula rasa in the field of science and technology, as portrayed by various British historians.

SCIENCE IN COLONIAL INDIA

The advent of British rule in India, through the activities of the East India Company in the nineteenth century, led to a great many scientific surveys and explorations in India. Many scholars have argued that they were "of high scientific value yet they only symbolized the 'colonial science' and tended to accelerate the expansion of British imperialism" (Sangwan, 1984, p. 172). In 1813, the British rule decided to invest a sum of at least one lakh rupees (approx. $2000) for the purpose of the introduction and promotion of the knowledge of science among Indians residing in the British territories in India (Sangwan, 1984). Interestingly, until 1813, the East India Company had pursued a defensive policy with an oriental bias, but failed to embed the oriental educational practices in the newly emerging

Indian educational system, supported and perpetuated by the British government. These failures were due to many educational practices forced on the Indians by British administrators such as Lord Macaulay and Charles Wood. The practices "were not aimed at making them [Indians] scientist or inventors, but to create a loyal class of Indians, a class of Indian in blood and color, but English in taste, and opinions, and morals, and intellect" (Sangwan, 1984, p. 179).

It is, however, evident that the East India Company *government* did impart some education in medicine and technical matters to its Indian subjects. However, scholars such as Sangwan (1984) have argued that the colonial and commercial interest mired the real essence of medical and engineering education from the Indian students. It has been argued that the increasing pressure of imperial designs necessitated training and education of Indian students. For example, the usefulness of natives in various surveys and public work projects led to their training in these branches, hence survey schools[2] and engineering institutions[3] came into existence. The increased enrollment of Indian students in the engineering and medical colleges led to molding of students more into assistants and subassistants in the concerned departments.[4] The consistent argument that has emerged out of this discussion is that the imparting of scientific-technical education among Indians was not an end in itself, but a means of attaining specific interests.[5] Thus, preference was given to such branches of science and technology that could yield immediate results in abundance.[6] It can therefore be safely concluded that the education that the company decided for India, while it led to the overflow of job seekers in government departments, caused a paucity of talent in science.[7]

Prakash (1992) has also argued that, to the British, India was an ideal locus for science: it provided a rich diversity that could be mined for the knowledge and, as a colony, offered the infamous "elbow room" for an unhindered pursuit of science.[8] Equally important in the rise of these institutions was the conviction that India needed a new form of knowledge. Furthermore, it appeared that the company officials deliberately neglected the Indian classical sciences. They started denouncing and criticizing Indian (both Hindu and Muslim) heritage of science and science education (Sangwan, 1984). The British stated the matter plainly in 1874: "Local officers must be able to recognize with precision the various grains and other products of their districts, to enable them to deal with agricultural statistics in an intelligent manner. At present it is almost ludicrous to observe . . . how often the same things are called by different names, and different things by same names."[9]

The crusade launched by Charles Grant in 1872[10] reached its climax in 1835 when Macaulay completely sidelined the claim of oriental learning. It is thus apparent that the East India Company did not pursue a coherent and cohesive science policy. Consequently, science failed to emerge as a formidable force, 'an organized institution', but rather developed in fragments, again depending on the politicocommercial needs of the imperialists. In addition, an absence of an internal organization in science made it dependent on individualistic enterprise and ability; hence science remained an "individualistic romance with nature" (Prakash, 1992).

This leads us to believe that what the company government had aimed at was "production science," that is, science for profit and maximum exploitation of local resources (Alam, 1977, p. 5). Applied science and the new science-based-technology in fact became indispensable tools in the creation and consolidation of Britain's economic hegemony (Macleod, 1975), hence the steering wheel of the imperial ship. Focusing on the development and application of the biological and geological sciences in the colonies therefore became the clearest example of colonial science.[11] Furthermore, the British adopted a definite bias against the Indian scientific heritage. In the subsequent uneven interaction of the two cultures, India lost its originality with the sad consequence of intellectual colonization (Rahman, 1983).

Abraham (1998) has presented a development schematic model by George Basalla that addresses the important issue of the status of colonial science as a result of intellectual colonization. Basalla's diffusionist model suggests that the growth of Western science in different national settings was characterized by three phases, each marked by the degree of autonomy reached by local scientific institutions. The model argues that from its origins in the West, science spread over the world as a by-product of Western expansion and imperialism. "Colonial science," the intermediate phase, was a period when some scientific activity took place in the colonies, but was still dependent on metropolitan institutions and scientists. "Basalla's typology has helped reinforce the idea that the science practiced in most non-Western settings—read colonial science—is derivative, inferior, and has yet to reach acceptable—read Western—levels of quality" (Abraham, 1998, p. 35). India therefore lost on both fronts, whereby its own scientific tradition was discarded and the new science remained the privilege of the whites with colonial ethos and color-consciousness[12] eclipsing the evolution and proliferation of Western science in India.

SCIENCE IN PRE-AND POST-INDEPENDENT INDIA

There were three basic reasons for furthering the interest of scientific research in India before independence. First, the political community involved in the freedom movement was conscious of the role and value of science and technology in development (Qureshi, 1984). Second, the aftermath of World War II had created the conditions for scientific research in India. The British empire has successfully rooted out the local resources and industries and made the country more or less dependent on finished products made with the industrialized production. However, there were widespread protests against the use of imported goods and materials in order to generate employment opportunities for the local people. In addition, the war interfered with the international communication and it became difficult to get finished products from Britain. Third, the British had already known fully well that they would have to leave the country soon and a base for science in India to develop and produce certain strategic materials within India was necessary for their own interest.[15] The emergence of organized scientific policy with the participation of the enlightened Indians facilitated the process.

The practicing of scientific research in India after independence, however, faced major problems. Some of these problems were lack of research facilities in general; in particular, widespread neglect of scientific research in the universities because they were ill equipped and understaffed; the poor state of the traditional industry that had suffered greatly at the hands of British policy of discouraging local industries; and the trust and continued dependence of Indian political leaders on the British empire. The leaders sought help of the British as advisors, offered them important positions, and even preferred the British scientists to continue as the heads of some of the scientific research institutes with the most tangible benefit to the British being the import of British technology by India. This was possible because there was strong base of science and technology in India. The point to keep in mind is that an overlay of British values and traditions and their dominant manifestations of the behavior of Indian intelligentsia continued even after independence. Chatterjee (1986) has also recognized the fact that "nationalist thought in India challenged the claim that the colonized were inferior, but concurs that nationalists nevertheless accepted the premises of modernity on which colonialism was based" (p. 20).

Abraham (1998) has pointed out that despite the presence of financial stringency, lack of technical experience, and the lack of traditions in experimental sciences the cosmic-ray research started to instill confidence in young Indian scientists, as observed by Bernard Peters.[16] This confidence was gained by the fact that "they could achieve scientific results, of the very first order, in no way inferior to those obtained elsewhere, by means of hard work and devotion and by means of their own ingenuity" (Abraham, 1998, p. 45) and thus were able to establish deep scientific traditions in India. In other words, the idea of international credible self-reliant experimental science slowly became the conceptual possibility for the young physicist(s) and mathematicians working with the renowned scientist

Homi Bhabha. As a result, their practices coincidentally provided a convenient and consistent point of entry into political debates around the needs of self-reliant national development (Abraham, 1998).

The impact of the first cosmic-ray experiments in Bangalore made it possible for the scientists at the Indian Institute of Science to construct an image of their own work that mapped perfectly on to a dominant image of the nationalist thought (Abraham, 1988). Laboratory practice in the scientific world was given tangible expression in political terms—it could be as self-reliant, autonomous, and Indian, operating under harsh conditions of financial stringency and lack of institutionalized and laboratorized traditions, and finally, it was successful according to objective (international) standards. In other words, the line between the laboratory and the world got reformulated in a completely different way. As Abraham (1998) candidly comments, "so successful was the mapping that it may be legitimately asked who seduced whom" (p. 46). Abraham (1998) has further presented a strong argument that developing independent colonial science has more to do with establishing the legitimacy of an independent nation-state rather than the development of deep scientific traditions:

> The laboratory in colonial India was now producing the concrete expression of the scientific state that was yet to be. The metonymic move from the laboratory to the state produced a state that could work like a laboratory—it appeared to give a hard proof to the idea that all that was needed for the strong independent post-colonial state was, adopting Nehru's evocative phrase, to 'make friends with science'. . . . The irony of this powerful move from the laboratory to state is that in their foregrounding of India's physical resources and geographic location as the stimulus to the ingenuity, the Bangalore scientists could be described as doing 'colonial science'. . . . While writing a different script for their work, both Bhabha's and the colonial scientists' scientific raw material was of the same qualitative essence: their common question, 'what could 'India' do for science?' (p. 46)

This analysis is further supported by the final stage of development in Basalla's diffusionist model, called national science, when national institutions acquire sovereignty over local scientific practices, academics, and journals. Basalla's diffusionist theory helps produce the idea that the same thing—science—can exist in different places and can look different. In other words, in the metropolis they 'do theory' and in the colony they gather data. This reinforces the existence of difference, a difference between colony and metropolis, yet we know that science, by its own self-representation, is a unified field of knowledge. Overcoming this contradiction is possible only when we realize first that Basalla's model helps to create the categories of 'colony' and 'metropolis' as places where different rules apply to the same object, science. We then realize that if the same thing, science, is practiced in both places and yet science looks different in the colony and metropolis, it can only be due to the scientists themselves. Through this argument, Basalla falls back on and reinforces the impression of colonial scientists as derivative practitioners, not quite up to the standard of their metropolitan colleagues, valued more for the data they provide than the possibility of theoretical breakthroughs. Indeed, Abraham (1998) states that "once scientists enter the frame, 'colonial' becomes a euphemism for inferior" (p. 35).

The other theme that needs closer scrutiny is the perception that science is seen as inherently neutral, even if ambivalent, which brings to the fore the individual responsible for its production. In India and elsewhere, even though science was presented as the necessary instrument of national power and a vehicle of development, we find the institution of science and its agents made less credible. While Nehru (the first Indian prime minister after independence) embraced science and its impact on national development, there was s a strong sense of self-sacrifice. The paradox of embracing science and the scientific culture for national development and yet being cautious about the role of science and the scientist arises from the recognition that "the power of science, which was meant to remove the fetters of underdevelopment, is now seen to need a facilitator of its own" (Abraham, 1998, p. 46). Noted scientist Vikram Sarabhai shared his mentor's (Homi Bhabha) view of science as the primary symbol of modernity and privileged means of transformation, but saw science as an elite activity thus needing a facilitator of its own. Taylor (1995) has also used Fanon's[17] central argument in *The Wretched of the Earth* that speaks to transformation of decolonization into neocolonialism with the emergence of new national elites dependent on metropolitan economic linkages (p. 18).

INSTITUTIONALIZATION AND DOMINANCE OF WESTERN SCIENTIFIC DISCOURSE

In order to understand the prevailing nature of dominant discourse in science, it is important to understand the historical development of institutionalization of science as a discipline. Norman (1988) provides a detailed background of the institutionalization of science by way of the Royal Society in England and other academies in Europe. These institutions rendered science a powerful force in Europe's hegemonic projects. It was the scientific establishment that reinforced the widely held notion about the lower status of marginalized groups (women, the lower classes, and the colo-

nized masses). Furthermore, it legitimized and consolidated the dominance of the position occupied by European males at the top of the gender, class, and race hierarchy. As Norman (1998) articulates, "the almost
unassailable position of prestige and the influence attained by science
through its institutionalization was used to legitimize the tendencies of exclusion and dominance manifested in the wider society" (p. 367).

As a result of the institutionalization of science and its dominance, the
claims of scientists were deemed timeless, beyond the influence of culture
and history. The relative inaccessibility of science to would-be critics allowed science to legitimize race and gender inequality and provided objective evidence of the inferiority of marginalized groups (women, lower
class, colonized, enslaved, and homosexuals) by providing an impartial au-
thoritative basis for their semantic encodement (Norman, 1998).

In providing justification for the prejudices and the hierarchical notions of the day, science left no stone unturned. Invoking the common-
place philosophy of the day, the eighteenth-century philosopher Hume
(1740) declared that "the skin, pores, muscles, and nerves of a day laborer
are different from those of a man of quality." Beginning in the eighteenth
century, science constructed race as biological and then proceeded to provide the cephalic indices and other quantitative measures of race superior-
ity and inferiority (Gould, 1981, 1993; Livingston, 1993).

Harvard professor Louis Agassiz (1807–1873), a leading naturalist
and the most prominent American scientist of his day, was an ardent cham-
pion of polygeny. His writings on race, like those of Linnaeus and other
scientists of that period, "expressed popular racial prejudices in scientific
terminology, representing these beliefs as the outcome of dispassionate scientific inquiry" (Norman, 1998, p. 367). The question is whether the current scientific discourses unequivocally present these important and crucial
themes to practitioners and students of science as well as how presentation
of science as an inherently neutral enterprise and devoid of all historical
and cultural biases reinforces and perhaps perpetuates the status quo of
Western science.

AM I BEING FACILITATED TO REENACT AND REPLAY SIMILAR THEMES IN THE UNITED STATES?

The current central theme of science education in the United States is "scientific literacy" or "Science for all Americans." Scientific literacy defines
"what a public should know about science in order to live more effectively
with respect to the natural world" (Rodriguez, 1997, p. 594). Recognizing the importance of cultivating early interest in science, several U.S. reports have been generated for new directions in science education

(National Research Council [NRC], 1996; American Association for Advancement of Science [AAAS], 1993). The National Research Council (NRC, 1996) developed National Science Education Standards (NSES) for grades K–12 (NRC) and the American Association for Advancement of Science (AAAS, 1993) produced Benchmarks for Science Literacy (Project 2061) specifying guidelines for scientific literacy. Both documents have focused on the science knowledge and skills that a literate citizen should possess (Hammrich, 1998).

However, scholars such as Deboer (2000) have cautiously brought our attention the fact that the embodiment of themes for Science for All Americans (AAAS, 1989) are what Western science counts as science, and therefore, scientific literacy is defined solely in terms of Western science. Although, National Science Education Standards (NRC) recognize the contribution of other cultures, they nevertheless reinforce the understanding that Western science is the prominent—read dominant—domain of science, thus bringing with it all the presumptions, assumptions, attributes, and discourses that have been traditionally held by white European males. Lee (1997) has argued that, though 'scientific habits of mind' include a worldview based predominantly on Western tradition seeking to understand how the world works (i.e., describe, explain, predict, and control natural phenomenon), it differs from other ways of knowing, such as personal beliefs, myths, religious values, and supernatural forces.

Lee (1997) has argued that the norms of science instructional practice have significant implications for students from diverse cultures and languages. These students bring with them their own ways of looking at the world that are representative of their cultural and language environment that may be incompatible with, or even contradictory to, the Western science tradition and the mainstream cultural norms. Thus, although the development of scientific knowledge and habits of mind are demanding for most learners, the challenge is probably even greater for students from diverse language and cultures (Lee, 1997). Lee (1997) has further asked very pointed questions such as: "Does the western science tradition count as the proper, or the only domain of science? Do mainstream cultural norms determine instructional practices in science classroom? Do alternative views of science and norms of instructional practice count and, if so, to what extent and in what contexts?" (p. 220).

The key principle guiding the National Science Education Standards (National Research Council [NRC], 1996) is that science is for all students. This principle is one of equity and excellence (Lee, 1997). However, Rodriguez (1997) has questioned the lack of a well-articulated rationale behind that the principle of equity. In other words, he has argued that the NRC deliberately chose a more ambiguous language about the central theme of equity, instead of explaining the need for equity in today's schools and how various minority groups (e.g., women, the poor, and students of first nations, African, and Latino/a ethnic backgrounds) have traditionally been prevented and/or discouraged from pursuing science-related careers. In their present form, the NSES provides no arguments or compelling evidence that would encourage teachers and administrators to reflect critically on how well their students are learning, on how relevant the curriculum is, on the lack of ethnic and gender diversity in their advanced science courses, or on the socioeconomic impact of discouraging diverse learners to pursue science-related careers.

Rodriguez (1997) has further strongly argued and warned us to be aware of the underlying conceptual themes behind the NSES and other policy documents, and urges us to be:

> Aware of how a conservative ideology embodied by 'A nation at risk report' has little to do with school reform and more with school conformity when this ideology equates effective schools with the production of the required elements to sustain a strong military, an oppressive capitalist economy, and the ethnocentric illusion that the predominant cultures values are everyone else's values. (p. 23)

Similar sentiments were echoed by scholars (Prakash, 1992; Sangwan,1984), who argued that the impact of implementation of Western science based on similar themes (survey work needing descriptions, explanations, predictions, and controlling natural phenomenon) led to the emergence of predominantly "production science" that facilitated the consolidation of Britain's economic hegemony and thus led to intellectual colonization in India.

As a science educator working primarily with undergraduate students preparing to be elementary teachers and secondary science teachers, I recognize that radicalized and gendered science exposed by these marginalized discourses has implications not only for who participates and who is excluded from science, but also for the kind of science that is done (Schiebinger, 1993). I understand the stance that mainstream science adopted toward women and non-Western people "perpetuated a system in which those who might have brought new perspectives to the study of nature were barred from the enterprise at the outset, and the findings of science crafted in their absence were used to justify their continued education" (Schiebinger, 1993, p. 70). My gradual transition from being a practitioner of science to an educator is partly due to a firm belief that there should be a clear commitment to increasing the participation in science of hitherto underrepresented groups. For that purpose, we need to understand the historical basis of that exclusion and then we may be able to demonstrate that science has indeed made a break from the practices and ideological commitments that made such exclusion possible.

I feel, however, that my ongoing and future experiences as a science educator in the US academia are and will be more or less influenced and directed by the policy documents such as the NSES. To me, for good or bad, the significant advantage of having to use these policy documents as guidelines in my methods courses is the legitimization of my postcolonial experiences of studying and practicing "colonized science" and now reenacting them in the context of the Western academia. I find it astounding that these policy documents demand and almost give no other choice to me other than the fact that I fall back on my academic experiences and preparation in postcolonial India and thus am able to facilitate the reenactment and replaying of similar themes in the undergraduate science methods courses. As a result of my postcolonial experiences of doing science I do not feel marginalized in these classes; in fact, I feel empowered because of my skills, expertise, and experiences of doing colonized science during my educational training and later as a practitioner. My experiences get further legitimized in these classes when my students look at me in wonder when I demonstrate how most of NSES can be met by practicing the so-called familiar domains of colonized science.

I truly wonder, however, whether my undergraduate students in the science methods course (guided by NSES) will be able to provide viable experiences to their students in their science classrooms in order to transform them into credible producers or consumers of science with a degree of scientific literacy that will enable them to be effective agents of change who will influence science to serve progressive rather than regressive cultural ends. I question the fact that the standards-driven science education will give opportunities to students to see how science had become appropriated by various cultural agendas in the past, whether they will be able to assess the extent to which modern science is still beholden to such agendas. With the experiences of doing standard-driven science, will the students as both consumers and producers of science be in a position to recognize and, if need be, resist modern attempts to appropriate science for undesirable cultural agendas (Norman, 1998)?

Basalla's diffusionist model helps reinforce this perspective of mine further, affirms my understanding, and reinforces my meaning making of this process (Basalla, 1967). The stability of Basalla's diffusionist model depends on the direction of the flows, raw facts, and data moving from the colony to the metropolis, while accomplished scientists and developed institutions flow from the metropolis to the colony. As we have seen in the discussions in an earlier section, colonial science eventually becomes national science—it could not sustain the idea of border crossing during the existence of a hierarchy of scientific spaces. Yet, as we know, these borders are and were crossed often, especially from the colony to the metropolis. In particular, colonial scientists moved from the colony to the metropolis and did not always go back. In the current scenario with respect to scientific research institutions in the United States, we know that many of these top scientific research organizations are run successfully due to continued presence of scientists from postcolonial societies. The question to be asked is that "once these scientists reach the metropolis, what did they do? Can colonial science be performed in the metropolis? How do we know it is still metropolis if there are colonial scientists present" (Abraham, 1998, p. 35)?

I am not a practicing scientist anymore. I am an educator who was trained as a scientist in postcolonial India. I teach the science methods course to undergraduate students and find it rather disillusioning that the presence of standards in the course enhances my level of comfort. I want to rejoice in the feeling as this brings together my past educational training and current professional expectations. However, when I pause to think, I squint my eyes, I rub my forehead, and when I tap my head, I truly want to believe that it is my heightened sense of imagination that I am being the facilitator of reenactment and replaying of the themes of colonial science in a college classroom in the Western academy. I want not to believe my imagination. Should I feel marginalized because I am an immigrant woman of color beginning to operate in the Western academy or should I feel empowered since my training as a scientist in a postcolonial country places me in an advantageous situation in this case?

Perhaps I should feel marginalized because the current reform movements in science education in the United States facilitate my ongoing engagement with colonial science and do not help me make the transition from 'colonial' to 'metropolis' science. Perhaps I should feel empowered because my past experiences place me in an advantageous position compared to my metropolis-educated science educator colleagues, as I feel I am very much at ease with the implementation of standards in my science methods courses. However, I am positive that the feeling of marginalizaton and empowerment in my case will always have a sense of duality and reversibility and that I am never going to feel them at the same time or maybe with the same intensity.

NOTES

1. Baber, 1995, p. 153.

2. The first survey school was founded by Michael Topping, the famous astronomer and surveyor of the eighteenth century, at Guidy (Madras) in 1794. But

it failed to supply the required demand. Consequently, the education in mathematics and trigonometry was started in different colleges. In 1824, a Surveying School was founded in Bombay and courses were added by Lord Auckland in 17 September 1837. Home Public Proceedings (HPP), 24 August 1836, No.14, Public Works Department, P.W.D. (Railway), *Letters from Court*, LFC dt. 16 March 1853. No. 5.

3. Between 1842 and 1847 some attempts were made to add engineering classes at the Madras High School; Hindu College, Calcutta, and Elphinstone Institute, Bombay, but could not materialize due to Court's reluctance and lack of qualified teachers. The first Engineering Institution was founded at Roorke with the initiative of James Thomason, the Lieutenant Governor of the North-Western Province in 1847. Another Engineering College was established in Calcutta in 1856. The Madras and Bombay Engineering Colleges came into existence in 1858.

4. The famous Thomason College of Civil Engineering (Roorkee) allowed Indian students to be admitted only to the lower class (meant for assistants and subassistants), Home Public—*Letters from Court* (HP-LFC) dated 2 June 1852. Likewise, medical education was imparted to Indians only to make them capable of working under European Doctors. HPP, 6 January 1841 No. 37A.

5. The individual exponents of the cause of education in India had specific motives at the back of their plans. While men like Charles Grant Wilberforce, Holt Mackenzie, Elphinston, and John Malcolm wanted to 'civilize' Indian people, there were some like Trevelyan and Cameron who wished to be relieved of the 'old debt' by civilizing the natives. Adam, Trevelyan, and Macaulay had political ambitions, yet some, like Lord Ellenborough, opposed the idea on political grounds. A few in fact wished to diffuse the idea of self-consciousness and liberty among the Indians

6. Introduction of subjects like botany, geology, chemistry, mathematics, and medicine in various colleges and the opening of survey, industrial, and engineering schools and colleges speak of the real motives and policy of the government.

7. Sir Richard Temple observed in 1882 that the undue and disproportionate attention devoted to the literature and philosophy caused the legal, judicial, and administrative professions to be overcrowded, while the scientific and practical professions were starved and neglected

8. Speaking for the opportunity that India offered for scientific inquiry, George Campbell, the governor of Bengal and a noted colonial ethnologist, remarked in 1866: "In fact, it is now evident, that as this country, in a far greater degree than any enquiry, presents an infinity of varieties of almost every one of the great division of the human race, so also there is no lack of able and qualified men to reap this abundant harvest"; *Proceedings of the Asiatic Society of Bengal*, January to December, 1866 (Calcutta, 1867), 46

9. Government of Bengal, Financial Department (Industry and Science), Proceeding no. 2.1, May 1874, India Office Library and Records, London (IOLR), P/186.

10. Charles Grant stated that "Hindus err because they are ignorant, and their errors have never fairly been laid before them. The communication of our

light and knowledge would prove the best remedy for their disorders"; Charles Grant; *Observation on the State of Society etc.* written chiefly in the year 1792; dated 16 August 1797.

11. The late eighteenth- and early nineteenth-century colonial science had development with slight regional variations in the new colonies like New England (America), Canada, Australia, and India. Commercial and military considerations worked as a modus operandi of science policy there.

12. For an interesting account of the development of color-consciousness see Lord Cromer; *Ancient and Modern imperialism* (1910), pp. 123–43. New York, Longman.

13. Sir Francis Bacon, *Advancement of learning* (Everyman's Publications, 1973).

14. Peters was an émigré German-American physicist from the University of Rochester who had left the Unites States after being denounced by Robert Oppenheimer before the U.S. House of Representatives Committee on un-American activities. Bhabha had given him a position at TIFR.

15. Fanon, Frantz, *The wretched of the earth.* Trans. Constance Farrington. (New York: New York University Press, 1968).

REFERENCES

Abraham, I. (1998). *The making of the Indian atomic bomb: Science, secrecy and the postcolonial state.* London and New York: Zed Books.

Alam, A. (1977, December). Imperialism and science. *Social Scientist,* 65, 5.

American Association for the Advancement of Science. (1989). *Science for all Americans: A project 2061 report on literacy goals in science, mathematics, and technology.* New York: Oxford University Press.

American Association for the Advancement of Science. (1993). *Project 2061: Benchmarks for science literacy.* New York: Oxford University Press.

Baber, Z. (1995). *The science of empire: Scientific knowledge, civilization, and colonial rule in India.* Albany: State University of New York Press.

Basalla, G. (1968). *The rise of modern science: external of internal factors?* Lexington, Mass.: Heath.

Bernard, P. (1966). Bhabha and cosmic rays. *Science Reporter,* 3 (10), 455–457.

Bhabha, H. (1994). *The location of culture.* New York: Routledge.

Chatterjee, P. (1986). *Nationalist thought and the colonial world: A derivative discourse?* London: Zed Press, 1986.

Deboer, G. E. (2000). Scientific literacy: Another look at its historical and contemporary meanings and its relationship to science education reform. *Journal of Research in Science Teaching,* 37 (6), 582–601.

Gould, S. J. (1981). *The mismeasure of man.* New York: Norton.

Gould, S. J. (1993). American polygeny and craniometry before Darwin: Blacks and Indians as separate, inferior species. In S. Hardings (Eds.), *The racial economy of science*. Bloomington: Indiana University Press.

Hammrich, P. L. (1998). What the science standards say: Implications for teacher education. *Journal of Science Teacher Education, 9,* 165–186.

Hume, D. (1740). *A treatise of human nature.* (Ed. P. H. Nidditch, 1978). Oxford: Clarendon Press.

Lee, O. (1997). Scientific literacy for all: What is it, and how can we achieve it? *Journal of Research in Science Teaching, 34* (3), 219–222.

Livingston, F. B. (1993). On the nonexistence of human races. In S. Harding (Ed.), *The racial economy of science*. Bloomington: Indiana University Press.

McCarthy, C. (1998). *The uses of culture. Education and the limits of ethnic affiliation*. New York: Routledge.

Macleod, R. M. (1975). Scientific advice for British India, Imperial perceptions and administrative goals. *Modern Asian Studies, 9* (3), 343–384.

National Research Council. (1996). *National Science Education Standards,* Washington, DC: National Academy Press.

Norman, O. (1998). Marginalized discourses and scientific literacy. *Journal of Research in Science Teaching, 35* (4), 365–374.

Prakash, G. (1992). Science "gone native" in colonial India. *Representations, 40,* 154–178.

Qureshi, M. A. (1984). Science and technology in post-independence era: Some issues and problems. In A. Rahman (Ed.), *Science and technology in Indian culture: A historical perspective* (pp. 219–236). New Delhi: National Institute of Science, Technology, and Developmental Studies.

Rahman A.(1983). *Intellectual colonization: Science and technology in West-East relations*. New Delhi: Vikas Publishing House.

Rodriguez, A. J. (1997). The dangerous discourse of invisibility: A critique of the national research council's national science education standards. *Journal of Research in Science Teaching, 34* (1), 19–37.

Sangwan, S. (1984). Science policy of the East India Company in India. In A. Rahman (Ed.), *Science and technology in Indian Culture: A historical perspective.* New Delhi: National Institute of Science, Technology, and Developmental Studies.

Schiebinger, L. (1993). *Nature's body.* Boston: Beacon Press.

Taylor, P. (1995). Rereading Fanon, rewriting Caribbean history. In G. Rajan and R. Mohanram (Eds.), *Postcolonial discourse and changing cultural contexts: Theory and criticism* (pp. 17–32). London: Greenwood Press.

CHAPTER FOUR

Always Already Colonizer/Colonized: White Australian Wanderings

LISA J. CARY

Always Already Colonizer/Colonized
Always Already
Both Colonizer and Colonized
Blurring the boundaries
Unhomed and deterritorialized

From teaching for social justice
To studying the holy trinity
Race, class and gender
Critical theory and pedagogy

Moving countries
Privileged knowing/traveling
Ideas, people, places
High theory consuming

The establishment position
Working to interrupt dominant ways
Creating Other spaces/homes
Present/Past/Post Colonial days

There have been numerous treatises under the umbrella label of post-colonial theory that suggest that only those who are colonized or have been historically subjugated may use this tool authentically. This desire for authenticity highlights the importance of postcolonial theory work for those who have been silenced—although as Spivak (1995) suggests, it is an im/possibility for the subaltern to speak, to be heard in the 'Master's House.' So where does this leave us? By bringing together my studies in poststructural and psychoanalytic theories with my personal/professional wanderings through postcolonial theory I move the emphasis away from the study of the victim to an analysis of the messy terrain the history of colonization left behind that we are all embedded in. I find *me* in the story, in the present manifestations of colonization (institutionally, culturally, socially, and spiritually). With the best of intentions, the idea that postcolonial theory might 'provide' or 'create' space for Other voices and Other theories is as dangerous as the critical guys and gals saying, "We'll give voice to the voiceless." We still exist within institutionally dominant and oppressive colonizing structures. And so I find the notion of working within and against and using strategic essentialism as suggested by Spivak (1995) as well as moving beyond reductive notions of that concept to 'what we can not think without' as an important move (1993).

This work (my personal/profession work) makes use of Spivak's (1993) notion of a 'new politics of reading'—a strategy that does not excuse, or accuse but establishes critical intimacy. "This is the risk that one must run in order to understand how much more complicated it is to realize the responsibility of playing with or working with fire than to pretend that what gives light and warmth does not also destroy" (Spivak, 1993, p. 283).

The risk business is important business and subjectivities change with time, geographic space, and position. We add to our 'selves' as we wander through life. Now, as a 'legitimized' academic, in a valid institution I get to play different games—self-regulating no doubt, but also with more power. I no longer need to authorize my work by overtheorizing (trying to prove to my advisors, search committees, and publishers) that I 'know' the theory. This is why postcolonial theory is so important to me at this point in time. This is why I agreed to write this chapter. I now need to bring my theorizing and my subjectivities together in work that addresses the regimes of truth and the technologies of power while interrupting hegemonic practices and highlighting the way the historical colonial project shapes the spaces we find ourselves inhabiting today. This brings my multiple subjectivities to bear on my personal/professional life.

> The wider significance of the postmodern condition lies in the awareness that the epistemological 'limits' of those ethnocentric ideas are also the enunciative boundaries of a range of other dis-

sonant even dissident histories and voices—women, the colonized, minority groups, the bearers of policed sexualities. For the
demography of the new internationalism is the history of the diaspora, the major social displacements of peasant and aboriginal
communities, the poetics of exile, the grim pose of political and
economic refugees. (Bhabha, 1994, p. 5)

It is who I am, my subjectivity, that led me to postcolonial theory. As
both a literal colonial subject and a white academic in the United States. I
am colonized and colonizer. The multiple places I inhabit within the U.S.
academy are all framed by my alien status and my intellectual vagabondage
(Gilroy, 1993).

What is theoretically innovative, and politically crucial, is the need
to think beyond narratives of originary and initial subjectivities
and to focus on those moments or processes that are produced in
the articulation of cultural differences. These 'in-between' spaces
provide the terrain for elaborating strategies of selfhood—singular
or communal—that initiate new signs of identity, and innovative
sites of collaboration, and contestation, in the act of defining the
idea of society itself. (Bhabha, 1994, p. 2)

Colleagues, even casual acquaintances, ask without hesitation, "How
did you get here?" And whenever I begin to answer (sometimes brutally
short answers, sometimes a narrative), I begin to wonder at the way this innocent inquiry resituates 'home' and reinscribes the center because under-
neath is the assumption that 'here' is the best place, the only place, the
most democratic space to be. However, for the sake of this piece I'll
describe my journey.

Why would anyone leave the pristine ancient wilderness of Australia
(read here the fixed sign of 'Australia as the bush/outback') to live in a
large U.S. city? The fact that I have lived, studied, and taught in three different countries makes me an exotic strange/r. Yet, because I am from an
exoticized, romantic, crocodile-infested (!) place I am a 'desirable' wan-
derer (on walkabout). I grew up in a comfortable upper-middle-class
home surrounded by a loving, humorous, large Catholic/Protestant family. I spent my time reading books—I have always lived in/through books.
I attended Catholic schools and I think it was the 1970s that are to blame.
The theme of the many Catholic candle-lit vigils (picture guitars and im-
provisational prayer) was social justice—we were encouraged to make a difference. The Church politicized me. At a very young age I became
obsessed with issues of justice and equity. However, I wonder now:

CATHOLIC EXCLUSIONS

The Father
(When did I notice the exclusion?)
The Mother
(Is that the only role available?)
The Son
(Hello? What about Daughters?)

Upon completing my undergraduate studies in social studies, English, and world religions, I started teaching in 1986 in a Catholic high school and I often framed my classes around issues of justice and equity. I don't know how many times I showed *Cry Freedom*. At that time apartheid South Africa was the evil colony. However, although I was supportive of aboriginal land rights and other indigenous issues in Australia, I truly didn't realize how successfully Australian society had instituted an informal apartheid, or the effectiveness of ongoing genocidal governmental policies. Looking back, I am sure I was a typical privileged white teacher, with the best of intentions, seeking to save the children from society. I totally removed myself from the equation and worked from the outside, battling societal ills. Of course, at the end of the day I went home to a comfortable house.

CRY

Cry Freedom
        Cry Home
            Cry Silently
                Cry Indigenous Death
                    Cry Australia

In 1994, I left Australia to follow my dream of graduate study and moved to Regina, Saskatchewan, in Canada. From 1994 to 1996 I completed my Master's of Education degree in curriculum, focusing on social studies education. I began to immerse myself in literature and scholarship that supported my 'critical' questioning of society. I found the work of Paulo Freire (1970). I see it in my students now and I remember it myself—the epiphany for students from the dominant culture that comes from reading Freire's work. For me it was the beginning of a journey toward understanding power. He invites us in to consider the subjectivities of the oppressed and the power of the oppressor. I began my interrogation of colonial power through Freire's work. I found myself a most comfortable space in the critical pedagogy realm of thought. I could continue to believe in saving the world, I could continue to believe that I had the answers and that I could lead the sorrowing masses (the poor, women, the homeless) to enlightenment. I shudder to think of this now. But I do re-call my discomfort on numerous occasions when talking with first nation people in the university setting how they generally saw me as an outsider and therefore not as dominant as a white Canadian. Yet, I am white and I always already carry colonial/colonizing power. That was one of my first realizations that as a foreigner I had different spaces to 'talk about race' but that it also meant that the history of genocide and racism I carried with me as a white Australian was erased. This was dangerous stuff—I could be a radical and not have to carry my own subjectivity around with me!

THE CRITICAL CABARET

I am the truth
And maybe even the way
And I'll lead you toward the light
Me and My Critical Mates
Freire, Giroux and McLaren
(Excuse me: Why aren't there any women listed here?)

Anyway, I got really turned on by my studies in social studies education to save the world—critical thinking, democratic citizenship forever. Along the way I had started to read some stuff in feminism but generally I happily immersed myself in unproblematic notions of critical pedagogy. And then I began to collect data for my thesis on the life histories of preservice social studies teachers and how this influenced their decision to teach in this sub-ject. I was 'into' the idea of good teachers and what made them tick. How-ever, I was immediately interrupted in my comfortable space, once again, by one of the participants. Irene was a thirty-nine-year-old, mature student completing her undergraduate degree in social studies education. She stopped me in my tracks and made me think about where I was in all of this? What about my unquestioned position of authority and power as re-searcher? Instead of a 'normal/ized' expected story, she told me a story of abuse and hardship. I was blown away. And long after the thesis was fin-ished I worked on Irene's story as a way into the unarticulated assumptions that had framed my journey to this point (Cary, 1999). She raised in my mind the issue of power. Everything kept coming back to power.

I had a choice of staying in Canada or moving to the United States to do my doctoral work (talk about white privilege). I had not really consid-ered the United States before, because from a colonial point of view, Canada was thought to have a better educational system. Of course, the ul-timate would have been Cambridge or Oxford. But I chose to move coun-tries one more time and found myself in Columbus, Ohio. I'll never forget the four- day drive (yes, I took my time) from Regina, Saskatchewan, to Ohio State University in Columbus, Ohio—marveling at the wealth of this country and its enormous population. So many people and so much noise. OK—Regina was freezing most of the time but it was still a relatively comfortable, sparsely populated colonial/commonwealth type of space. Now I had to negotiate all sorts of new cultural spaces—the most frightening being the health insurance system and the huge monolithic university (the largest in the country). I was exhausted in those first few weeks, spending time at the international students office and walking all over campus to get paperwork, assistantships, enrollment, and so on.

THE KNOWLEDGE FACTORY

An Educational ruin
Negotiating in English
With welcome white skin
An Australian delight
A Diasporic vagabond
Saved by the . . . accent

It was soon clear that the critical theory/pedagogy perspective was not enough. I had more questions than answers now that I was beginning to see myself in all of this—as woman, heterosexual, colonial subject, English language/culture subject. I began to write about notions of citizenship from a postcolonial perspective, highlighting the ways the social construct excluded through gendered and raced discourses (Cary, 2001). Delgado (1999) historicizes exclusionary practices in the social construction of citizenship in his discussion of the raced nature of the citizen as part of a national community:

> In the United States, the current community—the institution to which the argument would hand unfettered discretion regarding immigration policy—is deeply affected by racism and exclusionary practices. For much of our history, a national-origin quota system and, before that, anti-Asian and anti-Mexican laws, kept the immigrants of color low. . . . For much of our history, women and blacks were denied the right to vote or hold office. Higher education was virtually closed to both until about 1960, and in Southern states, Black Codes made it a crime to teach a black to read. . . . 'The community,' then, is deeply shaped by racism, sexism, and xenophobia. This is not only in terms of its demography and makeup but also its preferences and values. (p. 250)

I was most fortunate and privileged at Ohio State University and was encouraged to create a space in the doctoral program within the College of Education to work in both social studies/global education and cultural studies in education (a new program that brought the Birmingham School type of cultural studies approach to education in the United States drawing on feminist, poststructural, psychoanalytic, and postcolonial theories). The Birmingham School (Birmingham, England) was a group of intellectuals and scholars whose work moved the study of society/culture from a structural perspective toward the study of culture (cultural Marxism) and popular culture—thus creating one of the first schools of thought in the field of cultural studies.

I was drawn toward postmodern theories of education. I studied qualitative research and was exposed to the study of folklore. I started to see ways of addressing my colonial self in my work. Postcolonial theory became an integral part of my personal/professional journey toward understanding my multiple subjectivities.

> It is in the emergence of the interstices—the overlap and displacement of domains of difference—that the intersubjective and collective experiences of *nationness*, community interest, or cultural value are negotiated. How are subjects formed 'in-between', or in excess of, the sum of the 'parts' of difference (usually intoned as race/class/gender, etc.)? How do strategies of representation or empowerment come to be formulated in the competing claims of communities where, despite shared histories of deprivation and discrimination, the exchange of values, meanings and priorities may not always be collaborative and dialogical, but may be profoundly antagonistic, conflictual and even incommensurable? (Bhabha, 1994, p. 2)

I was drawn into issues of cultural performance within and against hegemonic structures. I went into my poststructural phase, living through theory about self-regulation, total institutions, and regimes of truth (Foucault, 1980). All this connected nicely to reading postcolonial theory as it was all about 'power'—circulating, fluid, negotiated yet never innocent. A number of theorists have discussed the ways in which culture is sociohistorically constructed and performed through social interactions often involving experiences of domination and subordination within the enlightenment project of colonization and imperialist territorialization. Clifford (1997), Bhabha (1994), Pratt (1992), Kaplan (1996), and Gilroy (1993) have discussed in different ways how the culture is a performative act that is socially and politically inscribed.

Bhabha (1994) in *The Location of Culture* highlights the reinscription of hegemonic discourse through the relativistic discourse of diversity. He suggests that by highlighting the hybridity of cultural performance we may move beyond essentialist discussions of race and culture. Culture, according to Bhabha, is developed performatively through discursive processes. Bhabha aims to disrupt the epistemological assumptions of the hegemonic discourse that silences and erases issues of race from any discussion of culture. He especially highlights the need to focus on difference rather than on diversity that has become a culturally relativistic position—a white solution to the black problem.

Gilroy (1993) discusses the diasporic nature of the construction of the Black Atlantic and disrupts the notions of cultural holism or racial essentialism through a discussion of the ways in which cultural performance is influenced by sociohistorical conditions and political and economic influences—using music to discuss the multiple origins of the music in the "West." His is an anti-anti-essentialist discussion that attempts to trouble realist ontologies and also interrogate the binaries that influence the social construction of race. And a number of other theorists also discuss the socially interactive performative nature of culture as a place from which to disrupt the colonizing mentality of Western knowledge. Pratt (1992) talks of contact zones as another concept of cultural performance in which the social interactions of colonialism and imperialism shaped and continue to shape the cultures of those colonized and the colonizers. Kaplan (1996) talks of various theories that deterritorialize culture as one way of moving beyond static and holistic discussions. In all these re-presentations of culture, a move is made (or attempted) to move any discussion of difference beyond relativistic and reductionist discussions that remain mired in the realist and marginalizing discourses of essentialist traditional discourses.

TRAVELING SUBJECTIVITIES

White Woman as Privileged Position
Colonial Monarch-of-all-I-survey
In Deterritorialized Spaces
Within/Against Colonizing Total Institutions
What interruptions can I make?
Perform my colonizer/colonized self
Witness my Personal/Professional journey
Light the fires and heat the water.

Now, I am in a tenure-track position within the U.S. academy, in a highly respected research institution, on an H1-B (temporary residence visa), working toward permanent residency. The facts about my immigration journey are important as we so often 'race' other foreign students and immigrants as third world people of color (even more dangerous since 9/11). I am 'raced'—but my white self is so privileged that it is almost hidden in its coercive dominating power. I am a colonizer by the very nature of my privileged position within the academy. I am a colonizer because I am white. I am a colonizer because I am a white Australian. I am a colonizer because I only speak one language and that is the language of the historic colonization project. However, this chapter is not meant to present any sort of confessional moment. Rather, I have attempted to tell you how I came to immerse myself in postcolonial theory as a way of negotiating and understanding my colonizing position and to work toward revealing how I myself am colonized.

One of the main ways postcolonial theory has influenced my research has been to trouble my own desire for claims to authentic knowing/experience within colonizing projects (e.g., multicultural education projects and education reform projects—see Cary, 2001). Everything is in danger of colonizing—everything is suspicious. I call this researching postcolonial/ity or postcolonial/ly. It's all about power and colonizing in research and reducing Others (research participants) into knowable subject positions. So I always ask the dangerous question: What work does it do to claim postcolonial authentic spaces? How does race play out in postcolonial theory?

Lather (1996) uses 'trouble' as a move "to problematize or deconstruct a commonsense meaning, in this case, the assumed innocence of transparent theories of language" (p. 543). This is a move away from a realist focus on authenticity and experience in research: "This does not mean that experience does not exist or that it is not important, but rather that the ways in which we understand and express it are never independent of language" (Gavey, 1997, p. 51). By focusing on the ways I have come to know and speak about postcolonial theory/research, this chapter has attempted to both highlight and complicate the foundational assumptions that frame the field of educational research. For example, I have studied the discursive practices surrounding the institutionalization of this theoretical positionality, and I think it is vital that we continue to probe the manifestations of the relations of the power of 'truth' (regimes of truth) as distinct from the forms of dominance. "A discursive structure can be detected because of the systematicity of the ideas, opinions, concepts, ways of thinking and behaving which are formed within a particular context, and because of the effects of those ways of thinking and behaving" (Mills, 1997, p. 17). The study of discourse practices in this project utilizes both a poststructural perspective and a postcolonial perspective to shift the focus away from the critical realist interpretation to a more complicated study of the formation of the subject/culture by looking at the way we live out our lives in this contested terrain of contradictory positions and symbolic exchanges (Lather, 1996).

Mills (1997) talks about the legitimization of knowledge and 'truth' as occurring from a position of dominance when she says, "Colonial power enables the production of knowledge, and it also maps out powerful positions from which to speak" (p. 115). If we then further complicate this with the conceptualization of power as discursive and fluid, using the work of Foucault (1980) and Serres with Latour (1995), we may produce a 'text' that highlights the messy and dangerous construction of subject through the PDS model as discourses shapes our interpretation of text (Mills, 1997).

Research issues include an interruption of the redemptive project of social and educational research (Popkewitz 1998) that so clearly mirrors the salvation projects of Western missionaries in native cultures. The dogma that one must make practical claims that research is useful and will empower is embedded within the unquestioned assumptions of social science and educational research. Popkewitz (1998) goes on to argue that "the particular ideas of progress and redemption inscribed in the social sciences are the effects of power which, when they go unnoticed in contemporary research and policy, may inter and enclose the possibility of change by reinscribing the very rules of reason and practice that need to be struggled against" (p. 3).

Thus, we need to consider Other methods of research and historicize ethnographic claims—to highlight the way power works in research. A number of respected anthropological and sociological scholars have sought to challenge the metanarratives that surround ethnographic representations (Clifford, 1986, 1997; Marcus and Fischer, 1986; Van Maanen, 1995). They believe that by questioning the ethnographic canonical assumptions of truth and reality, traditional practices may be altered and a new ethnography (postmodern ethnography) may arise. However, just what is this new postmodern ethnography? According to Van Maanen (1995):

> the point driven home in these re-presentations is that the group portrayed is anything but isolated, timeless, or beyond the reach of contemporary society. The wistful assumption of 'one place, one people, one culture' no longer holds the ethnographic imagination in check. This is made quite clear in what Marcus (1994) calls the 'messy texts' of a deterritorialized, open-ended, and 'new' ethnography that attempts to foster an idea of how lives around the globe may be contrasted yet still interconnected. Important messy texts do not lament the loss of the anthropological object but, in fact, invent a more complex object whose study can be as revelatory and as realistic as the old. (Van Maanen, 1995, p. 19)

Therefore, postmodern ethnography is about living within the tensions of the 'messiness' of the social text. Ethnography in this light is seen as cultural translation and never fully assimilates difference and thus raises issues of just what is good ethnographic research and the impossibilities of fully 'knowing/knowable' a subject. "The postmodern idea of radical or surplus difference counters the liberal concept with the idea that difference can never be fully consumed, conquered, or experienced, and thus any interpretive framework must remain partly unresolved in a more serious sense than is usually stipulated as 'good manners' in doing interpretive work" (Marcus, 1994, p. 566).

By conceiving of time and space as fluid, with fluctuating boundaries and edges, the new postmodern ethnography may move beyond simplistic representations and respond to the ethnographic crisis. This epistemological transformation requires a state of flux philosophy, such as described in the work of Michel Serres. Destabilizing and disrupting essentialist assumptions provide possibilities for other ways of knowing. Bringing together time and 'networks of knowing' challenges ethnographers to an increased awareness of the fluctuation and bifurcation of cultural understanding. In this way progressivist notions of culture that have been immersed within linear time analyses are deconstructed and the search for an authentic truth is interrupted (Serres with Latour, 1995):

> We conceive of time as an irreversible line, whether interrupted or continuous, of acquisitions and inventions. We go from generalizations to discoveries, leaving behind us a trail of errors finally corrected—like a cloud of ink from a squid. "Whew! We've finally arrived at the truth." It can never be demonstrated whether this idea of time is true of false. (p. 48)

Once it is accepted that cultures are not static but fluid and the im/possibilities of fully knowing the subject are highlighted, cultural representation is complicated (Serres with Latour, 1995):

> Time does not always flow according to a line . . . nor according to a plan but, rather, according to an extraordinarily complex mixture, as thought is reflected stopping points, ruptures, deep wells, chimneys of thunderous acceleration, rendings, gaps—all sown at random, at least in a visible disorder. Thus, the development of history truly resembles what chaos theory describes. Once you understand this, it's not hard to accept the fact that time doesn't always develop according to a line and thus things that are very close can exist in culture, but then line makes them appear very distant from one another. Or, on the other hand, that there are things that seem very close that, in fact, are very distant from one another. (p. 57)

Therefore, the new postmodern ethnography sees time as a chaotic percolation that raises the possibilities of multiple, fluctuating ways of knowing, in multiple locations (a discursive culture). And cultures become "an object, a circumstance, is thus polychronic, multitemporal, and reveals a time that is gathered together, with multiple pleats" (Serres with Latour, 1995, p. 60).

So, Other ways of doing research is one way of looking at this. However, more important, the way I research, framed within a postcolonial perspective and coupled with poststructural theory, has led to a constant reflexivity on how power plays out in research. And more important, it highlights the impossibility of the subaltern speaking. Thus, it goes against the current desire for voice and the call for a return to realism seen in recent meetings of the American Educational Research Association. Another way of looking at research *for* change might be to look at subjugated knowledge and normative narratives. "The narrow epistemic violence of imperialism gives us an imperfect allegory of the general violence that is the possibility of the episteme" (p. 28).

I have also relied on the work of Popkewitz (1998) and his work to interrupt the desire for redemption in research that highlights the im/possibility of the call for empowerment and transformation in critical research. This does not mean we should give up our desire for social change, equity, and an end to colonization—rather it highlights the difficulty of the work and the place of the work. The Western academy is a safe space from which we call for change. It is a powerful place. But it is still a colonizing institution, a total institution, a technology of power. So, when we do our work informed by postcolonial theory we must constantly be aware of place and privilege and power.

As Spivak (1995) states:

> When we come to the concomitant question of the consciousness of the subaltern, the notion of what the work *cannot* say becomes important. . . . 'The subject' implied by the texts of insurgency can only serve as a counterpossibility for the narrative sanctions granted to the colonial subject in the dominant groups. The postcolonial intellectuals learn that their privilege is their loss. In this they are a paradigm of intellectuals. (p. 28)

Race and gender are central to this rethinking of research through a postcolonial lens. Consider the epistemological space of the subaltern female—if the subaltern (male) has no history and cannot speak, then "the subaltern female is even more deeply in shadow" (Spivak, 1995, p. 28). We need to complicate the ways we use and learn from postcolonial theory to encompass race, gender, and heteronormativy. We must be aware of the dangers of relativism in postcolonial theory and the accompanying threat of depoliticizing colonialism. We must refocus on imperialism's ideological aggression (Parry, 1995, p. 38).

Finally, Slemon (1995) reminds us that postcolonial theory has become the tool within a "heterogeneous set of subject positions, professional fields, and critical enterprises" (p. 45). He goes on to suggest that by becoming more tolerant of methodological difference and reflecting on the concept of the postcolonial within the university institution, a more sophisticated and complex approach should emerge.

> However, it is vital to consider the need for material presence of the 'local': so the research and training we carry out in the field of post-colonialism, whatever else it does, must always find ways to address the local, if only on the order of material applications. If we overlook the local, and the political applications of the research we produce, we risk turning the work of our field into the playful operations of an academic glass-bead game, whose project will remain at best a description of global relations, and not a script for their change. There is never a necessary politics to the study of political actions and reactions; but at the level of the local, and at the level of material applications, post-colonialism must address the material exigencies of colonialism and neo-colonialism, including the neocolonialism of Western academic institutions themselves (p. 52).

However:

REMEMBER

It is more than
Local made Global
Or
Global made Local

It is more than
'knowing' colonialism
And
'giving voice' to silenced subalterns

It is
Seeing yourself as colonizer
Colonized.
It is
More.

REFERENCES

Bhabha, H. K. (1994). *The location of culture*. New York: Routledge.

Britzman, Deborah P. (1998). *Lost subjects, contested objects: Toward a psychoanalytic inquiry of learning*. New York: State University of New York Press.

Cary, L. J. (1999). Unexpected stories: Life history and the limits of representation. *Qualitative Inquiry*, 5 (3), 411–427.

Cary, L. J. (2001). The refusals of citizenship. *Theory and Research in Social Education*, 29 (3), Summer, 405–430.

Clifford, J. (1986). Introduction: Partial truths. In James Clifford and George E. Marcus (Eds.), *Writing culture: The poetics and politics of ethnography* pp. 1–26. Berkeley: University of California Press.

Clifford, J. (1997). *Routes: Travel and translation in the late twentieth century*. Cambridge: Harvard University Press.

Delgado, R. (1999). *"Citizenship."* In R. D. Torres, L. F. Miron, and J. X. Inda (Eds.), *Race, identity, and citizenship: A reader*, pp. 247–252. Malden, MA: Blackwell.

Foucault, M. (1980). *Power/knowledge: Selected interviews and other writings, 1972–1977*. Ed. Colin Gordon. New York: Pantheon.

Frankenberg, R. (1993). *White women, race matters: The social construction of whiteness*. Minneapolis: University of Minnesota Press.

Freire, P. (1970). *Pedagogy of the oppressed*. New York: Seabury Press.

Gavey, N. (1997). Feminist poststructuralism and discourse analysis. In M. M. Gergen and S. N. Davis (Eds.), *Toward a new psychology of gender: A reader*. New York: Routledge.

Gilroy, P. (1993). *The Black Atlantic: Modernity and double consciousness*. Cambridge: Harvard University Press.

Kaplan, C. (1996). *Questions of Travel: Postmodern Discourses of Displacement*. Durham, N.C.: Duke University Press.

Lather, P. (1996). Troubling clarity: The politics of accessible language. *Harvard Educational Review*, 66: 525–545.

Marcus, G. E. (1994). What comes (just) after 'post'?: The case of ethnography. In N. K. Denzin and Y. S. Lincoln (Eds.), *Handbook of qualitative research* pp. 563–574. Thousand Oaks, CA: Sage.

Marcus, G. E. and M. J. Fischer. (1986). *Anthropology as cultural critique: An experimental moment in the human sciences*. Chicago: University of Chicago Press.

Mills, S. (1997). *Discourse*. New York: Routledge.

Parry, B. (1995). Problems in current theories of colonial discourse. In B. Ashcroft, G. Griffiths, and H. Tiffin (Eds), *The post-colonial studies reader*, pp. 36–44. (Reprint of *Oxford Library Review*, 9, 1 & 2, 1987). New York: Routledge.

Popkewitz, T. S. (1998). The culture of redemption and the administration of freedom as research. *Review of Educational Research, 68,* 1–34.

Pratt, M. L. (1992). *Imperial Eyes: Travel Writing and Transculturation.* New York: Routledge.

Rosaldo, R. (1999). Cultural citizenship, inequality, and multiculturalism. In R. D. Torres, L. F. Miron, and J. X. Inda (Eds.), *Race, identity, and citizenship: A reader* (pp. 253–261). Malden, MA: Blackwell.

Serres, M., with Latour, B. (1995). *Conversations on science, culture and time.* Ann Arbor: University of Michigan Press.

Slemon, S. (1995). The scramble for post-colonialism. In Bill Ashcroft, Gareth Griffiths, and Helen Tiffin, (Eds), *The post-colonial studies reader,* pp. 45–52. (Reprint from Chris Tiffin and Alan Lawson (Eds.), *De-scribing empire: Post-colonialism and textuality,* London: Routledge, 1994.) New York: Routledge.

Spivak, G. C. (1993). *Outside in the teaching machine.* New York: Routledge.

Spivak, G. C. (1995). Can the subaltern speak? In Bill Ashcroft, Gareth Griffiths, and Helen Tiffin (Eds.), *The Post-colonial studies reader* pp. 24–28. (Reprinted from Cary Nelson and Lawrence Grossberg (Eds), *Marxism and the interpretation of culture.* London: Macmillan, 1988.) New York: Routledge.

Spivak, G. C. (1999). *A critique of postcolonial reason: Toward a history of the vanishing present.* London: Routledge.

Van Maanen, J. (1995). An end to innocence: The ethnography of ethnography. In John Van Maanen (Ed.), *Representation in ethnography* pp. 1–35. Thousand Oaks, CA: Sage.

PART II

*Critical Personal Narratives on
Decolonizing Research Methodologies*

CHAPTER FIVE

"Tell me who you are": Problematizing the Construction and Positionalities of "Insider"/"Outsider" of a "Native" Ethnographer in a Postcolonial Context

DUDU JANKIE

This chapter problematizes the dilemmas and challenges I confronted and worked through in doing my dissertation research (Jankie, 2001), particularly as evident in my role as an "insider" and "outsider" in a postcolonial context. I problematize my role as a Motswana (citizen of Botswana) researching a context that I was an insider to, but at the same time an outsider to. What did I represent in the eyes of the participants? Was I part of them? Was I an outsider? Did I have one foot in Kgololo senior secondary school[1] and another outside as an educator and researcher belonging to a community of educators and researchers beyond this social context? Within this context, was I viewed as an outsider doing insider research? I conclude this chapter by considering the role of an insider/outsider binary in efforts to decolonize the research process.

The primary aim of my dissertation study was to describe and interpret whether Setswana teachers create classroom environments that build on students' personal and community experiences; and whether and how its incorporation or marginalization affected the perspectives of both teachers and students toward incorporating knowledge about the community and community ways of knowing into the curriculum. I further problematized Setswana literacy practices within the current educational reforms in Botswana by examining (a) students' and teachers' perspectives toward incorporating knowledge about the community and students' experiences in the curriculum, and (b) the practices of teachers who are considered "experts" to the discourses that are constructed, acknowledged, and marginalized in Setswana classrooms.

The two secondary classes that formed the focus of this study were selected on the basis of teacher participation. In addition to both teachers being experienced secondary school Setswana teachers, one of them participated at the policy-making level through membership in the Ministry of Education teacher committees. Mr. Tumelo, one of the teachers, was a member of the task force that designed the Setswana senior secondary school teaching and examination syllabi. Similarly, he was a member of the committee that prescribed textbooks for use in secondary school classrooms.

Positioning myself within my study pushed me to consider the pedagogical practices of the two teachers and my interactions with all the research participants in relation to the positionalities I assumed during my dissertation research. This is essential because, although researchers like myself might enter classrooms primarily as learners, seeking to observe, learn, and interrogate classroom discourses, their interactions with participants contribute to the identities that are bestowed on them in the process. It is within the context of the identities bestowed on them, how they perceive themselves and the participants, as well as the roles they assume, that doors are opened or closed for researchers to gain access to the knowledge they are seeking. Participant-observations, semistructured interviews, feedback from participants, and document analysis formed an integral part of the larger study that is the basis of this chapter.

POSITIONING AND REPOSITIONING AS INSIDER/OUTSIDER IN SETSWANA [AND U.S.] CLASSROOMS

Problematizing my positionality/ies pushes me to adopt a self-reflective stance in my research by acknowledging the multiple roles, identities, and experiences I have in relation to the teachers, students, education officers, and community members who participated in my dissertation study. For instance, as a student in Botswana's primary and secondary schools, I experienced the privileged status accorded to English at the expense of Setswana and other local languages. I also observed that Setswana culture and language were not really valued as part of school-based knowledge. Part of these discourses denied my classmates and me opportunities to celebrate and acknowledge our identities by restricting our communication in "native" languages in school, while reinforcing the privileged status of the "queen's language."

Similarly, as a Setswana teacher educator, some of the teachers and prospective teachers I have had conversations with over the years have voiced concerns for being in classes rife with students' negative attitudes and resistance to learning Setswana. English's privileged status as a highly prized commodity was and is still normalized through the roles it is authorized to perform (Bourdieu, 1991) in Botswana's education system. My discursively constituted hybridized identities stem partially from my language or linguistic experiences. Language is a means of identity as much as it is a tool of empowerment and representation. Not only is language central to how knowledge is constructed, authorized, and the purposes it fulfills, it is essential in "working the hyphens" that separates and, at the same time, shapes the relationships, experiences, and interactions of the colonizers and the colonized.

English was a key instrument in the expansion of the British empire and this made it a cornerstone for formulating language education policies. In the process, traditional knowledge systems were "supplanted" by colonizers' knowledge systems such as through the education system. Thus, language is situated in power relations. In theorizing about the role of language in the construction of the African persona/image in postcolonial contexts, Ngugi wa Thiong'o speaks to the African sense of identity and representation as "insiders" and "outsiders" to their "native" languages that they should seek to value as highly prized commodities in authorized national linguistic markets.

Moreover, Ngugi wa Thiong'o (1986) reminds us that African languages are the cornerstone of cultural preservation and the process of decolonizing the mind. Similarly, he cautions us to decenter educational practices that both deny students opportunities to speak their home languages in school and marginalize their experiences and community ways of knowing. In the process, African children might stop seeing the universe from the perspectives of European culture and history. Yet, schooling experiences of individuals like Ngugi wa Thiong'o and his peers who were severely punished for speaking home languages in school and their out-of-school experiences marginalized at a time when most African countries were under colonial rule, serve to illuminate the circulation of discourses on linguistic identities in postcolonial contexts as reflected in my personal experiences and that of many students in Setswana classrooms, including the ones in my dissertation study.

Acknowledging that colonial powers not only marginalized "ways of knowing and the languages for knowing" (Smith, 1999, p. 68) in colonial contexts and further used their languages to marginalize the colonizeds' "cultures, their values, and hence their minds" (Ngugi wa Thiong'o, 1993, p. 31) necessitated that I make choices on the languages to use for my interactions with participants in my study. The choice of language for conducting interviews in particular focused on the questions: should I use Setswana or English or should I let participants choose? Is there a way to use both languages? Do people move back and forth between languages? Do they have a strong preference for using one language? If so, what are their reasons? The complexity of this issue was masked, in that using English meant that I might be less likely to distort the views of participants in writing up the dissertation. In that way, I would avoid the complexities of translation. Yet, at the same time, doing that would privilege English over Setswana, a phenomenon I was problematizing in my dissertation. Consequently, I requested participants to choose language(s) for our interviews. The linguistic currency that most participants legitimated in this context was Setswana for a variety of reasons. They expressed that: (a) Setswana and not English is their mother tongue; (b) they are able to express themselves freely in Setswana; (c) as teachers they teach Setswana; (d) they are more confident in conversing in Setswana than in English; (e) English is a foreign language and there is no need to privilege it over their mother tongue; (f) they have their own language and there is no need to use English in this context; and (g) the interviews sought knowledge related to Setswana education and so it was proper to use Setswana in our interactions. For these participants, choosing to use Setswana was part of naming and constructing their identities through the medium of the national language. In some instances, this was done against the presence of English and thus gave a sense of double consciousness (DuBois, 1994). On the other hand, participants—particularly the students, teachers, and education officers—chose code-switching between Setswana and English as the legitimate discourse for conducting the interviews because it allowed them to articulate ideas or concepts they found challenging in the language they deemed favorable for that purpose. Some attributed this to the fact that code-switching is part of their everyday communication. I believe that the choice to code-switch from Setswana to English or vice versa may also be interpreted as a recognition by the participants of their multiple hybridized identities and realities, some of which may be manifested through language.

My professional identity intersects with my identity as a parent in that, as a mother to two adolescents in secondary school classrooms during the inception and actualization of this study, I learned from my talks with them that students' perspectives about Setswana paralleled some of my own educational experiences in that social context. Likewise, they paralleled the students' views about Setswana literacy instruction as reported by researchers who have examined Setswana literacy practices in secondary school classrooms (Martin, 1990; O'Mara, 1994; Tlale, 1991). Therefore, as a parent and educator, I was (and am still) continuously struggling with inquiring and understanding why there appears to be consistency in terms of students and teachers' views about Setswana education over the years.

As a graduate teaching assistant in Madison schools, I observed that instructional practices in elementary, middle, and high schools were learner-centered as compared to the teacher-centered ones in most Botswana secondary school classrooms. Moreover, as a graduate student, I was exposed to postcolonial theoretical perspectives, which subsequently provided a foundation for my dissertation's conceptual framework. This, together with my graduate courses that promoted equity, social justice, culturally relevant pedagogy, multicultural education, and multiple literacies, made it possible for me to develop perspectives that I used to make problematic Setswana literacy instruction. Moreover, these suggest that I have a foot in two worlds, as a native educated in the West and who is attempting to use the "master's tools to dismantle the master's house" (Lorde, 1984, p. 112) and, in the process, contribute to efforts of decolonizing research in postcolonial contexts. Therefore, in my research, the interpretations of life in Setswana classrooms were partially influenced by my experiences in U.S. educational institutions and thereby contributed to my sense of double consciousness in this regard. One tension evident in this is superimposing values from the U.S. culture into the Botswana culture. Hence, the need to position myself as a participant-observer who believes that her work stands in relation to the research participants and the discourses in which they participate, by interrogating the relationship between my dual role as an insider and outsider in Setswana classrooms.

The sense of double consciousness (DuBois, 1994), partially arising from my outsider status because of my Western education (Smith, 1999), often made me feel uncomfortable, vulnerable, and cautious in my attempts to interrogate Setswana education through the lenses of the knowledge and experiences I was acquiring in graduate courses. "Working the hyphens" (Fine, 1994) partially arose from the cautioning voice inside me, as I continuously crossed educational borders, warning me to take heed of superimposing values from the U.S. "culture" into the Botswana "culture." Similarly, as a result of my experiences as a Ph.D. international student, I often felt that my identities, experiences, and voice were marginalized. As the only African/international student in most of my graduate courses, I had to attempt to connect the knowledge taught with my educational experiences, needs, and expectations. In the process, I felt frustrated, uncomfortable, and marginalized, and never knew whether my efforts to interrogate Botswana's education system through my Westernized eyes/experiences would be legitimated.

Two incidents stand vividly in my memory illustrating this phenomenon. A weekly requirement in one of my graduate courses was to submit written questions based on assigned readings. Naturally, I submitted questions that aimed at helping me to interrogate and understand better educational practices in Botswana's education system. In response to one of my questions, the professor expressed that it was extremely difficult to find space for my questions since the group knew little to nothing about Botswana specifically and Africa in general, and that it was almost impossible to expect a whole class discussion of the topics I raised. In another graduate course, for one of the readings the students had to write a response journal focused on language and literacy practices within Britain's educational system. I could easily identify with the chapter assigned for this purpose because the practices that were examined are evident in Botswana's education system. This came as no surprise considering that Botswana is a former British protectorate. Thus, I was looking forward to the class discussion. My feelings of frustration resurfaced during the lesson when my perspectives were treated as inappropriate and irrelevant to the U.S. education system. Most white American students rejected the chapter, claiming that it addressed foreign educational issues and, thus, wished to concentrate on readings relevant to their educational system. Although I tried to explain why I appreciated the perspectives raised in the assigned reading and was interested in a discussion on it, my efforts were in vain. The professor and students chose to ignore my voice and consequently, the chapter was not discussed. I felt alone in my efforts to interpret what I was learning through the lens of my educational experiences, needs, and expectations as a native teacher educator. Reflecting on episodes of this nature, I realize that although I was formally part of that academic setting, I was often the inappropriate other, whose task was to bring non-relevant issues into a well-arranged system.

These incidents suggest that, although international students enter graduate programs primarily seeking to observe, learn, and interrogate their "discursively constituted experiences" (Scott, 1992), their positionality/ies as outsiders may close doors to the academic knowledge they seek. Historically constructed, my educational experiences positioned me on the margins of discourses privileged in some graduate courses my professors and classmates were insiders to. Yet, as Fine (1994) reminds us, Self and Other are joined by the hyphen that simultaneously divides and unites multiple identities and realities. Thus, part of the forced dichotomy of insider/outsider that created a binary between us simultaneously acknowledged my negotiated insider status as a member of the graduate school community who had to be a participant in learning institutionalized "Western knowledge" to fulfill program requirements. To achieve this, I needed the guidance of my instructors, who were in a privileged position to influence the situated identities I could develop as a graduate student. While being a graduate student at the University of Wisconsin—Madison who had to learn Western knowledge, provided me with multiple perspectives for interrogating practices in Setswana language education, this depended on the power of the professors to cross educational borders to provide interactional contexts that legitimated complex, competing (and often contradictory) local and global social, political and knowledge systems that influence education/educational discourses.

In retrospect, by "working the hyphens" to promote these discourses, some professors recognized the dual, often conflicting roles of graduate students as insiders and outsiders to institutionalized academic knowledge. Similarly, I learned that the educational discourses and experiences that contribute to our multiple, hybridized images, identities, and subjectivities in reality, rather than pushing insiders and outsiders in opposite directions of the forced binary interactions, often occur lower to the midpoint of this binary.

"HOW NATIVE IS A 'NATIVE' RESEARCHER"?

"How native is a 'native' anthropologist" (Narayan, 1993, p. 671) or researcher? Narayan's analysis of a 'native anthropologist helps understanding the relation between knowledge and power, researchers and researched in colonial and postcolonial contexts. Narayan indicates that researchers use their own sense of identity and image as insiders as well as outsiders to construct themselves and the researched. In this sense, all the researchers—including the natives of a culture—bring to the field acquired knowledge and experiences that shape the researcher-researched relationship, the specific roles each one assume, the knowledge obtained, how it is interpreted and used. The following narrative explains how positioning myself as a learner and being perceived as one by participants affected my role as a participant-observer.

Mrs. Boitshwarelo's image stands vividly in my mind; I remember the first time I walked into her house. She looked at me with her penetrating black eyes and with a smile on her face asked, "Why don't you tell me who you are." I explained that I was a University of Botswana teacher educator entrusted with the preparation of preservice and inservice secondary school Setswana teachers. I am a "native" of Botswana, currently studying in the United States and working on my doctoral dissertation related to Setswana education in Botswana secondary schools. Once I provided this information to Mrs. Boitshwarelo's satisfaction, she invited me to explain the purpose of my study. I did and praised her exceptional educational work that I had learned about from other educators who were familiar with her pedagogical practices. I concluded with a humble request for interviewing her concerning her professional experiences in order to learn from and to understand the relationship between students' academic literacies with their personal and community experiences.

Mrs. Boitshwarelo nodded. "Well, I am glad that you consider your-self to be a learner my child. It is unfortunate that some of you schooled young persons think that you know everything and that there is nothing you could learn from elderly people like myself. You know, you need to ac-quire knowledge from your elders to understand your society better. You cannot learn everything from all those books you read. I might not know everything, but tell me what you wish to know about Setswana education and I will share my knowledge with you. I have been around for a long time, you know." Then, I understood that positioning myself as a learner worked positively for me as a researcher and participants were more recep-tive to my questions and open to dialogue as they strove both to educate me and shared their knowledge about Setswana education.

Positioning myself as a learner also opened doors for me in another context. Mr. Tshomarelo viewed me as a learner and a member of a gen-eration lacking in cultural knowledge. The following vignette illustrates my positionality in this regard:

Mr. Tshomarelo listened attentively as I explained to him the purpose of my study. He nodded occasionally to acknowledge my explanation. "I hope to learn a lot from you as one of the individuals knowledgeable about Setswana education and cultural discourses," I said. "I will share with you my knowledge and experiences that are relevant to your research," he re-sponded. Part of our interview focused on educational policy matters. "The *Revised National Policy of Education of 1993* stipulates that the gov-ernment has taken the decision to improve the status of Setswana as a school subject and national language. Mr. Tshomarelo, if you were to ad-vise the government on how to achieve this decision, what would you say?," I inquired. Mr. Tshomarelo pondered my question for a moment. "The way Setswana was taught in the past did not really teach the students the relevance of this language in their daily lives. As such, most students lack knowledge and experiences of the discourses legitimated in different social contexts. Emphasis should be placed on increasing students' knowl-edge of Setswana as a living language that is relevant to their lives," Mr. Tshomarelo explained.

"Well, it is interesting though that most secondary school students feel that learning Setswana is a waste of time because they communicate in this language daily. Again, they feel that it is inappropriate to learn cultural val-ues, beliefs, and practices they consider outdated," I explained. "It is a pity that most teachers and educators like yourself have limited knowledge about the cultural knowledge you are expected to teach. One of the key challenges facing Setswana education is that individuals teaching this lan-guage do not really know Setswana," he said. "Can you explain what you mean by that, Mr. Tshomarelo?," I asked promptly. "I am not saying that teachers are not educated. They have satisfactorily fulfilled their professional requirements. Yet, most teachers like their students are not familiar with the cultural discourses legitimated in specific social contexts."

Mr. Tshomarelo paused for a moment and continued. "It is important for Setswana to be taught in schools. Listen to me carefully, Dudu; teaching cultural knowledge does not mean that students or even your generation should perform traditional practices and customs. It is more about knowing who you are. I am not saying that cultural knowledge should not accommodate current lifestyles. Although these often clash, I believe to bring these together; we have to project Setswana cultural values and knowledge into current lifestyles. Setswana cultural knowledge is part of the past, present, and future. As I nodded my head to acknowledge his perspective, Mr. Tshomarelo added, "For example, most of you are not familiar with the practice and social significance of age-regiments." He looked at me and said, "What do you know about that?" Although I felt awkward then and at other times during the interview doubting my knowledge in the eyes of someone so knowledgeable, Mr. Tshomarelo incorporated my views into the knowledge he shared with me. In the process he guided me in learning and relearning the role of cultural knowledge in improving the status of Setswana as a school subject and national language.

I understood Mr. Tshomarelo's actions as an acknowledgment of my status as a learner who could benefit from knowledgeable community members like himself who have "discursively constituted experiences" (Scott, 1992) of Setswana cultural knowledge.

My status as an insider and outsider was also evident in how I was positioned in the school setting. The nature of my participation was negotiated with the Setswana teachers whose practices I was observing. I believe I was viewed as an insider when I was invited to co-teach a topic, share instructional strategies, participate in whole class discussions, fill-in for an absent teacher, provide feedback on students' essays, and record students' performance. To some degree, when participant teachers, school principal, and education officers hoped that my research would provide useful information to address teachers' professional needs and students' views about Setswana education, I was also identified as one of "them." Furthermore, as a known teacher educator, my participants recognized that I shared similar concerns about Setswana education and identified or positioned me as a colleague and resource.

One of the double-edged features of classroom research is that the same practices that contributed to my role as an insider also contributed to my positioning as an outsider. For example, although grading and providing feedback positioned me as an insider in the eyes of one teacher, these practices illuminated my position as an outsider in the eyes of another:

Mr. Tumelo, one of the teachers whose class I was observing for my ethnographic study, walked into Mrs. Lesedi's office while I was conversing with two of his colleagues. Following his greetings, he informed me that he recently attended a meeting with other Setswana teachers from neighboring senior secondary schools on writing "test items" for the Form Four mock examination. This he explained was essential since most teachers were struggling with the interpretation of the communicatively-based Setswana teaching syllabus and its assessment requirements. I thanked him for the information and promised to get in touch soon to get the details about the meeting. "How are you progressing with the marking of the mid-term examinations?," I inquired. "I have so much work to do that I definitely need assistance to complete marking all the scripts on time," Mr. Tumelo responded as he looked for a moment at the papers in one of his hands. "If you were familiar with the marking schemes of the current Setswana syllabus, I would give you some of the scripts to grade," he continued.

My heart leaped for joy at Mr. Tumelo's words for I viewed them as an opportunity for me to learn more about the discourses in Setswana classrooms. "Grading students work would give me insights into the nature of their written responses, more so because Mr. Tumelo was dissatisfied with their performance in the literature test earlier," I thought. "Well, I can assist you with the grading of the examination scripts for the class I am observing for this study. I am familiar with the official marking schemes for specified topics in the syllabus such as translation, summary, and essay and I can easily unravel them for purposes of this examination," I explained. "Therefore, you can confidently give me some of the scripts to grade on your behalf," I continued. After pondering my response momentarily, Mr. Tumelo responded, "It is very challenging, particularly for someone who has not taught the current Setswana senior secondary syllabus to assess its items. So, I think it would be better to do all the marking myself." "Even if you feel that I cannot unravel the marking scheme to your satisfaction, I believe that I can assist you with the examination questions that do not require a predetermined criterion provided by the Ministry of Education," I stated. "You know, I really feel that you have a lot of work to do for your research project. So, I will just grade all the scripts. It won't be fair to give you additional work," Mr. Tumelo stated. "In fact, grading students' scripts fits into the activities that I can engage in as a participant-observer in Setswana classrooms," I explained. "No, I think it would be better if I graded all the scripts. As it is, you have a lot of work to do," Mr. Tumelo reiterated.

As Mr. Tumelo walked out of the office, I found myself struggling to understand why he rejected my help to grade students' papers. Later, I reflected in my researcher's journal, "Is my role as a university teacher educator and researcher a contributing factor in Mr. Tumelo's decision? Even if I confronted challenges in unraveling the predetermined criterion provided, wouldn't I have learned and benefited from his "expertise" as a member of the Task Forces that designed the Setswana senior secondary teaching and assessment syllabuses?

In all, I understood Mr. Tumelo's decision as an identification of my outsider image and the lacking of expertise or knowledge regarding syllabus requirements. Similarly, his decision was a positive reminder that, although as a "native" researcher I was striving to examine life in Setswana classrooms from an emic perspective, I was in part an outsider to the "discursively constituted experiences" (Scott, 1992) of participants.

On the same vein, my identification as an outsider was extremely clear when I was not invited to a meeting focused on the department's annual report. The Head of the Department indicated to me that teachers needed to feel free to express their ideas about it and it would be in the interest of the teachers if I did not attend the meeting. I believe that as the institutional gatekeeper the Head of Department was probably guarding the interests and vulnerability of her colleagues from researchers/outsiders.

Reflecting on those experiences, as a researcher, I had a privileged position to observe, interpret, and make judgments about the participants. However, the knowledge that as a researcher I had access to was controlled by the participants, who were privileged to choose what to tell or not to tell researchers/outsiders about the researched social contexts. The following narrative illustrates this phenomenon.

The staff room was full of teachers, either sitting alone or chatting excitedly with one another as they enjoyed a cup of coffee or tea. I greeted some of them and they in turn greeted me warmly as we waited in line to get our beverages. As I glanced through the room, looking for a seat, I saw Mr. Tumelo and walked toward him. I occupied the seat next to him and between gulps of hot, delicious coffee inquired how his lessons were progressing that day. "They are fine," he responded with a smile on his face. "Is it possible to have copies of your students' written artifacts?" I inquired. "I do not have much in terms of students' written work. The lesson I observed today will be helpful because I was able to audio and videotape one of the groups working on the translation activity you assigned. Similarly, I was able to record the whole class discussion afterwards," I added.

Mr. Tumelo pondered my request and responded, "Well, the only written tasks the students in the class you are observing have up to now focus on speech writing and the "common" literature test written by all Form Four students. Actually, they have not written a single composition/essay. That is why I informed them in class today that it is a possibility that they will write a composition/essay in the end of year examinations before I teach them how to write it. But I plan to have them compose one essay before then. I would definitely make available to you the students' examination scripts for purposes of your study." "I wonder how this fits into the Setswana Department's system of common scheming/planning," I said. As

I looked keenly at him, Mr. Tumelo stated, "Our instructional practices have to fit within the Department's common scheming framework." After a moment of silence, I probed, "How does this fit into the Department's agenda of monthly tests? The reason why I am asking this is partially because Mrs. Lesedi's students have written two individual essays/compositions and two group ones up to now." Following a short silence Mr. Tumelo responded, "O botsa dipotso thata" (you ask a lot of questions).

Mr. Tumelo's response completely disarmed me in that it made me feel uncomfortable to probe for any more details. As the bell rang and I walked out of the classroom to get ready for my upcoming interview, I was worried and uncertain as to the appropriateness and sensitivity of the questions I asked Mr. Tumelo. Did I make him feel uncomfortable? Was I intruding too much into his pedagogical practices? Although I kept reminding myself that getting an emic perspective was part of my role as a native researcher, I felt like an intruder prying too much into other people's lives. Consequently, I felt guilty that I might have turned Mr. Tumelo against me. I found myself thinking of Behar's (1996) explanation that both the researcher and the participants, or observed, are vulnerable. Thus, Mr. Tumelos' response might suggest his vulnerability at what he might have seen as an intrusion and passing of judgment on his pedagogical practices, more so since he had indeed not given the students any written essays/compositions up to this time.

Participants often positioned me as an insider in terms of the collective experiences, knowledge, and beliefs we have in common. Instead of providing me with the information I sought, their responses to my questions were "O a itse" (you know). My positionality in this regard is evident in my interactions with some of the educators who participated in my study.

As I walked into the Ministry of Education headquarters I couldn't help pondering on the interview I was going to conduct with Mr. Mosireletsi and Mr. Tshwaragano, two senior education officers. "I cannot wait to hear their perspectives of the ongoing process of localizing the senior secondary school syllabuses and examination system. This is important for understanding and interpreting the discourses I am observing in Setswana classrooms at Kgololo senior secondary school," I thought. "One of the recommendations stipulated in Government White Paper Number 2 is that Setswana teachers should be familiarized with a variety of teaching methods, with emphasis on communicative approaches.[2] Closely related to this is the production and implementation of the current senior secondary school Setswana teaching syllabus. Could you describe for me the process that was followed in producing this document?," I asked Mr. Mosireletsi and Mr. Tshwaragano shortly after the interview started. "As education officers, one of our major responsibilities is to interpret government policy in order to ensure that the objectives and goals of the education system are met. Within this context, we were given deadlines and were informed by our supervisors that the Setswana, physics, biology, English, chemistry, and mathematics syllabuses were to be ready for implementation in 1998. We had to convene a Task Force to start producing the syllabus. The whole syllabus was produced within a limited period of time in order to meet implementation deadlines. You know, things are never done the way they should be," Mr. Tshwaragano stated. "Now, we are beginning to talk about practices and experiences you know of," he continued. "What did I really know about this issue?" I thought.

Although Mr. Tshwaragano's comment acknowledged and privileged the common experiences we shared as participants in varied Ministry of Education teacher committees, as well as educators entrusted with the professional development of Setswana secondary school teachers, I struggled to take this insider status for granted. "As a researcher, it is important that I don't make assumptions. I have to hear your stories," I explained. "She is right," Mr. Tshwaragano responded. Mr. Mosireletsi nodded and reiterated, "She is right." "You have to tell me all that you know about this issue because your knowledge will help me clarify what I already know. Again, as education officers, you definitely have knowledge that I do not have concerning the complexities and challenges of policy-making and implementation processes." Mr. Tshwaragano smiled and said, "Okay, I will share with you my knowledge." As Mr. Tshwaragano shared his in-depth knowledge of the educational reform process in Botswana with me, I was grateful that he and Mr. Mosireletsi were part of my dissertation study.

My positionality as an insider in the eyes of Mr. Tshwaragano was reminiscent of an earlier interview with one of the educators who participated in my study. Part of our interview focused on the meaning and significance of the communicative approach to language instruction as an educational reform strategy in Setswana senior secondary school classrooms.

"What the students learn is also relevant to their lives beyond the classroom; they apply what they learn to their daily lives. So, this is an approach that provides opportunities for changing students' negative attitudes toward Setswana as a school subject," she explained. I looked up at her warm smiling face and requested, "Well, you continue to inform me about the communicative approach." "What about it?" was her immediate response. "Well, what you think it is and its significance to the teaching of Setswana or just anything you wish to add to what I have already learned from you," I explained. She looked at me intently for a moment and said, "O a itse" (you know). We both laughed softly. "Well, it is important that you don't assume that I know or have the knowledge that you have about this approach. I cannot assume what you know because in the process I might misinterpret your own perspectives." "Okay, Dudu, I will tell you more about this approach."

In all, participants' responses alerted me to the knowledge and experiences we shared and that they assumed I should take for granted in our interactions. Although acknowledging our collective experiences acclaimed them (Smith, 1999), it was my responsibility as a researcher to interrogate these assumptions in order to learn from the participants and interpret their stories appropriately. In the process, I realized that emic perspective often provide "native" researchers with opportunities to learn and relearn what they are already familiar with. Moreover, experience is a contested phenomenon (Scott, 1992) and hence the importance of not taking it for granted.

An important part of the researcher's presence in the field is that as an outsider he or she may influence how and in what ways students and teachers interact with one another. Open Day activities at Kgololo senior secondary school exemplify this phenomenon. As a forum for teacher-parent conferences, Open Day provided parents and guardians with opportunities to discuss and raise concerns related to their children's academic performance. Mr. Tumelo encouraged students to participate in this event by inviting them to tell parents or guardians how they viewed their performance in Setswana, their role and feelings of the group work strategy, and how they hoped to improve their performance. Similarly, he invited parents to share ways in which they helped their children learn Setswana, as well as their perceptions of Setswana as a school subject. At the end of the parent-teacher conferences, Mr. Tumelo explained to me that he structured conferences this way to give me insights into parents and students' views about Setswana.

The normal practice is to inform parents about the students' performance, mostly based on their internal examination performance—a phenomenon I observed in Mrs. Leasedi's teacher parent-teacher conferences. In all, an advantage of being viewed as an outsider who had to be familiarized with parents' attitudes towards Setswana is that it provided me with opportunities to get their perspectives toward Setswana as a school subject. This provided insightful research data since I had not included students' parents as participants in my study.

My status as an insider and outsider in the two Form Four Setswana classrooms suggest that being a native to the culture or context that is researched or studied does not guarantee the researcher treatment as a complete insider. My positions as an insider and outsider suggest that researchers and participants play a significant role in structuring power relations in the research process. Within this context, teachers used their power to accommodate me as an insider and thus as part of the discourses in Setswana classrooms. At the same time, teachers used their power to position me on the margins of the discourses in this setting. Moreover, teachers, education officers, and community members used the knowledge and experiences we shared and did not share to position me as an insider and outsider. Similarly, interrogating my position as both insider and outsider in my study also pushes me to acknowledge that my account of life in Setswana classrooms is in a sense, not *the "truth."* Hence, my interpretations may differ from those of the participants themselves as complete insiders to the context I was researching.

WHAT COUNTS AS A DECOLONIZING RESEARCH AGENDA?

One of the challenges that face researchers is the manner in which they are positioned in their dual, often conflicting roles as both insiders and outsiders to the lives and "discursively constituted experiences" (Scott, 1992) of the research participants. To some degree, DuBois' (1994) notion of double consciousness can be equated to representations or images of native ethnographers (Narayan, 1993) or indigenous researchers (Smith, 1999) working in postcolonial contexts. They strive to look at and problematize the lives, experiences, or cultures they are researching through the eyes of the participants themselves; yet they cannot achieve this without drawing on their own images and multiple identities. Failing to do so renders or positions them as colonizers of research participants (Fine, 1994; Villenas, 1996).

Yet, at another level, DuBois (1994), Fine (1994), and Villenas (1996) speak to the images, identities, and (im)possibilities of researchers whose primary intention is to decolonize research in postcolonial contexts. They remind us that researchers' hybridized selves and realities influences the research agendas they seek to promote. Research as an "imperial tool" was used to construct and represent the colonized in ways that their identities, realities, and ways of knowing were marginalized (Smith, 1999). Decolonizing research provides a site of agency for decentering colonial knowledge, and "working the hyphens" as part of an agenda of native researchers to use the "master's tools"(Lorde, 1984) such as acquired or learned Western education, knowledge, languages, and theories to produce and legitimate research knowledge from insider perspectives.

Yet decolonizing research does not imply totally rejecting Western theories and research-based knowledge (Smith, 1999). It invites deconstruction of Western research traditions and essentialist perspectives through collaboration between native researchers themselves as well as between native researchers and non-native researchers. Collaboration pushes researchers like myself to acknowledge and consider the relevance of our academic knowledge and hybridized identities and experiences in the construction of research knowledge. Collaboration in this regard entails making problematic the relation between knowledge and power, researchers and researched in postcolonial contexts.

Similarly, collaboration as part of decolonizing research reminds us that as insiders and outsiders the selves we bring to the field even as natives of a culture are relevant to the researched for it shapes their relationship with us, the specific roles we assume, the languages we use, and the knowledge we obtain as well as how we interpret and report it. Again, as researchers we have research agendas that we seek to promote, which are shaped by our interactions throughout the research process. Within this context, collaboration as part of decolonizing research invites me as an insider and outsider to acknowledge and at the same time treat cautiously the Western academy as part of the fields that contribute to the academic and research knowledge that I tap from as I strive to decolonize my subjective positions in the academy in a postcolonial context. Embedded in this is the necessity for using research methodologies that open doors for native researchers and participants to speak for themselves by both telling their stories from their perspectives and making them problematic.

What did I learn from doing my dissertation research that informs efforts to decolonize research in postcolonial contexts? As a novice researcher, my dissertation research, which was grounded on postcolonial theoretical perspectives, provided insights for recognizing in particular the political nature of research as well as the complexities and (im)possibilities for decolonizing research in pursuit of culturally appropriate scholarship. Similarly, my dissertation research provided realization that doing insider research may be problematic for natives who often find themselves in the outside as inappropriate others in the social contexts they are part of. My academic knowledge influences my teaching in that I am more conscious of the relationships between issues of equity, social justice, culturally relevant pedagogy, and multicultural education and educational discourses in Setswana secondary school classrooms in particular. Botswana teacher educators—including myself—are expected to adequately prepare preservice and inservice teachers for their professional lives in the country's multilingual and multicultural classrooms.

The challenge for me is how to incorporate these positively in my teacher education courses. Studying my own practices, in part to provide teachers with a firm knowledge base concerning their professional lives, can guide me in engaging in these issues more productively. Action research based on my own pedagogical practices has the potential to guide my interrogating the intersections between my multiple identities and realities, and issues of equity, social justice, culturally relevant pedagogy, and multicultural education.

Similarly, action research can promote the process of self-actualization and reflexivity that is necessary for fostering engaged pedagogy and holistic learning that is rooted in interrogating our subjectivities and multiple realities. Participating in collaborative research as part of an agenda to decolonize research can also yield positive rewards in this regard. To collaborate with others is to acknowledge and interrogate theories that inform our research agendas and the ethical and moral issues embedded in them as part of making this a reality. It also entails collaboration from the inception of research projects up to their completion. Moreover, it involves conducting research in ways that are sensitive and culturally appropriate for both native researchers and research participants.

Interrogating my status as an insider and outsider in Setswana classrooms as well as the possibilities that exist for colonizing research has also led me to consider the following challenges as I journey into my life as a researcher in the Botswana postcolonial context:

- How can we deal with the complexities of double consciousness when indigenous or native researchers more than often use colonized knowledge, including western languages like English and French to "dismantle the master's houses"?
- In what ways do postcolonial theoretical perspectives provide (im)possibilities for dealing with the ethical and political challenges and complexities brought about by the colonized knowledge native researchers have attained as part of their Western education or training?
- What role do researchers and participants' multiple identities play in postcolonial research considering that indigenous researchers are often considered outsiders in contexts where researchers and participants have common identities, such as ethnicity, social class, and race?

It is my hope that my journey into the research world would nourish my professional experiences in part by helping me to understand the complexities, contradictions, and (im)possibilities of the insider/ outsider binary as I strive to create pedagogical contexts that guide prospective and inservice teachers to continuously examine the impact of their philosophies of teaching, theories that inform them, and their overall teaching in Botswana's multilingual and multicultural classrooms. I have a lot to learn from the experiences of researchers and educators locally and globally as well as from individual and collaborative research projects in which I hope to engage.

NOTES

1. I use pseudonyms to protect the confidentiality of research participants.

2. Although the National Commission on Education report of 1993 explains that teachers should be introduced to communicative *approaches* and other teaching methods as a way of making the teaching of Setswana interesting, the syllabus on the other hand refers to the communicative *approach* as a basis for teaching Setswana in senior secondary classrooms. Drawing from the teaching syllabus, participants in this study also refer to the communicative approach instead of approaches. To honor the voices of the participants, I refer to the communicative

approach in reporting and discussing their views as well as in making reference to the syllabi. I use communicative approaches where appropriate as an acknowledgment of what the National Commission on Education report expresses or states.

REFERENCES

Behar, R. (1996). *The vulnerable observer: Anthropology that breaks your heart.* Boston: Beacon Press.

Bourdieu, P. (1991). *Language and symbolic power.* Trans. G. Raymond and M. Adamson. Cambridge: Harvard University Press.

DuBois, W. E. B. (1994). *The souls of black folk.* New York: Random House.

Fine, M. (1994). Working with hyphens: Reinventing self and other in qualitative research. In N. K. Denzig and Y. S. Lincoln (Eds.), *Handbook of qualitative research* (pp. 70–82). Thousand Oaks, CA: Sage.

Government of Botswana. (1994). *Government paper No. 2 of 1994: The revised national policy on education.* Gaborone, Botswana: Government Printer.

Jankie, D. (2001). *Rethinking Setswana literacy practices: Towards incorporating community-based and students' experiences in senior secondary classrooms.* Unpublished doctoral dissertation, University of Wisconsin–Madison.

Lorde, A. (1984). *Sister "outsider": Essays and speeches.* Freedom, CA: Crossing Press.

Martin, M. M. (1990). *A comparison of attitudes about English and Setswana reported by selected secondary school students and teachers.* Unpublished master's thesis, University of Wisconsin–Madison.

Narayan, K. (1993). How native is a "native" anthropologist? *American Anthropologist, 95(3),* 671–686.

National Commission on Education. (1993). *Report of the national commission on education.* Gaborone, Botswana: Government Printer.

Ngugi wa Thiong'o. (1981). *Writers in politics: A re-engagement with issues of literature and society.* Oxford and Nairobi: Heinemann.

Ngugi wa Thiong'o. (1986). *Decolonizing the mind: The politics of language in African literature.* London and Nairobi: Heinemann.

Ngugi wa Thiong'o. (1993). *Moving the centre: The struggle for cultural freedoms.* London and Nairobi: Heinemann.

O'Mara, L. C. (1994). *Factors that influence the teaching and learning of Setswana in senior secondary schools.* Unpublished master's thesis, University of Botswana, Gaborone, Botswana.

Scott, J. W. (1992). Experience. In J. Butler and J. W. Scott (Eds.), *Feminists theorize the political* (pp. 22–40). New York: Routledge.

Smith, L. T. (1999). *Decolonizing methodologies: Research and indigenous peoples.* London, New York, and Dunedin, New Zealand: Zed Books and University of Otago Press.

Tlale, I. (1991). *An analysis of Botswana's secondary school classroom practice: The case of Setswana language*. Unpublished master's thesis, University of Wisconsin–Madison.

Villenas, S. (1996). The colonizer/colonized Chicana ethnographer: Identity, marginalization, and co-optation in the field. *Harvard Educational Review, 66*(4), 711–731.

CHAPTER SIX

Multiple Layers of a Researcher's Identity: Uncovering Asian American Voices

SUSAN MATOBA ADLER

THE RESEARCHER'S IDENTITY

Who can hear the voices of the colonized? Who might listen with authenticity, with sensitivity, with an open mind? Ethnographers have meticulously studied groups from the "outside," hoping to interpret what is on the "inside," through the voices of informants. But why are there such dichotomies, when, in reality, researchers are insiders in some contexts and outsiders in other situations?

In conducting qualitative research, the identity of the author and his or her subjectivity is of concern for establishing authenticity. But there are few "standards" for revealing these contextual parameters. The late Alan Peshkin's personal subjectivity audit of the multiple "I" gives us a template to address the issue. Peshkin (1988) writes:

> When researchers observe themselves in the focused way that I propose, they learn about the particular subset of personal qualities that contact with their research phenomenon has released. These qualities have the capacity to filter, skew, shape, block, transform, construe, and misconstrue what transpires from the outset of a research project to its culmination in a written statement. If researchers are informed about the qualities that have

emerged during their research, they can at least disclose to their readers where self and subject become joined. (p. 17)

Before beginning a research project, I attempt to apply Peshkin's concept of the multiple "I" and define myself as: the midwestern Japanese-American "I," the scholar/researcher "I," the middle-class, middle-aged "I," the female feminist "I," the ethnic multicultural "I," and the Sansei (third-generation Japanese-American) daughter/mother "I." This situates me as different from younger Japanese-American scholars reared and working in areas such as Los Angeles or Honolulu, where there are large Asian-American populations. My cultural values and beliefs are based on post–World War II, European-American midwestern society, mediated through a Japanese-American family and household that included elderly grandparents.

When researching Asian-American families, I see myself having a changing, negotiated identity, sometimes as an insider, sometimes as an outsider, but not necessarily one or the other. I situate myself as a U.S. citizen (nationality), as a monolingual (English speaking), as a Japanese (ethnicity, heritage), as an Asian (racial ascription), and as a midwesterner (regionalism), although I have also lived in New York State, Colorado, and North Carolina. My roots and my family are in Wisconsin and my career positions in higher education have been in Michigan, Wisconsin, and Illinois.

Narayan (1993) discussed the "native point of view" suggesting that "native" researchers consider themselves in terms of "shifting identifications amid a field of interpenetrating communities and power relations" (p. 671). She explains her approach of negotiating both personal narrative and anthropological scholarship as follows: "Tacking between situated narrative and more sweeping analysis, I argue for the *enactment of hybridity* in our texts; that is, writing that depicts authors as minimally bicultural in terms of belonging simultaneously to the world of engaged scholarship and the world of everyday life." (p. 672)

In my research I have experienced the tension between the academic world and the everyday world of my participants. The women in my study on midwestern Japanese-American mothers were predominately middle-class, educated women who endorsed my scholarship, perhaps even trusting me too much to interpret their words accurately as an insider. In contrast, even though I am using a Hmong parent as a research assistant and translator in my current study, there are Hmong parents who have expressed skepticism about giving answers to an outside researcher, wary that I am aligned with the school as an institution of power. According to the Hmong school district liaison for Hmong parents, many of these parents were educated in Laotian schools run by the government. There is concern that the public assistance they receive or their cultural ways of disciplining their children could be affected by answers given to a researcher. My personal knowledge of their life as refugees is limited to the available research and few interviews that I have personally conducted with Hmong families in my Detroit study.

THREE STUDIES OF ASIAN-AMERICAN FAMILIES

This chapter is based on the theoretical orientations and research methodologies used in three of my studies on Asian Americans. I draw from the literature of postmodern feminists, such as Nicholson (1990) and Hekman (1990) and from racial and ethnic identity development theories (Cross, 1991; Helms, 1990; Phinney and Rotheram, 1987; Sheets and Hollins, 1999; Tatum, 1992). I have used a feminist interview method of conversations between interviewer and interviewees (Oakley, 1981). I situated myself by openly sharing my own experiences as a Japanese American reared in the Midwest. This allowed me to establish an authentic trust with most participants.

My dissertation study and book, *Mothering, Education, and Ethnicity: The Transformation of Japanese American Culture* (1998), is a three-generational study of the beliefs of midwestern Japanese-American women about education and childrearing. The postwar settlement of Japanese Americans coming from the internment camps to the Midwest created a new generation of children who had little contact with ethnic communities, and, for political reasons, were often not taught much of their ethnic heritage. "Be 100% American" was the motto at the time. The study examines mother-daughter dyads and one triad, of Nisei (second-generation American born), Sansei (third generation, mostly assimilated and generally non-Japanese speaking), and Yonsei (fourth generation, including biracial women due to the high rate of interracial marriage of Japanese-American women). The immigrant generation of Issei have mostly passed away but left a legacy of family involvement living in multigenerational households of Issei grandparents, Nisei parents, and Sansei children.

Methodology included an open-ended survey on race and ethnicity, in-depth individual interviews, mixed generation group interviews, responses to literature written by Japanese-American women, and gathering documentation (mostly photographs) of the families' lived experiences. Findings indicate that there are Japanese cultural concepts, such as "gambare" (hard work), "gaman" (endurance and perseverance), and "amae" (the parent-child interdependency) that have been transformed by Japanese Americans.

The group interviews and responses to literature allowed my study to be "less colonial" by providing opportunities for participants to co-create perspectives on various issues. There were lively exchanges at the group sessions between older and younger women as they tried to learn about and from each other. Differing reactions to the literature selections illustrated the diversity within this ethnic group. One particular poem, "Masks of Woman" by Mitsuye Yamada, provoked strong and opposing responses by two participants. One felt that it helped her define boundaries for herself and understand her own mother's behavior, while the other saw it as a negative façade, masking real feeling and open communication (Adler, 1998).

My two-year study of Japanese, Chinese, Korean, Filipino, and Hmong families in the Detroit, Michigan, area focused on parents' view of how they socialize their children to understand race and ethnicity and develop a sense of racial and ethnic identity. Nineteen families participated in the original survey; twelve individual interviews with families were conducted along with follow-up interviews. In addition, parent-child interactions reading picture books with Asian-American characters and themes were observed. Follow-up interviews (some by phone), including questions about parental perspectives on their own racial and ethnic identity (referring to Helms and Cross Identity Development Scales), were also conducted.

Data indicated that parental racial identity development was weaker than ethnic identity. For example, when asked about both race and ethnicity, participants' self-identified in terms of ethnic culture, language, and heritage more frequently than in terms of race. Parents tended to discuss issues of race and ethnicity when incidents (usually stereotyping) occurred for their children in school or other social settings. There was tremendous within-group diversity, especially among Korean families due to family immigration history as well as desire and opportunity for assimilation.

My current study of Hmong children in an elementary school in Saint Paul, Minnesota, with a population of over 50% Hmong students, investigates how teachers (and staff) construct racial and ethnic identities of their Hmong students, and how the school provides parent involvement for the Hmong families. It also attempts to give voice to Hmong parents about their children's education. Observations in the classrooms were conducted during five school visits of three to four days each, and during one parent-conference day. Interviews with the school administrators and Hmong administrators and counselors were also conducted. Newsletters and minutes of the Hmong Parent Teacher Organization meetings, and special parent programs such as "Mother Reads," were documented by the parent coordinator and PTO president. Follow-up questions for parents and staff will be conducted by the Hmong research assistant and through e-mail with participating staff members.

Preliminary findings indicate that school personnel view the Hmong children as neither "model minorities" or "at risk" for socioeconomic reasons, but as academically behind, due primarily to linguistic differences. They rely heavily on the ELL (English language and literacy) program and on interpreters in the school. The staff members who participated in the Lickert survey felt that they knew a lot about the Hmong culture and were providing positive multicultural education for their students. Individual interviews, especially with the three Hmong teachers and the ELL teachers, indicated that the multiculturalism provided in the school curriculum was at best superficial. Hmong parent surveys indicated that they were generally happy with their children's progress at school, felt that they were limited in helping their children due to language barriers or heavy work schedules, and that they didn't feel that the school staff knew much about their culture.

SILENCED VOICES AND INVISIBILITY

It has been said that Asian Americans are the "invisible" minority (as well as the "model minority") and have been silenced by both cultural socialization (primarily women) and a collective attitude of maintaining privacy and group harmony (Adler, 1998). Zia (2000) writes:

> Internalizing their invisibility, Asian Americans sometimes enforce a self-imposed silence, in a sense 'closeting' the community, especially when issues are tinged with a perception of shame or stigma. For years, Asian women activists around the United States struggled to ignite a broad community response to issues of domestic violence and sexual assault. . . . Their progress was hindered by the lack of support from Asian American male leaders who saw such issues as 'dirty laundry' that shouldn't be aired in public. (p. 237)

Public assistance for Asian Americans tends to be limited (except in the case of refugees from the Vietnam War era), based on this invisibility, assuming that Asian communities will take care of their own and do not want or need public services for mental health problems (Sue and Sue, 1975). Over the years domestic violence has become more public, leading to the coalition between some Asian American community groups and mainstream women's groups (Zia, 2000).

Ironically, Asian Americans have also been considered "visible minorities" throughout history, based on racial ascription, but this was countered by the "model minority" myth that paints Asian Americans as successfully assimilated and high-achieving Americans, rather than an underclass. (See Wu, 2002, for an extensive discussion of the model minority thesis.) This misconception applied to early immigrants and recent high-tech industrial immigrants, but not to some of the Vietnamese "boat people" and Hmong refugees. The diversity among Asian groups in the United States is tremendous. Very little research has been done on specific Asian ethnic groups from their cultural perspectives.

The *voice* of minorities in the United States has been silenced for political reasons and those in positions of power often speak for them. Howard (1999) writes about white privilege and voice:

> Even in our postmodern rhetoric related to the deconstruction of dominance, Whites often speak of 'giving voice' to marginalized groups, as if *their* voice is *ours* to give. From the position of privilege, we have often attempted to construct the stage on which other people's dramas are enacted. We have even tried at times to play their parts. And of course, we have usually sold the tickets. (p. 62)

As a Japanese American growing up in post-internment years in the Midwest, and later as a professional (teacher, professor), I was silenced as a child, a woman, a teacher, and a scholar. I was expected to circumvent problems rather than confront them directly, especially in the public sphere. The impetus for this behavior was both cultural and political in that drawing attention to oneself could bring shame (or pride) to the family and Japanese-American community. Only through my poetry, journaling, and academic writing have I been able to express my inner thoughts and interpretive analysis. It is for these reasons that I chose to give *voice* to Asian-American families in my research.

An interesting situation arose while I was recruiting participants for my mothering study. Two Nisei women indicated that I should speak with their husbands about Japanese Americans, assuming that they knew more about the history, socioeconomic status, and politics of this ethnic group. When I explained that the study was about childrearing and education, they were still reluctant, indicating that they had little to contribute. This was my first experience with internalized oppression, as manifest by gender roles intersecting with ethnicity. I began to wonder about reasons why other siblings of some of my participants chose not to participate. Was it a factor of limited time, lack of interest in things Japanese, and or low ethnic and racial identity? As one participant said of her sister, "She thinks she's pretty white" (Adler, 1998).

Ladson-Billings and Tate (1995) speak of "naming one's own reality" as a significant part of Critical Race Theory that serves as both interpretive structures by which we organize our experiences and as a "psychic preservation of marginalized groups" (p. 57). I use postmodern feminist theory to allow Asian Americans to name their own reality and share their view of American society through their cultural lenses. We can learn much by listening to the "silenced minorities" and reconstruct U.S. society as truly multicultural.

When I explored the research and literature on Asian-American women, I realized that few entries honor self-constructions by these women, while various identities have been imposed on them through stereotypes. For example, when I asked participants in the mothering study if they considered themselves "exotic" and "subservient" Asian women, several Sansei participants laughed and dismissed the myth as the "white man's" fantasy. Yet when this was discussed in the context of obligation to husband, children, and family, some indicated that they might be considered "subservient" because they had been socialized to consider the good of the family first before their own personal interests and to avoid confrontation. Others felt that both the stereotype and the cultural socialization caused confusion as well as mixed messages from peers and family for acceptable behavior. My study allowed the women to express their frustration with these contradictions when their ability to fight stereotypes was thwarted by their ethnic group behavioral expectations. "We know how to act Japanese, even when we want to be our free liberated selves," said one participant (Adler, 1998).

LISTENING TO AUTHENTIC VOICES

One of my major goals in each study was to uncover the participant's lived reality and to share mutual insights that could open new and multiple perspectives about being Asian American in U.S. society. I often began with sharing my background and ethnic childrearing in order to situate myself. This was an informal process. The following are some interesting occurrences from my studies that indicated a "connection" or a "contrast" with participants that led to further investigation of the diversity within a racial (Asian) group. I will refer to the studies as: the mothering study, the Detroit study, and the Hmong study in this chapter.

There are many examples from my three studies that echo the perspectives of my participants. In order to give them a forum from which they can speak, I need, as a researcher, to establish a connectedness to them as people. I attempt to engage in a dialogical process in which they have ownership of their words and I elicit and interpret *their* meanings. I may use my insider knowledge and behavior patterns to build rapport, but I must be careful to honor their words.

In my first study on Japanese-American mothers, I used the insider perspective of Japanese-American anthropologist Dorine Kondo (1990). In her ethnography of the Japanese workplace she allowed her Japanese heritage and knowledge of interactional style to assist her in areas of access and communication. She spoke Japanese, but found herself being defined in differing ways in different contexts. Similarly, Mirza (1998) in "Same Voices, Same Lives" revisited black feminist standpoint epistemology, and described the concept of "placing" in the research process. She was not readily accepted as an insider with her interviewees who were of the same race, ethnicity, and gender. Class and educational level often become other variables that can counteract other similarities.

In the mothering study, women of my mother's generation (Nisei) who knew my grandmother (Issei) often used the phrase "You know . . ." to signal my understanding of their cultural message. I tried to decipher on the spot or later from the transcripts whether these were just colloquial phrases or if there was an inherent assumed knowledge base that they expected me to have. In most cases, I believe it was the latter, so I had to be careful to acknowledge that information, either by an example of my own (conversational interview methodology) or by some verbal or nonverbal acknowledgment. For example, if a Nisei woman said, "It was hard for my mother to get around and get to know people, you know," I might respond, "Yes, my grandmother could understand a lot of English but hesitated to speak to 'white' people." The conversation might then lead to a discussion about either language barriers or embarrassment in public, or both. At a recent presentation of this chapter, a colleague shared that her Japanese-American in-laws often used the response "neh" after statements in Japanese, indicating a colloquial phrase meaning "Isn't that so?" This comment challenges me to consider the former as a reasonable interpretation.

The Sansei participants in my own generational group often asked if my experiences were similar to theirs after describing an incident. This was particularly rewarding to me since I had never discussed some of these issues about race and ethnicity with others (especially not with another Sansei woman who grew up in the Midwest). It gave me an emotional sense of belonging that I had to keep balanced with the research content I was receiving. It could be easy to wander off on a mutually reminiscent journey of identity development, but there was always a tension between the rapport building and the clarity of data gathering in my mind.

In the Detroit study, especially during the initial phase, when I contacted Asian American organizations for referrals, participants of other Asian ethnicities seemed to be more receptive when I told them I was Japanese American born and raised in the Midwest. I believe that even if they had lived in cities with high populations of Asians and Asian Americans, there was a general consensus that life was "different" for minorities in the Midwest. If anything, there was less overt racism, although all believed it still exists. During the interview process it was common to hear phrases such as, "I don't know if this is how the Japanese do it, but we Chinese (Koreans, Filipino, Hmong) do . . . or think. . . ." It was easy to talk about cultural norms that crossed different ethnicities such as the importance of family and respect for teachers and elders. Of course, everyone had stories of exceptional cases that didn't fit the perceived "norm."

One Korean mother described a particularly disturbing incident of a lesson on racism taught in her daughter's second grade class. She indicated that she could share her anger about it with me since I would understand her frustration, being an Asian-American mother and a former teacher. The classic school study conducted in the 1960s in an Iowa classroom that arbitrarily divided children into groups of privileged "blue eyes" and minority "brown eyes" was replicated in her daughter's classroom. The blue eyes were given preferential treatment by the teacher while the brown eyes faced discrimination throughout the day of the experiment. This mother's child was in the brown-eyes group, and at the end of the day, she was told by a child in the blue-eyes group that the Korean daughter "was black, so she was the slave" of the other privileged child. This comment was internalized and thereafter her daughter worried about getting too much sun, too tanned, so as to not appear too "black" (Adler, 1998). When the Korean mother contacted the teacher, she was told that it was a lesson and the children should know it wasn't real. This was not her daughter's experience.

During a preliminary visit of my Hmong study, I found that the few staff members who were Hmong and Vietnamese seemed to easily open up, indicating that they were pleased that Southeast Asian families in their school were to be the focus of this research. I was invited into the classroom of the three Hmong teachers anytime during my four-day visit to the school. One of the first impressions about the Hmong culture came from a Hmong teacher who said, "We Hmong don't easily assimilate." Later she asked if I knew about the story (myth) that the place of origin in China where the Hmong were said to first live was actually inhabited by Japanese and that each year many Japanese tourists come to that city to honor their relatives. Thus, Japanese and Hmong may have the same "roots," possibly genetically as well as culturally. I was amazed and grateful for her openness and perceived racial connection to me.

As I attempted to set up a group gathering of Hmong participants, I learned that there was a strong division in the Hmong social hierarchy between men and women. Because there was one male Hmong teacher, I was told that he probably would not attend the evening dinner at the home of a colleague. Indeed this was true, and it took me several trips to begin to develop a relationship with him, which may or may not have been a function of my being an Asian-American woman. It may have been the dynamics of the group of females (two of whom were European American) or the nature of the research itself. These are interesting dimensions of this research I am currently pursuing.

MUTUAL INSIGHTS AND SHIFTING IDENTITIES

There have been times during dialogues with participants that I have felt that their words have enlightened my thinking and enriched my perceptions. One such incident was in the mothering study when a Sansei mother, whom I knew as a child but had not seen in some forty years when I interviewed her, spoke of the differences she saw between herself and her European-American husband. "I always thought the differences were individual rather than cultural, but the more I participate in your study, the more I think they ARE cultural" (Adler, 1998). This struck me as exactly how I had been interpreting my marriage of thirty-two years, while my parents were well aware of the cultural differences between us and were trying to accommodate their son-in-law's ways of interacting. Perhaps I interpreted his ethnocentrism as the norm, and accommodated him in order to "fit" into his worldview. While growing up I did not have a sizable ethnic community by which I could compare behavior, expectations, and interaction styles. This could have contributed to a weaker ethnic identity as a Japanese American, compared to a more dominant ascribed identity as a visible racial minority. I always knew that racially I was different from most of my peers, but I assumed a cultural connectedness in terms of mainstream "American" culture. This research gave me the opportunity to probe for specific cross-cultural examples, to inventory my own family relationships, and to ponder the salience of my racial identification.

A particular interview conducted during my Detroit study made me aware of my desire to connect with my own "Japaneseness." The woman I interviewed was from Japan and considered herself Japanese in terms of values and beliefs. But, since she intended to stay in the United States, she assumed her children would become Japanese American, picking up more Western styles of behavior as they readily acclimated to American schools and society. She was a bilingual teaching assistant in her children's public elementary school. What first struck me as interesting was that on entering her home, you could not tell from the decor that a Japanese family lived there. My own home had many more artifacts of Japanese origin and design than I had while growing up. My sister pointed out that this might have been a function of the time, politically (post–World War II), when we as a family did not draw attention to ourselves as Japanese Americans. But as I furnished my own homes over the years, I find myself including a more Asian flair than a Western motif. The environment we create for our family life represents our attitudes and self-identities. It reflects who we are at that time in our lives.

Another personal insight that I gained from my research came as a result of conversations with a Hmong administrator, a European-American counselor, and a Hmong counselor, both assigned to schools with high Southeast Asian populations. Usually being in minority positions all my life, I celebrated the possibility of having Hmong professionals in positions of power. I had always campaigned for the recruitment of people of color into the teaching profession. Not being part of an ethnic community on a daily basis, I was unaware of the strong influence ethnic communities have over the families they serve. This community influence is particularly true of the Hmong in the Twin Cities of Saint Paul/Minneapolis. "Even though I am now in the administration building, I have limited power," said the parent coordinator for Hmong families, "They (community leaders) want results and I cannot deliver because of political systems" (Adler, 2002). Parents want results while they generally do not understand the political constraints of U.S. institutions. Hmong counselors, teachers, social workers, and translators are sometimes caught in the precarious position of having to report negative incidents to school authorities, private and delicate information about families in the community, that might include members of their immediate or extended families. How does one balance professional responsibility with the honor of the community (not bringing shame)?

MAKING THE RESEARCHER'S VOICE PART OF THE STUDY

In conducting research, I try to carefully delineate my narratives from those of my participants. I am as explicit as possible about how our conversations evolved and carefully code my probes differently from their responses. If there appears to be agreement, at least at the conceptual level, I indicate it by using both codes (mine and those of my participants). I take ownership for any of my own reactions and opinions, and make certain they are clearly separated from the words of the participants. But I do not shy away from interpreting the influence we have on each other during the research process. I also rely heavily on member check, having participants read transcripts and some parts of the written interpretation. I may frame similar questions or issues in a different manner or context to help clarify my views from that of my participants. Or I may restate what appears to be a point of agreement between us, allowing the participant to reaffirm it. Sometimes this leads to deeper meanings and specific differences. I ask for examples so that additional data confirms a stated viewpoint. I also look for and document signals of connectedness and tension in my field notes. These are written primarily as observed behaviors, but sometimes are "gut feelings" of uneasiness or shared awareness.

Earlier in this chapter I spoke of the problematic dichotomy of "insider" and "outsider" research stances. I still see myself as having a changing, negotiated identity as a listener, a recorder, an interpreter, and a co-constructor of data. Sometimes the data represents the voice of the participant. At other times it may be our voices as we interact, agree, disagree, support each other, and negotiate positions. Sometimes I play the set director, or the motivator. At other times, I play the receptor/receiver, who may throw the ball back to the sender with new challenges or words of support and acknowledgment. It is dialogical and therefore interconnected. It is a mutually engaged interaction, though I make it a priority to take the participant's lead, trying to uncover her perspectives first.

Sometimes I set the stage by opening with a story of my own, from my experiences. This has provoked responses and stories of their own that may or may not be similar to mine. From there we discuss differences in context or personalities involved. For example, when discussing gender expectations of our fathers, one Sansei woman commented, "Your father was very traditional Japanese." I had not thought of that description, but, in contrast to her father, I could understand her comment. Sometimes, when discussing a particular topic common for Asian Americans, participants might ask me the background or experiences of my family. In a sense, they were seeking commonalities by which we could better communicate. This occurred most often concerning my fluency (or lack of) in the Japanese language. There was concern about the loss of language, and cultural underpinnings, across the generations.

While situating myself in the research process, I had to be cognizant of how I differed from the person I was interviewing. One example of this situating occurred when one of the participants in the mothering study shared her experiences as a member of the Nisei Drum and Bugle Corps. She showed me the video of their reunion and explained how the elder Nisei parents used the corps membership for their Sansei children to teach the cultural lesson of working your hardest for the benefit of the group. Individualism was secondary to membership within the group, and excellence was a group goal (Adler, 1998). I had never experienced this kind of group cohesion and responsibility to others within the context of competition. Her story gave me another perspective on how we had been socialized as Japanese Americans.

In all three studies, I learned from my participants in unique ways. They helped me see multiple perspectives by both inquiring about and challenging the personal experiences I shared with them. For example, the Japanese woman in my Detroit study helped me acknowledge my connectedness to a Japanese worldview, and some of the elder Nisei participants in the mothering study helped me recall the richness of my heritage as well as the struggles of my Issei grandparents. Communication with Hmong teachers helped me recall my identity as an elementary teacher in the 1970s when I was just beginning to identify with being Japanese. Interactions with women in my studies who have interracial marriages caused me to ponder the complexities of childrearing within mixed cultural contexts. These are only some of the examples that have led to the construction of my own identity as a Japanese (Asian) American. I suspect they were as liberating and confusing to the participants as they were to me. They did lead to reflexivity by all of us about our lived experiences in the Midwest and the effect our environments had on our beliefs and identity development. They are ongoing, shifting identities.

CRAFTING THE RESEARCH PRODUCT

Researching from an "insider" perspective some of the time is fruitful and challenging and forces me to situate myself, both to the participant and in the written analysis. It gives me great satisfaction to know that I am facilitating the *voices* of these Asian-American participants. Their messages can help others learn about the multiple ways in which knowledge is constructed and experiences are interpreted. In this research process, we play various roles and are ascribed various positions while interacting. The honesty by which we as researchers describe this "placing" (Mirza, 1998) and the trustworthiness of our interpretations are critical. It is a delicate literary process.

I take full responsibility for the written document, yet it represents multiple voices and co-constructions. I feel as if I have in some way contributed to the empowerment of the women in my studies by having given them both permission and encouragement to speak, while attempting to protect their personal privacy. The data can be reported as a consensus of the group, the "us," as well as the representation of specific individuals. There is a collective *voice*, as well as multiple *voices* in the final product. This is particularly relevant since, for many Asian Americans, verbal expression of one's opinions or viewpoints is carefully monitored in the context of interpersonal relationships. I believe this results from both cultural norms and internalized oppression, depending on the speaker's experiences with discrimination, age and generational level, and fluency with English and mainstream culture. I wonder how these research experiences have helped me understand my own internalized colonization and allowed me to serve as a model for other participants. The research process has been liberating for me and the writing of our stories has been psychologically rewarding.

REFERENCES

Adler, S. M. (1998). *Mothering, education, and ethnicity: The transformation of Japanese American culture.* New York: Garland.

Adler, S. M. (2001, April). *Racial and ethnic identity formation of Midwestern Asian American children.* Paper presented at the American Educational Research Association Annual Meeting, Seattle, Wash.

Adler, S. M. (2002). Racial and ethnic identity formation of Midwestern Asian American children. *Contemporary Issues in Early Childhood.* United Kingdom: Triangle Journal. (www.triangle.co.uk/ciec).

Cross, W. E. (1991). *Shades of black: Diversity in African-American identity.* Philadelphia: Temple University Press.

Hekman, S. J. (1990). *Gender and knowledge: Elements of postmodern feminism.* Cambridge: Polity Press.

Helms, J. E. (1990). *Black and white racial identity: Theory, research, and practice.* New York: Greenwood Press.

Howard, G. R. (1999). *We can't teach what we don't know: White teachers, multiracial schools.* New York: Teachers College Press.

Kondo, D. K. (1990). *Crafting selves: Power, gender, and discourses of identity in a Japanese workplace.* Chicago: University of Chicago Press.

Ladson-Billings, G., and Tate, W. F. (1995). Toward a critical race theory of education. *Teachers College Record, 97*(1), 47–68.

Mirza, M. (1998). "Same voices, same lives?": Revisiting black feminist standpoint epistemology. In P. Connelly and B. Troyna (Eds.), *Researching racism in education: Politics, theory and practice.* Philadelphia: Open University Press.

Narayan, K. (1993). How native is a "native" anthropologist? *American Anthropologist, 95,* 671–686.

Nicholson, L. J. (1990). *Feminism/postmodernism.* New York: Routledge.

Oakley, A. (1981). Interviewing women: A contradiction in terms. In H. Roberts (Ed.), *Doing feminist research.* Boston: Routledge.

Peshkin, A. (1988). In search of subjectivity—one's own. *Educational Researcher,* October, 17–22.

Phinney, J. S., and M. J. Rotheram. (1987). *Children's ethnic socialization: Pluralism and development.* Newbury Park, CA: Sage.

Sheets, R.H., and Hollins, E.R. (1999). *Racial and ethnic identity in school practices: Aspects of human development.* Mahwah, NJ: Lawrence Erlbaum.

Sue, S. and D. W. Sue. (1975). Chinese-American personality and mental health, *Amerasia Journal, 2,* 158–202.

Tatum, B. D. (1992). Talking about race, learning about racism: An application of racial identity development theory in the classroom. *Harvard Educational Review, 62,* 1–24.

Wu, F. H. (2002). *Yellow: Race in America beyond black and white.* New York: Basic Books.

Zia, H. (2000). *Asian American dreams: The emergence of an American people.* New York: Farrar, Straus and Giroux.

CHAPTER SEVEN

Decolonizing Research on Gender Disparity in Education in Niger: Complexities of Language, Culture, and Homecoming

HAOUA M. HAMZA

Ninety percent of the population in Africa today speaks only African languages (Ngugi wa Thiong' o, 1986, p. 27).

Buro Hawul man, yalla n'dawu suro kerye Diffa yen keraza fuwu ro leza? Mbeji yaye , gana ma nya? Yalla mewun luko uwun, au biya findi so kozein wa suro fiwu yen. Attye nognena. Wonnye yal fiakku, au biya fidiyau, suro yal miya yen kangurno sawandin. Ngewunza so walta leza cida kotaranza ye sadin. Jire dero, wu koronyi fuwumandero genakin mbeji. Fuwuma cidi nde ye dema kerye nde dea ngurnozanyi wo yen nongenyi, au biya fuwuma kerye so dema Diffa ro chissanyi wo yen nongenyi, kuru ala ma yallande dema hangal kuttuwa wo yero nongenyi. Ndasoson yaye, kerye'a gade de Diffa wa fuwunbuin kozana. Ade nankaro, awo dono fuwumande ro gullukkin ade shima; ciza tarai ro daza lamar ilmu yallaye kerye ade yero. Shima a'a raksainba ada'a daji sandya kollo fatoro isa banasa. Alamanza de lokkol de yen fuwuro lezainba , fato yen yanza' a awanza'a banazanyi. Daji akai do yim lokkol den saiya duzai ya, shi fero ye dember nze zane lan mit serye ya zawal nem zawar ye sedain. Shima tada konga dea, nasartya, leze kulo kotara yen tattachi chidajin , au biya yalla bela

123

ye wa kela keljya; daji zuwut so kela lai yen shayi kenza au, tafa kenza'a kasun afima gade kendo ye sadanyi. Fuwumande deye muradenza chissa'a ande ya kerenta ye mbeji wa wo? N'gela! Wande mbeji wa, sowori do yikkin ade shima ande'a samno ro bowosa, kawuri anden, kamanden ye kerenza, daji delefu donyi kaziyi ade'a kerenta ye de ande samman fandiyowe. Ade nyi ya, to shi wane ye fanzein napkata, wu ye dina waras wayi ya shana ram nyin demba ni kelan na, buni keri n'juwo ro lengin, ya wane ye samno demaro lezenyi, kele futu fin kela kaziyi nde ye bui yen? (Hamza, 2001, p. 181)

The above lines represent an answer of a non-formally educated female participant in Kanuri, her mother tongue, to the following question: "If you were in the presence of: The minister of education . . . the representatives of donor agencies . . . the school administrator . . . a teacher . . . an opinion leader . . . or your traditional chief, and you had the opportunity to be heard, what suggestions would you make to help narrow the gender disparity in educational outcomes in your region?" The following is the English translation of the participant's answer.

To begin with, how many graduates or educated people does this city have? There is but a handful of them. We are aware that there are not more than fifteen or twenty children who succeed out of fifty. May be 30 or 40% succeed when you take a total of one hundred children and the majority goes back to work in their family garden. I will frankly ask these authorities some questions; for I wonder whether it is our national leaders themselves who do not want to foster growth and progress in this region, or if it is the regional and local authorities themselves who lack concerns for Diffa, or if the children themselves are too dumb. In any case, other regions fare better than Diffa. I will tell them that if they don't promote our children's education, then they should let them come back home because they don't seem to progress at school and are not helpful at home. Once expelled, some girls tie the wrapper tightly up, ready to hit the streets for prostitution. As for the boy, if he is lucky enough, he will go and cultivate red pepper in the family garden, or else chances are he will join a group of young delinquents who sit and drink tea and blow cigarettes on the streets. Do the authorities care to listen to us parents? Well, if they do, I would suggest that they convene meetings and involve us in sharing and exchanging ideas and take steps backed by their support to address those issues. But when Mrs. X. is sitting in her home, and me on my way to buy fresh fish, and Misses Y and Z's mothers did not attend the meeting, how can ideas and actions be developed and applied?

I will come back to my interpretation of this answer, and will address the following questions. How knowledgeable are we about our issues? Can we listen to one another to problem solve? Are we collectively and uniquely involved in fostering growth in our communities?

SOME LESSONS ON DESIGNING AND CONDUCTING RESEARCH AS AN INDIGENOUS SCHOLAR: COMPLEXITIES AND CONTRADICTIONS

Embarking for research in my country, Niger, to collect data on gender disparity in secondary education was a passionate and significant decision that I made because of my commitment to understanding the issue and contributing to its solution. It was inspiring. This process became more exciting when I resolved to expand the pool of participants to girls (since it is about their educational experiences) and their parents, whether the latter were formally educated or not. The process in itself is full of contradictions, not only with regard to the choice of language or languages of research, but also because the research took place in a context of a postcolonial, predominantly Muslim sub-Saharan African country. Like many other African countries, Niger has what Mazrui (1986) describes as the triple heritage: African, Euro-Christian, and Islamic. The country has ten officially recorded national languages. Not many, one may say, compared to its southern neighbor, Nigeria, with over two hundred languages. This reality in itself is complex and full of contradictions.

In Niger, in which 75% of the population is illiterate and where the illiteracy rate is highest among females, who constitute slightly over 50% of the population (Rabo, 1994), the real questions then came to my mind. How many languages would I need to use? Are there any instruments developed in these languages? If not, who would translate the instrument back into English? Who would transcribe the data? And, the main concern, how true to the original meanings could the transcribed data be?

In a context where French is the official language, and as a doctoral student in an American university, the choice of language started to loom as an issue as I developed the research proposal. These questions, in combination with the multilingual context, constituted the complexities and contradictions in my research experience, a reality that confirmed Smith' s (1999) concern that, as an indigenous researcher carrying out research with other indigenous people, there was little to no help regarding issues an insider would encounter in the standard

methodological guidebooks (p. 196). As a multilingual indigenous researcher, however, there was an opportunity for using my linguistic skills
in my dissertation research. It was a challenge to conceive the instrument
in French (which in itself raised some concerns) and translate it into two
other national languages, Hausa and Kanuri, then back into English for
data analysis and final write-up. It became even more challenging to
transcribe the data from each of these three languages into English before proper analysis began.

Despite my graduate university's significant initiatives in advancing international education, its Bureau of Research was not equipped to help international students and scholars who may conduct research in different
languages. Although the transcription process was time-consuming and
frustrating at times, it was also fulfilling. There were some fun—and
fond—moments too, as I heard those voices in the tapes and a sheep bleat-
ing in the background, or children playing and being rebuked for disrupting the interview, or when hearing the voices of impromptu neighbors
announcing themselves through their *laalewos*. And I remembered how
they would quickly hold their mouths and disappear for a later visit.

THE QUEST FOR SIGNIFICANCE

The question of significance to me has primarily been a lifelong quest and
an academic goal in this whole process. My research interest relates to gender disparity in educational access, persistence, and achievement at the secondary level in Niger. The purpose of the research was to identify state
strategies and interventions in terms of policy, programs, and projects that
appear to improve girls' educational outcomes. Though the study took
place in a context traditionally fraught with gender inequity, I needed to
investigate the nature of efforts undertaken by the government, including
multilateral efforts by non-state agencies or NGOs. The immediate objective was to identify such efforts, with a long-term goal of analyzing policy
impact. My reasons for investigating this issue go back to the image of my
early years as an elementary schoolgirl among many in my hometown, yet
one of the very few who made it through high school and graduated to
college. Like most of my schoolmates, I also come from a family background in which both parents are not formally educated, a factor that, according to many researchers, contributes to the lack of persistence in the
girl child's educational experience in developing countries (c.f. Tietjen,
1995). Therefore, I was inspired to know how much of this picture has
changed since I was a child, by investigating various stakeholders' roles in
and perceptions of girls' schooling in Niger. Although the senior high
school girls constituted my primary source of data, it was crucial for me to

interview their parents, especially their mothers, in addition to their teachers, their male classmates, and policy-makers.

Interviewing some of the parents, especially the mothers, led me to integrate several national languages because several participants cannot speak
French, which is the official language, let alone English. I needed to include these mothers in the dialogue. I needed them to confirm what I
knew deep down—that these women may not have any formal schooling
but they discern the issues that surround them. The long quote at the beginning of this chapter testifies to the good grasp of the issue by an "illiterate" female participant. So would I hope to gain a more balanced
understanding into the issues, concerns, values, and visions of more than
50% of a population that is female, among which the level of illiteracy is
known to be higher?

DECOLONIZING RESEARCH METHODOLOGY

A CULTURALLY SENSITIVE APPROACH

In her book *Decolonizing Methodologies,* Smith (1999) states, "When indigenous peoples became the researchers and not merely the researched,
the activity of research is transformed. Questions are framed differently,
priorities are ranked differently, problems are defined differently, and people participate on different terms" (p.197). Smith's position is crucial in
research by indigenous scholars.

How meaningful was my methodology? First, going back into my
community to conduct research made me see the necessity of a culturally
relevant method, as well as my limitations in not finding an appropriate
one. Although this was my first major research project, I yearned for a
topic that begs our attention in the field of education and in society. The
topic, which is very current and a common issue to many developing
countries, emerged from my personal reflections on gender inequity in the
Nigerien society about which I wrote eight years prior to developing the
dissertation proposal. Second, meaning to me also lies in the way I framed
the research questions. For instance, do the questions focus on the people,
their issues, and their experiences? Third, does my approach advance
meaning making by having respondents actively participate through the
use of their mother tongue as they comfortably answer questions throwing
in a proverb here, a saying there? And how significant is the content of
such a study to the indigenous community while fulfilling the requirements of a doctoral program in a Western university?

Niger's formal education system as we know it reflects and embodies
its colonial legacy. It is a heritage fraught with inequities and challenges,

with goals that neither the Addis Conference of Ministers of Education of the 1960s, nor the post-independence era, or even Niger's most recent and historical 'Conference Nationale' has been able to address effectively (Hamza, 2001). Among instances of challenges are what Phillipson (1996) calls " linguistic imperialism [which] is monolingual" (p. 163). According to him, " 'the straight for English' [and I might add or 'for French'] policy, promoted not by the colonial government, but the newly independent African governments who wanted to deemphasize 'ethnicity and build a sense of nationhood'" promoted linguistic imperialism. Another example pointed out by several policy-makers in my research is the issue of gender gap in formal education, historically created during the colonial era. Moreover, as argued by Mikell (1997), the issue of female marginalization in education reflects existing forms of gender inequity that colonization reinforced. The sociocultural and religious environment has successfully marginalized women both economically and politically, and the formal education system has been among the effective tools that reproduce these practices (Charlick and Ousseini, 1996).

My inquiry into an issue rooted in the historical and sociocultural fabric of the society and the choice of languages spoken by the participants suggest initiatives for decolonizing my research. The issue of gender inequity in education is both a sociocultural and colonial construction that I need to approach both critically and sensitively. Thus, it was imperative that, as a native researcher, I sought to "decolorize my mind," as suggested by N'gugi wa Thiong'o (1986) by beginning to deemphasize the sole use of colonial languages. I revisited my national languages in order to meet my participants where they are. At the sociocultural level, both my collaborator (my brother) and I enjoyed a great support for this study and adopted what Smith describes as a "culturally sensitive" approach to ensure, for instance, that I interviewed female parents while my male collaborator conducted interviews with male parents, according to the cultural norm in the community.

RECONNECTING WITH A WORLDVIEW: AN INTEGRATIVE APPROACH

The challenge of decolonizing research methodology exists for those of us indigenous/African researchers who have imbibed Western methodologies and may not seem to relevantly frame the questions and issues in terms that reach out and apply to the indigenous worldviews and contemporary realities and experiences. Likewise, our non-indigenous counterparts, who do not educate themselves about the African languages and worldview, may face the same limitations. The very word "decolonizing" suggests a reality with several legacies to indigenous people. Discussing

African cultural identity, Ali Mazrui (1986) proposes two routes for Africa's redemption:

> One is the imperative of looking inwards towards Africa's ancestors. The other is the imperative of looking outwards towards the wider world. Indigenous culture has been the foundation of the inward imperative towards ancestry. Islam and Western culture have constituted the beginnings of looking outwards towards the wider world of humanity at large.

The Western African setting where I conducted my research is rich with all three cultures: indigenous, Islamic, and Western. Decolonizing research in such a context to me is a process with two facets: On the one hand, such an approach needs to be relevant to its indigenous environment; on the other hand, because of its foreign cultural legacies, the relationship of indigenous research methodologies with other forms of methodologies can be celebrated.

In this postmodern and globalized era, Mazrui's argument suggests vast possibilities enabling both indigenous and non-indigenous researchers to rethink their approaches. The inward imperative in the field of research points to the need to deemphasize the Western approach to research in indigenous setting and requires one explore and produce knowledge that is reflective of the African worldview. It is a worldview that Tournas (1996) describes as the *Tswana soul,* which "is the composite of every man, woman, animal and plant-in short, all life of which the Tswana individual was just one bull in a herd that acquired its identity as a collective unit." Here, Tournas introduces us to a pre-Cartesian worldview, in which interconnectedness is the theme, and cultural practices (and I must argue that research as a tool for knowledge production is one of them) help connect self to the environment, because one saw oneself as part of it. This worldview is present in traditional African societies from Nouakchott in Mauritania to Johannesburg, South Africa, from Yaounde, Cameroon to Antananarivo, Madagascar. This is a frame of reference, which, as stated by Moumouni (1964) in his book *L'Education en Afrique,* includes institutions such as tales, riddles, proverbs, and apprenticeship and initiation practices. These are teaching and learning practices that are among others, the African ways of knowing, and of engaging in research. As a tool for knowledge construction, research needs to look into these indigenous ways, not in essentialized or exoticized ways, but in ways that reflect their complex and often contradictory heritage.

In essence, it is worth pondering how the form and style of one's methodological approach draws from indigenous philosophies or belief systems to pave the way toward reasserting a common African cultural identity. The meaning embodied in African myths, cosmology, folklore, language, songs, proverbs, and oral literature, to mention only a few features of traditional African culture, and their philosophical connotations should be examined for a better understanding of the way Africans look at life and its issues. In a few instances in my research, participants who were fluent in both French and a national language or two, would comfortably code-switch to answer a question because they knew I understood those cultural nuances. These nuggets of knowledge are worth saving when they appear in our data and should be interpreted with a renewed interest. Research in such a context must present African worldview in its meaningful, highest, and broadest conception. (culture and civilization).

Decolonizing research methodology to me must represent a process that not only reaffirms formerly suppressed forms of knowledge, but also produces discernible indigenous models of research that integrate a broadened circle of diverse ways of knowing in a global and postmodern age. This by no means suggests provincialism in research methodology. It is essential, as Tournas (1996) suggests clearly, to understand the effect of the "deference" to Western research model on the African culture, while being careful to avoid what Said (1991) terms 'the logic of displacement' that seeks to replace "one set of authorities with another" (p. 311). Therefore, the task of decolonizing research methodologies needs to apply the lessons of decolonization itself, and African independences to guard us from what Fanon (1963) described as unchecked nationalism, and enable ourselves to raise social consciousness in the field of the indigenous research model in a sustained manner.

Mazrui's second imperative for Africa seems important for decolonizing research. While it is crucial for decolonized research methodologies to embody indigenous forms and styles as cultural works, indigenous cultures with a triple heritage like the one I belong to may not pretend to be pure and unchanging; hence, the significance of Mazrui's second imperative for looking outwards to humanity at large to make this a collaborative effort. This reinforces the theme of interconnectedness. Said (1991) calls it worldliness, which echoes Cesaire (1947) who asserts that "no race possesses the monopoly of beauty, of intelligence, of force, and there is a place for all at the rendez-vous of victory." Cesaire's vision suggests integration rather than exclusion. It is about broadening the scope, which in research will allow cooperation and the celebration of various forms of research.

A LESSON FROM THE 'ILLITERATE' MOTHER, HOUSEWIFE, AND BUSINESSWOMAN

Now back to the opening quote. I must confess that it was humbling, though I was not surprised, to listen to this mother who had no formal education, yet held a critical perspective in her response. She had a strong will, a sense of business, and a determination to succeed in life. She also has a vision for her daughter, whose schooling she fully supports. In another section of the interview she stated that she encouraged her daughter to major in business and clearly explained why. When asked about suggestions she would make to increase girls' educational participation in the region if she were before various political, educational, and community leaders, she cleared her throat, took a deep breath, and gave what I consider powerful reflections in Kanuri, her mother tongue. As an indigenous researcher, this experience confirmed that deemphasizing the primacy of the colonial language in my interview was an important step in stopping what Phillipson (1996) calls hegemonic practices in my approach.

This participant is remarkably eloquent in her language—Kanuri. She was aware of the issue as well as the obstacles in the community. Although she was unable to read any statistics in French, her figures regarding students' achievement rates, as she discerned them in her mind, were approximately correct. Her comments give us a glimpse into the socioeconomic reality of her community, the attitude that many uninvolved parents adopt, and the nature of her own occupation. She probed and was interested in understanding the leaders' roles and responsibilities, and then she stated their lack of accountability. Finally, the participant acknowledged the lack of involvement by parents and the need for authorities to reach out. Toward the end, she pointed at an important skill, that of listening and a collaborative approach to sharing and exchanging ideas and knowledge to address issues.

This quote highlights the capacity of the average 'illiterate' female parent to deconstruct old ways of doing business with school and reconstruct new approaches for addressing issues relating to their children's schooling by reaching back and drawing from our traditions. To do so, she invites us to look into the centuries-old African approach to collective problem solving. In light of Africa's postcolonial reality, native researchers need to create relevant and functional approaches that enable both the researcher and the participant to unleash their creative cultural energies and enthusiasm for cultural renewal. This respondent basically refreshed my memory of the Nigerien value of interconnectedness and its collective approach to problem solving, which I saw at work while growing up in Niger.

UNFORESEEN IMPACT

During data collection, many participants expressed their appreciation for seeing me come back to the community to conduct research, while some expressed cynicism about the tendency for many educated sons and daughters not to look back. Those fathers and mothers were proud and authentically interested in sharing about their sons, daughters, and themselves with "people who were just like them," to borrow from Smith (1999, p. 197).

On one occasion, an impromptu trip to the elementary school I attended to collect curricular documents became an opportunity for the principal to introduce me to these young faces in as many classrooms and grade levels as he could. It was the end of the morning classes, so we took fast steps toward the classrooms. The principal told me that he "wanted to inspire them and let them know how far they could go from these benches and yet come back." This is a metaphor that reflects how far I have gone (from these same classrooms years back, in a very rural Diffa), all the way to the United States and returning to the same community to collect data for a dissertation. The following day, mothers came home to comment on my short presence in their children's classrooms. Those schoolchildren who knew me talked to their parents about me, and those who were unsure of my identity (and wondered whether I was one of my sisters or my mother's sister, because we resemble one another) mentioned that they had a visitor in their classroom who looked like Djimai, Aisha, two of my sisters or Hadjia (my mother).

I discuss this occurrence among others because it finally hit me at the end of my interviews and just before I left my hometown that I had my minute of impact on these children, thus reminding me of the compliment a former classmate I had not seen in a long time gave me on the bus to Diffa, when he found out the reasons for my trip. He said "tu representes sans doute un modele a emuler et ton theme est d'actualitte," which suggests that I represent a role model and that my research topic is very current. Was this a prediction or what! Verily, I did not anticipate the impact I might have on these young elementary school students as I was struggling to develop my proposal, although I knew that my commitment to a group such as women and adolescent girls has been genuine from the time I started my literary writings.

CONCLUDING THOUGHTS

Africa has two imperatives—to avoid the trap of reductionism and exclusion (Mazrui, 1986). To encourage change, native researchers need to realize their own impact in conducting studies using their linguistic and sociocultural skills and the decision to include the 'illiterate' people's perspectives about the issue tackled. As a native researcher, my choice for the topic and inspiration derived from personal experiences evolving as a daughter, a rural schoolgirl, and later, as a wife and a mother in a society that marginalizes women in various ways and in an educational system that is slow to reconnect with its environment. Furthermore, though I am a teacher, I am also an avid student of my mother—a woman whose tremendous impact on her community I admire. Like millions of her counterparts on the continent, her lack of formal education is no barrier for active involvement at important levels in her community. I realize the importance of probing into meaningful ways of examining issues based on both my informal and formal education.

It was armed with a sense of reality that I adopted a multilingual approach to data collection, which constituted both a challenge and an asset. It was an asset because it drew me closer to the participants who were aware that their perspectives were understood. I believe that while the use of national languages in this study is an experience that is inclusive of the so-called illiterate's perspective, it is liberating for the researcher as well as the participants, both the illiterate and the formally educated. For the essence of the message is captured, and the needs are articulated because it is the participant's language that is used. This practice should become a powerful tool for the native researcher to begin the process of unlearning 'linguistic imperialism' in research, as argued by Phillipson (1996). I believe native researchers need to empower their language by reassessing its impact in their research design and methodology.

In an era of globalization and increasing knowledge, however, I concur with Mazrui's (1986) suggestion of two imperatives to the African in general. And to the native researcher I would suggest that while on one hand, she or he seizes the colonial language as a tool to fulfill the imperative of looking "outward toward the wider humanity," to disseminate the knowledge acquired about his or her background to connect globally; on the other hand, domestically, it is imperative that the native researcher looks "inward towards the ancestry" in order to begin the process of 'decolonizing the mind,' as Ngugi (1986) suggests, by making an effective use of one's mother tongue. The native researcher should feel at home code-switching along with her multilingual respondents to reframe issues, provide answers, and express authentic needs and feelings as did mine in this study. This process will bring the native researcher closer to his or her community. Although finding an appropriate methodology constitutes a serious limitation in conducting research in a native setting, we need to learn to reconnect despite our Western training.

I would, therefore, encourage a periodic "retour a la source," a return to the continent by researchers and scholars relocated and/or uprooted to other continents to avoid what a Hausa proverb suggests—"kowa ya bar guida, guida ma ya bar shi," simply meaning that whosoever abandons his root will be abandoned by it.

REFERENCES

Cesaire, A. (1947). *Cahier d'un retour au pays natal.* [Return to my native land.] Trans. A. Berger and J. Bostock. Baltimore: Penguin.

Charlick, R. and H. Ousseini. (1996). *Advancing the participation of women in Nigerien political life* [on-line]. Available: November 12, 1999, http://www.csuohio.edu/polisci/nigerwom.htm.

Fanon, F. (1963). *The wretched of the earth.* Trans. H. Kirkpatrick. New York: Grove.

Hamza, H. M. (2001). *State strategies and interventions that increase secondary school girls' educational participation in Niger.* Unpublished Ph.D. dissertation, Kent State University.

Mazrui, A. (1986). *The Africans: A triple heritage.* London: BBC Publications.

Mikell, G. (1997). *African feminism: The politics of survival in Sub-Saharan Africa.* Philadelphia: University of Pennsylvania Press.

Moumouni, A. (1964). *L'Education en Afrique.* Paris: F. maspero.

Ngugi Wa Thiong'o. (1986). *Decolonizing the mind: The politics of language in African literature.* London: James Currey.

Phillipson, R. (1996). *Linguistic imperialism: African perspectives. ELT Journal,* 50(2) Oxford University Press.

Rabo, M. (1994). *Seminaire national sur l'education des filles.* [National convention on girls' schooling]. Niger: Kollo.

Said, E. (1991). The politics of knowledge. *Raritan,* 11(1) 17–31.

Smith, T. L. (1999) *Decolonizing methodologies: Research and indigenous peoples.* London: Zed Books.

Tietjen, K. (1995). *Educating girls: Strategies to increase access, persistence, and achievement.* Washington, DC: Creative Associates International, Inc.

Tournas, A. S. (1996). From sacred initiation to bureaucratic apostasy. *Comparative Education,* Vol. 32(1) 27–43.

CHAPTER EIGHT

Education Research with Philippine Communities in Greece: Intricacies and Possibilities

Leodinito Y. Cañete

The primary focus of my dissertation for the Department of Primary Education of the Aristotle University of Thessaloniki was to investigate the conditions surrounding the basic education of children of Philippine communities in Greece. My research tasks were to describe Philippine immigrants' children's experiences in different learning environments, to gather the opinions and attitudes of their parents toward primary education, and to document the educational initiatives of Philippine communities in Greece. Issues that prevailed in the basic education of these children were identified and raised from these experiences, opinions, attitudes, and initiatives. These issues were grounded on the contextual relationship between pedagogy and sociology because the societal concerns that affected these communities had an impact on the issues that confronted schooling. In broad terms this was what my study was about.

In this chapter I will not delve into the results of my dissertation, but will focus on the details of my education research methodology with Filipinas and Filipinos living and studying in Greece. My research was made possible by a grant from the Greek State Scholarships Foundation (IKY). This financial aid provided the basis for my assuming the privileged role of *iskolar ng bayan* (state scholar) in the Philippine communities in Greece with all its intricacies and possibilities.

BASES FOR QUALITATIVE EDUCATION RESEARCH

The goal of investigating the conditions surrounding the basic education of Philippine immigrants' children in Greece was carried out using qualitative research for a number of reasons. Describing these conditions demanded a qualitative look at the sociological and pedagogical conditions of these communities.[1] Qualitative research methods were used because the conditions were studied in their natural setting and the issues were perceived and interpreted with the participants. I understood the events in the field because I shared some common perceptions and interpretations with them. Through my interactions and interviews with my compatriots, I discovered themes and together we suggested their meanings (Tuckman 1994).

I designed the study as naturalistic inquiry of real-world situations as they unfolded (Bogdan and Bilken, 1998). As such, I did not have predetermined outcomes and was nonmanipulative, unobtrusive, noncontrolling, and at the same time flexible to the field conditions. My research took a holistic perspective by studying the whole phenomenon of the education of the children of Philippine communities in Greece as a complex interrelated system. That is why the educational research agenda was contextualized within the living and working conditions of Filipinas and Filipinos in Greece (Charles, 1995).

The naturalistic inquiry called for the use of my own judgment instead of quantitative measuring instruments to accurately identify and depict existing variables and their relationships in order to discover and learn from the participants' experiences (Spindler, 1982; Spindler and Spindler, 1987). Thus, it raised more questions on the educational conditions of these children relative to racism rather than it answered.

Troyna criticized quantitative research as being "too crude to capture the subtle and complex nature of racism in education" (1991, p. 429) because it reports only what is happening while qualitative research methods look at the why's and the how's. Qualitatively looking at the why and the how's of the educational conditions of Philippine immigrants children meant that I had to explore the "tricky business" (Troyna, 1995, p. 396) of race relations. I looked not only for observable, clear-cut instances of racist abuse, harassment, and bullying either by teachers or pupils in verbal or physical forms but also in hidden or indirect forms. Although parental views were not legitimately accepted as accurate and reliable portrayal of racism in their children's schools because of the tenuous relationship between what children experience in school and parental perceptions of these experiences, I sought them out to provide me with a rough and ready guide to the extent and intensity of racism in children's everyday experiences at school.

Zuckerman (1990) also criticized the unreliability of quantitative research methods in investigating racism in schools because the scientific premises for looking for statistical differences between groups designated as *races* were questionable from the beginning. He expressed his doubts on explanations of such differences in strictly biological-evolutionary terms. There have been studies on temperament, basic personality traits, disorders (such as antisocial personality), and specific genetic markers that showed much more variation within groups designated as races than between such groups. Furthermore, he warned us about interpreting differences on the basis of limited sampling within the three broad racial groups (Negroid, Caucasoid, and Mongoloid) to carefully avoid selectivity and misinterpretation of data that serve racist ideology.

I considered these theories and principles in designing suitable and appropriate data-gathering tools. The basic tool to collect primary data was the semistructured interview schedule. Different sets of open-ended questions were formulated for different respondents (i.e., children and adults). The interview sessions were done in small groups to establish rapport and camaraderie. In addition to the semistructured small group interviews there were focus discussion groups. I also observed and recorded descriptive details about the actual life and everyday behavior of the participants. Another technique used was documentary analysis in which relevant printed materials were gleaned to reveal the educational status of Philippine immigrants' children. All the tools were originally formulated in English and translated/interpreted into the language that the participant was comfortable with.

INTRICACIES OF THE INVESTIGATION

With the tools in hand, I conducted a preliminary investigation with the aim of gaining access to the Philippine communities and determining the setting and participants of the study. My first contact with Filipinas and Filipinos in Greece as organized groups coincided with the visit of then president Fidel V. Ramos to Athens in 1997. His visit catalyzed the generation of a master-list of Philippine organizations in Greece. I represented one of them that was based in Thessaloniki in the meeting with Ramos.

A few months later, I formally contacted the Philippine embassy in Athens through the honorary consul of the Philippines in Thessaloniki to estimate the child population and identify key informants within the communities. In my personal meeting with the ambassador and his diplomatic staff I secured a list of possible key informants and got an unofficial estimate of school-age Philippine immigrants' children in Greece. After the meeting, I visited a Philippine community school in downtown Athens where I met

Mang Tom for the first time. He is a lawyer from Cebu, Philippines, who was a staunch critic of the oppressive Marcos regime. In 1983, he fled the Philippines and was granted political asylum in Greece. He was and still is passionately involved in the educational plight of the Philippine communities and proved to be a valuable resource person for my research. He shared the historical background of the educational initiatives of the Philippine communities in Greece. He was also instrumental in introducing me to parents with children in elementary schools. In addition he helped me determine the Greek schools with Philippine immigrants' children as observation sites and introduced me to the school principals.

The approval of my request to conduct research in Greek primary schools from the Greek Ministry of Education and Religious Affairs came in 1998. Following this, I began in earnest my fieldwork in Athens where I visited five schools where Philippine immigrants' children attended. Of the five, two were Philippine community schools; two were Greek public primary schools, and one was a private school. I had direct personal contact with all the participants and was able to establish a close rapport with them.

It should be noted that my personal experiences and insights were an important part of the inquiry and therefore critical to understanding the phenomenon. My privileged assumed status as *iskolar ng bayan* provided me the crucial standpoint as an "insider" looking on Philippine communities but not without difficulties.

Topping these concerns was the issue of language(s). I was aware of the challenges of conducting ethnography among Philippine communities in Greece because of our multicultural and multilingual nature. The Philippines are historically composed of peoples of different languages and cultures and remain so until today. There are over one hundred languages spoken all over the Philippines with three *linguae francae*—Tagalog-based Filipino,[2] Cebuano Bisayan and Ilokano (Gonzales, 1998). These *linguae francae* were largely determined by politics rather than culture, as reflected in the 1987 Constitution of the Philippines that provided for two official languages—Filipino and English.[3]

English, as the primary language of the study, was a practical rather than a political choice. It was the main language of interaction because of my fluency in it and my perception of the comprehendible level of English literacy of the participants. However, in the course of the fieldwork, I met respondents who were partially fluent in either English or Filipino and had to code-switch to Taglish combined with a sputtering of Greek. On several occasions, I had to rely on my key informants to translate/interpret the participants' discourse in their mother tongue that I did not understand.

In my observation of Philippine immigrants' children in Greek schools, I relied on my elementary Greek and a pocket Greek-English, English-Greek dictionary to understand the verbal transaction among teachers and pupils. A year before my fieldwork I completed a ten-month course in modern Greek for beginners at the School of Modern Greek in the Aristotle University of Thessaloniki. My elementary Greek proved to be a challenge in my dealing with the Greek teachers, but I overcame these difficulties by asking them for English translations of Greek words and idioms. The children were given the freedom to determine the language of communication to give them a sense of control of the discussion agenda. In their chosen language, I wove the research topic into their talk about daily lives and social worlds to respond.

The language issue compounded my difficulties as a researcher because I was at the same time an observer and a translator of some languages I did not fully understand. Although I was aware that words in different languages might have identical meanings, the way in which they are understood may be quite different partly because of cultural and historical experiences. I constantly shifted between what I understood and the way I understood it to echo the meaning of language spoken by the participants just as what Avalos and her colleagues found out in their ethnographic study of education in Latin America. In the constant shift the meanings as originally stated by the participants may have been lost and replaced by my own. The multicultural/lingual nature of the research participants was just one of the many intricacies that I had to address in my study.

POSSIBILITIES FROM THE PROCESS

Empathic neutrality was observed in the course of the study without much success on my part. However, it must be stressed that complete objectivity was impossible and my subjectivity was limited and thus did not undermine credibility of the research. My passion was to understand the case of the basic education of Philippine communities in Greece. Being a Filipino, I had my own personal experiences and emphatic insight, which formed part of the relevant data. But I took a neutral nonjudgmental stance toward content discussion that appeared in the course of the study.

As I had mentioned earlier, my personal experiences and emphatic insights were deemed part of the investigation, which in the course of interacting with the participants turned to be indigenous. Pe Pua (1989) expounded that indigenization "from within" implies that a methodology emerging from the experiences of the people from the indigenous culture requires full use of the indigenous language and culture. Indigenization is an increasing trend, particularly in the development of psychology in the Philippines as a reaction to the wave of "Westernization" sweeping the academe. Philippine psychologists have begun to feel the need to know more about Filipinas and Filipinos without really abandoning the long-cherished theories learned in a highly Western education.

Pagtatanong-tanong, a Filipino word that means "asking questions," has been identified as an indigenous research method in Philippine social science research. The repetition of *tanong* (question) to *tanong-tanong* indicates apparent casualness when the inquirer is truly determined to get answers to her or his questions. *Pagtatanong-tanong* is a behavioral trait that Filipinas and Filipinos ordinarily exhibit. *Pagtatanong-tanong* as a research method is sometimes interpreted as an informal interview or at best an "improvisation," which approximates the interview method, but this is not correct. Although there are some similarities, *pagtatanong-tanong* is basically different from the interview in general.

Additionally, the use of the local term *pagtatanong-tanong* highlights the importance of tapping culturally appropriate indigenous research methods without claiming exclusivity to it for the particular culture. It has four major characteristics: (1) It is participatory in nature; the informant has an input in the structure of the interaction in terms of defining its direction and in time management. (2) The researcher and the informant are equal in status; both parties may ask each other questions for about the same length of time. (3) It is appropriate and adaptive to the conditions of the groups of informants in that it conforms to existing group norms. (4) It is integrated with other indigenous research methods.

There are five underlying principles of *pagtatanong-tanong*. The first principle has to do with the level of interaction between the researcher and informant. The level of interaction or relationship that exists between the researcher and the informant significantly influences the quality of the data obtained. It must be noted that the level of relationship is not fixed. In fact, being a member of the group, although it served as an advantage, did not guarantee me the full confidence of my compatriots. But the social distance certainly was not very wide when I assumed the "insider" role of *iskolar ng bayan*, a highly regarded status in the communities.

The second principle calls for the full use of the native language of dialect of the ethnic minority group. It is necessary in *pagtatanong-tanong* for it is the language through which the members can best and comfortably express their ideas, emotions, beliefs, and attitudes. It is scientifically sensible to use the local language as source of theory, method, and praxis because the exclusive use of a mainstream language can according to Alfonso (1977 as cited by Pe-Pua) "lead to the neglect of the wealth of indigenous concepts and methods embodied in a language more meaningful to the culture." The use of several languages is the framework of the cross-indigenous perspective. Language and cultural barriers should be overcome in order to tap the indigenous psychologies of ethnic minority groups. Therefore, I had an advantage in doing research among Filipinas and Filipinos in Greece because I know the "official" language and appreciate the values, sentiments, beliefs, and experiences of my compatriots.

The third principle has to do with the cultural sensitivity (*pakiramdam*) of the researcher. Some characteristics of the researcher are bound to be scrutinized by the group being studied and have bearing on the research, for example, one's age, sex, educational qualifications, and most especially one's personality. In the Philippines or among Philippine communities abroad, one is socialized to pay attention to the *paramdam* (feelers), the *pahiwatig* (implied meaning), and the *parinig* (insinuation). *Pakiramdam* allowed me to explore the research situation and structure it according to incoming information. This called for a lot of improvisations based on the response and reaction of the informant to previous questions and/or situations. It was through *pakiramdam* that I knew when to ask or avoid personal questions, when to take my leave even if not directly told, or when to interpret a "yes" for a "no."

The fourth underlying principle of *pagtatanong-tanong* is on the issue of reliability and validity. Subjectivity or reactivity of the informant who wished to please me was avoided by establishing mutual trust. And the fifth principle deals with ethical issues. Following the principle of treating the informant as an active participant, I was able to establish equality. Inasmuch as *pagtatanong-tanong* is not an interview but a dialogue, the *kausap* (literally meaning the person spoken with) was treated as a fellow human being and was not exploited.

Nevertheless, collecting data with children proved to be a real challenge. Mauthner (1997) in a critique of the methodological aspects of collecting data from children in three empirical studies carried out in home and school setting using qualitative methods concluded that researching children's lives remains at an exploratory stage. Several factors had to be taken into account when devising an appropriate methodology: the research question, age, gender, and ethnicity of the children, the setting and context of the researches. Some methods such as interviews and self-complete instruments are more suitable for older children. Participant observation and small group discussions are particularly suitable techniques with five to six year olds. Small groups are ideal with children of the same age (peer groups) rather than different ages (sibling groups). Small groups allow children to set their own agendas and the research topic to be woven into children's talk about their daily lives and social worlds. The "draw and write" technique and structured activities can be effective when integrated into group discussions and interviews to provide a focus for children, especially where the research topic is abstract or not immediately salient in children's lives. Following these suggestions, I adjusted the initial open-ended interview schedule accordingly.

I had my share of difficulties in ethnographic writing when I had to sift out my opinions and inferences from my interpretations. But I had a stake in what I was describing and it was certainly demanding for me to remain 100% objective. This was why I used safeguards and techniques like triangulation (comparing multiple sources of data) to corroborate information and to check for discrepancies (Holly, 1989).

Gitlin and his colleagues (1993) emphasized that the question of method is of fundamental importance because it helps define relations between academics and the education community at large. I was far from being uncritical by re-tuning my original field guides in consultation with the participants and by injecting my own bias as a member of the community being studied. My study was a pioneer attempt to explore the educational realm of immigrant communities in Greece; it was important to establish trust and confidence among the participants. The choice of ethnographic methods was influenced by the limitations of economic determinist studies that cannot expose how schools reproduced inequalities or provided options, on the one hand, and the limitations of positivist paradigms, on the other (Gitlin, Siegel, and Boru, 1993). It was indeed a practicable bias for ethnography as a research method in which questions were raised on the way schools helped reproduce societal inequalities associated with class, race, and gender.

Ethnography requiring long periods of observation and participation in particular contexts has been vigorously criticized for its limitations on reliability and validity. The tacit purpose of my study was to foster emancipatory change—an innate potential of ethnography. My research was an attempt to trigger emancipatory change and thus employing qualitative research methods justified the means to this end. Again, Gitlin warned us that linking method and purpose as an approach to research could not by itself achieve emancipatory change at a societal level. He argued that wide-ranging changes in an inequitable class society are unlikely to occur without a basic change in its economic structure.

Furthermore, schools may not be the best and only site for such efforts. My study was concluded designed with the hope of establishing a "dialogical" community bound to democratic and egalitarian interests and with the further hope that it contributed rather than stood outside of the democratic and egalitarian interests. It was a study in and for education, not a study on or about education. Qualitative research method was used because it does not reproduce dominance structures.

I was aware of the limitations of my research methods, but one cannot have a perfect methodology and must be contented with what Lutrell called "good enough" methods for qualitative research. I was consciously aware of the difficulties in conducting qualitative research, but, rather than eliminate them, I have essayed here the tensions, contradictions, and power imbalances that I encountered in my study if only to prove that be-hind intricacies are hidden possibilities.

NOTES

1. A sociological profile of the Philippine communities in Greece at the close of the twentieth century is available in Greek (see Cañete, 2000).

2. Tagalog, Pilipino, and Filipino are the successive labels (grounded upon differing conceptualizations) for the Philippine national language (Salazar, 2000).

3. The bilingual education policy of the Philippines accounts for the absence of a truly monolingual class. Classes are multilingual with the vernacular, Filipino, English, and a code-switching variety (Taglish—from the hybrid mix of Tagalog and English). The use of Taglish and three instead of two languages for initial schooling were born out of necessity and represented a commonsense solution to the practical and real problem of communication in Philippine classrooms. This real problem is reflected in the semilingual capacities in either Filipino or English of many teachers and pupils in the Philippines (Gonzales, 1998).

REFERENCES

Avalos, B. (Ed.). (1986). *Teaching children of the poor: An ethnographic study in Latin America*. Ontario: International Development Research Center.

Bogdan, R. C. and S. K. Bilken. (1998). *Qualitative research for education: An introduction to theory and methods*. Boston: Allyn and Bacon.

Cañete, L. (2000). The Philippine community in Greece at the close of the 20th century. In S. Marvakis, A. Parsanoglou, and Pavlou, M. (Eds.), *Migrants in Greece*. Athens: Ellinika Grammata (in Greek).

Charles, C. M. (1995). *Introduction to educational research*. 2nd Ed. New York: Longman.

Gitlin, A., M. Siegel, and K. Boru. (1993). The politics of method: From leftist ethnography to educative research. In M. Hammersley (Ed.), *Educational research: Current issues*. pp. 191–210. London: Paul Chapman.

Gonzales, A. (1996). Using two/three languages in Philippine classrooms: Implications for policies, strategies and practices. *Journal of Multilingual and Multicultural Development, 17*(4), 210–219.

Gonzales, A. (1998). The language planning situation in the Philippines. *Journal of Multilingual and Multicultural Development, 19*(5/6), 487–525.

Holly, M. L. (1989). *Writing to grow: Keeping a personal and professional journal*. Portsmouth, NH: Heinemann.

Lutrell, W. (2000). "Good enough" methods for ethnographic research. *Harvard Educational Review, 70*(4), 499–523.

Mauthner, M. (1997). Methodological aspects of collecting data from children: Lessons from three research projects. *Children & Society, 11,* 16–28.

Pe-Pua, R. (1989). *Patanong-tanong:* A cross-cultural research method. *International Journal of Intercultural Relations, 13,* 147–163.

Salazar, Z. A. (2000). The *pantayo* perspective as a discourse towards *kabihasnan. Southeast Asian Journal of Social Science, 28*(1), 123–152.

Spindler, G. (1982). *Doing the ethnography of schooling: Educational anthropology in action.* Prospect Heights: Waveland Press.

Spindler, G. and L. Spindler. (1987). *Interpretative ethnography of education.* Mahwah, NJ: Lawrence Erlblaum.

Troyna, B. (1991). Children, 'race' and racism: The limitations of research and policy. *British Journal of Educational Studies, 39*(4), 425–436.

Troyna, B. (1995). Beyond reasonable doubt? Researching 'race' in educational settings. *Oxford Review of Education, 21*(4), 395–408.

Tuckman, B. W. (1994). *Conducting Educational Research,* 4th ed. Fort Worth: Harcourt Brace.

Zuckerman, M. (1990). Some dubious premises in research and theory on racial differences: Scientific, social, and ethical issues. *American Psychologist, 45*(12), 1297–1303.

PART III

*Cross-Cultural Collaboration
and Decolonizing Research*

CHAPTER NINE

Fall from Grace? Reflecting on Early Childhood Education While Decolonizing Intercultural Friendships from Kindergarten to University and Prison

Cynthia à Beckett, Denise Proud

Everything tells you that full mutuality is not inherent in . . . life. . . . It is a grace, for which one must always be ready and which one never gains as an assured possession.

Buber (1958, p. 164)

Denise Proud

I am a Murri woman born in the Wakka-Wakka area of southern Queensland. Indigenous Australian people from Queensland are known as Murries. I was born in the early fifties in Barambah, a government-run Aboriginal settlement later known as Cherbourg. After my secondary schooling I left my family on the settlement to take up studies in Brisbane. I returned to the settlement after completing an early childhood qualification to establish the first kindergarten at Cherbourg. After working there for two years I then left Cherbourg and worked in different early childhood settings in Queensland. For another ten years I continued to work in these settings, including working as an advisor for early childhood services.

At this point I moved to Denver in the United States and lived there for seven years; it was the place where my daughter was born. I worked for the United Way, supporting adults in various outreach programs and with children, staff, and families in a range of educational settings. I returned to Australia twelve years ago, but decided to extend my work beyond early childhood settings, to work with adults teaching life skills in various settings. I work in correctional centers, youth detention centers, high schools, women's centers, and universities as well as early childhood settings. Cynthia and I worked together first as early childhood program advisers and have over the years found special times of connection that have allowed our bonds to strengthen.

CYNTHIA À BECKETT

I am a fourth-generation non-indigenous Australian woman; my original family members migrated from England in the 1800s. I grew up in inner suburban Melbourne and rural Victoria. After my initial qualification as a kindergarten teacher, I worked for eleven years in various early childhood settings. I then worked as an advisor for early childhood services before moving into university settings where I have been working as a lecturer in early childhood education programs for the past eighteen years. Although I have moved away from direct work with children, I have maintained my core interest in early childhood education. My own continuing study program has grown from education to include a sociological perspective. My current research focuses on young children and families and how relations form. Denise has been a continuing support in all aspects of my work, from contributions to lecture programs to advice on my research.

This is our story, a story of mutuality of shared lives linked first through our work as early childhood educators then extended through our friendship. This work reports on the progress of an ongoing research project that examines the connections over the past twenty years considered as an ongoing conversation. The study considers the personal, professional aspects of the conversation with implications for teaching.

We first met when we worked together as early childhood advisors and we had each come from working with children and families in kindergarten settings. During the past twenty years we have each moved away from working directly with children, but in our current work with adults we feel we are still using early childhood approaches. We felt that we knew one another well; we have worked together, shared much socially and enjoyed connected friendship networks. A deep appreciation of one another existed, but we decided to explore this attachment in another way. We were interested in discovering more about our relationship of shared professional and personal experiences.

There are rich connections in the shared relationship at many levels, but some would argue that the key feature of this project is about contrast about cultural differences. We argue that this is only part of the story. Other storylines, other topics, came from the research and these combined with the cultural richness we each bring enables a sense of decolonizing previous research approaches.

The decision to explore our lives through a research process raises questions. Why investigate a shared relationship that gives much to each and continues to develop? We were encouraged to research ourselves after participation in the Reconceptualizing Early Childhood Education Conference in Australia in 2000. The approach of those attending the conference and the underpinnings of the reconceptualizers group support creative, innovative approaches to research. This encouraged us to use this style to discover more about our relationship. The work was extended through the presentation of the work at the Reconceptualizing Early Childhood Education Conference in New York in 2001.

Other long-term reasons also encouraged the decision to explore our lives through a research project. It seemed that there was an underlying desire in each of us to regain the pleasure of earlier professional collaborations. The opportunity, however, for regaining this connection has lessened over the years as each became more involved in work in the different settings of university and prison. During social times together work experiences provided regular conversation topics. There was ongoing encouragement for Denise to consider work in the university setting. The discussions did not include the converse—encouragement for Cynthia to consider work in the prisons since it seemed that Denise's work was becoming more specialized. Increasingly she held positions that few people regardless of their professional expertise could fill. Denise's work was also often a topic of discussion in professional and social settings as her work addresses life-and-death issues that concern all in her network.

The ongoing discussions and shared lives revealed some general understandings. It seemed that there were sharp contrasts between Denise's earlier work in kindergartens and the current work in prisons, yet many of these feelings were assumed and not made explicit. For Cynthia, the path to working in a university setting, supporting others to qualify as early childhood professionals, was more of an expected path. Over the years the conversations, the questions the issues always felt a little unfinished. There was an ongoing interest in each contributing in the work setting of the other, perhaps as a way of regaining the earlier work collaborations that seemed lost. This was realized more so with Denise when she provided guest lectures for students in early childhood preparation courses. The student response was very enthusiastic, which again led to encouragement for Denise to consider permanent work in the university setting.

These issues created a mixture of feelings that were spoken and unspoken, explicit and hidden, in some ways revisiting the underlying desire to regain earlier work connections. The richness and complexity of the issues encouraged informal ongoing research, although the word was never used to describe these connections. In a sense it was a decolonized, intercultural investigation of a deep friendship. The chance to understand more about our lives by adopting innovative approaches encouraged by the reconceptualizers group was taken on enthusiastically by each.

The underlying interests in our earlier shared professional history provided direction for the research approach. The professional links through early childhood education offered a framework for the research. We reflected on our lives since we moved away from our initial work with children in kindergartens. How did we each consider this change? Personally and professionally there have been a number of changes; we both now work with adults but in very different institutions. Denise teaches life skills in a correctional institutions and Cynthia is Program Director of Early Childhood Education at a rural university. We also live in different cities 500 kilometers apart. What has been the impact of these professional and geographic changes? As the work progressed, we decided that our initial work in kindergarten settings could be considered as a circumstance of grace and we wondered if we had maintained this sense of grace while working with adults.

After the decision to research our lives in a specific manner there was a sense of commitment and excitement about the process. It seemed that all was possible, but at the same time nothing was clear about how to proceed. It was as though the underlying desires for reconnecting were being answered but the way forward was taking each to unchartered territory. There was some fear about how a specific research process might change the nature of the relationship. These feelings were acknowledged before the research process commenced.

We decided to explore our relationship generally and our views about teaching through the use of an e-mail conversation. This research approach appeared initially in answer to the issues of living in separate cities. As the work progressed, the beauty of slowing down ideas through e-mail text became more apparent. The process was being invented together as things unfolded. We realized that the process required research guidelines to allow things to progress. As the e-mails continued, it seemed that various themes emerged. When the material was complete and the process of analysis under way, various themes were clarified. A research model entitled "The Knowledge Dreaming" helped consolidate the findings. The themes, the model, and even the research process provide ideas that can be applied to teaching.

E-MAIL: A RESEARCH TOOL

The research process was designed to explore more about our connections, to deepen our appreciation of one another's views and understanding of issues. It seemed that in some ways we made assumptions about one another's views and that perhaps we tended to take for these understandings for granted. An ongoing e-mail conversation was established to enable these issues to be investigated. We had not previously used e-mail as form of communication, but relied on face-to-face encounters, phone, and occasionally letters. The use of e-mail was a desire to use the text of the e-mail to examine our underlying feelings and ideas. The process involved fourteen e-mails, over a seven-month period. The process was one of turn taking, with one following the other and we each sent seven e-mails.

The process commenced with questions about teaching young children and this expanded. It seemed that during our twenty-year friendship we have shared so many things and felt we understood one another so well but we now questioned these assumptions. The questioning of the taken-for-granted assumptions commenced in a small way with the decision to research ourselves. The decision seemed to hold open a new space of understanding about one another. It seemed that there were new ways to find out more about the views of each other. This desire developed as the plans for the research progressed. As the e-mail conversation commenced, we were surprised how we held different viewpoints. It seemed that a deeper form of appreciation of this difference was created through the research process and it appeared that this had not been possible before. We found the difference exciting; it also allowed each of us to develop our own ideas through the other. This did not mean that we took over the ideas of the other but that we held the ideas of the other as a parallel theme. There was an interest in careful, detailed investigations of parallel and shared understandings.

We agreed on guidelines to support the process. We decided to use the text of the e-mail as our line of discussion on teaching issues so we did not discuss the content of the material while the process was unfolding. During the seven months of the e-mail communication we had four visits in three different cities. During those times we shared ideas about the process but not the content. We agreed that the e-mails were not quite a conversation and not quite a letter, but a combination of both. The e-mail process contained unique qualities that we found valuable. The process helped us to understand one another's thinking, to move below the surface. As the process unfolded, various conversation topics were repeated.

EMERGING THEMES

Many themes emerged, appeared, and disappeared, but four topics appeared more consistently than others:

- The meaning of grace and the application of this idea to teaching
- Definitions of education/teaching
- Parenthood
- Cultural issues and personal relations

MEANING OF GRACE AND THE APPLICATION TO TEACHING

We were interested in exploring what seemed to be a shared view of teaching. Teaching was viewed as times of connection in which things can be transformed in a moment of wonder. There was agreement that defining moments of wonder could be described as a position of grace. Ideas and views about grace appeared in a number of e-mails. It seemed that this was a core feature of our work as teachers. In some ways it seemed that our work revolved around notions of grace and this underpinned our work. We questioned and debated ideas of grace and what it means to our teaching. There were shared views that our initial work with children was grace filled. It seemed that the sense of grace might also exist in our current work with adults and we wondered if we had fallen from grace by leaving the world of kindergarten and young children.

We had been using the term grace and sharing some related notions of the term, but it was not until e-mail 10 from Denise that a more specific definition was developed. Denise defined grace as 'wisdom, strength, poise, empathy, and other things'. We each agreed with this as a helpful definition of grace and that it also involved a respect for others. The respect required an ability to listen and care, to be empathetic and compassionate and not to prejudge others. These definitions of grace also connected to ideas about human rights and social justice, which are key concerns for us in our current work.

The research explores definitions of grace in terms of working with children and adults in various settings. At the start of our journey we assumed that one could fall from grace. After our e-mail conversations it seems that this idea is flawed, or *bugell* as it would be described in Murri language.

It seems to me that we are using the word "grace" in two different ways—the first is our attitude and approach to life that we largely inherit from our parents and life experiences. The second is "working with children as a place of grace." But why is working with children a "place of grace"? Is it because teaching children is somehow felt to be a privilege, because you as a teacher are in a position of trust and influence. Is there more trust in teaching young children than in teaching adults? (Denise, e-mail 8)

We decided that grace had to do with our attitudes about teaching. It seemed that working with adults could also be a position of grace, but in a different form.

DEFINITIONS OF EDUCATION/TEACHING

As the research process unfolded, we discovered that we had different meanings for words such as teacher. Before this process there were assumptions about shared meanings for ideas such as definitions of teaching. The speed of everyday life requires a taken-for-granted view of key definitions and a sense that we defined things in the same way. The research process allowed time to dwell on certain words. The clear focus on a particular word produced the realization that we may be thinking of different things. These understandings of difference developed over time. The initial appreciation that we held different definitions and views about such key topics was surprising and exciting. The process of the e-mail and the use of the written word gave us a chance to understand more about the thinking of the other, to appreciated the differences. The appreciation of the difference of views was not about two views in opposition—it was about the different possibilities that each view held. It was a situation of seeing and knowing more of the other. Understanding differences in definitions allowed us to become closer. It enabled an appreciation of differences and a further sense of relation for one another.

The process of deeper appreciation of the views of the other seemed to allow each of us to extend our views by considering the position of the other. The difference was not in the form of a debate that required resolve—it was more like the discovery of the hidden treasure of difference. We could hold the view, the thinking, and feeling of the other. Although this provided a clarity of the other's views, we did not become the other. Rather, there was room to extend positions and dwell in the space of the other. It was a chance to extend a position through the understanding of another's view developed in another way. It was not about loss or debate or critique in that one had to change the previous view. It was about mutuality and closeness created through a better understanding of the position of the other. It opened up other views and gave a sense of a multiple perspectives.

> When I compare teaching in a university and teaching in an early childhood setting I feel that the chance to engage and be responsive often has many pressures and layers that work against direct response and real feelings about things. It seems that it is difficult to know if a tutorial or lecture has been useful because there are so many factors that impact on students and staff. (Cynthia, e-mail 5)

This analysis of teaching suggests that there are major differences between teaching children and teaching adults. The pressures of working with adults in a university setting appear greater that the pressures that may be experienced when teaching children. There was some sense that these views would be even more evident when considering the additional stresses when working with adults in prison. This was not the case with the views that were expressed.

> If you have the objective of achieving frankness and openness when teaching adults, you have to lead the group and be willing to disclose your personal feelings to the group. A teacher of adult students may have certain level of rapport with the class, but trust will only develop after self disclosure. (Denise, e-mail 6)

Working with adults in the prison system was considered in terms of a desire to be frank and open and to establish trust through self disclosure. It was not a case of feeling more pressured working with adults rather than children in early childhood settings.

CULTURAL IDENTITY AND PERSONAL RELATIONS

We discovered more about understanding of community. "My Murri heritage is based very much on a verbal history of storytelling. The use of written language is very alien to me. It places our thoughts in an almost abstract vacuum." (Denise, e-mail 14a).

We discussed the importance of heritage and community for each of us. This involved the exploration of differences such as the different approaches to written language. When Denise returned to Australia after living in the States for seven years she chose to work with aboriginal communities in different settings. Cynthia wanted Denise to come into the university setting and these issues were questions that had remained unanswered. Now with the e-mails there was clearer understanding of Denise's deep attachment to her community.

The e-mails extended our sense of mutuality with one another as they allowed opportunities to reflect on history such as the way we first related to one another.

> When we worked as preschool advisers I was new and you helped me to feel comfortable and to settle in. Through sharing our teaching stories we discovered that we both valued the sense of connection . . . with the communities that we worked with. Our discussions all those years ago about teaching with adults and children gave us pleasure, we both love that sense of connection and engagement that brings others in. (Cynthia, e-mail 3)
>
> It also added new ways for us to understand our connections. It has given a new dimension to our relationship which would never have been realized had we not been separated by distance. The very nature of this separation has enabled us to understand our relationship and how we stay connected even though we are separated by distance. We both feel comfortable with our own feelings and our own space. This is a type of grace that you refer to in your work. Many people spend their whole life without finding this comfortable space or feeling of "grace." Its very nature makes it almost impossible to put into words. It is not tangible. You can't touch it. You can't see it. But you can feel it. You know if it is there. (Denise, e-mail 14b).

PARENTHOOD

This has been something of great importance over the years. Cynthia was able to share in the upbringing of Monique, Denise's daughter who is now seventeen years old. This has been a further bond for both. For Denise the community raises the child and Cynthia has become part of that community.

The research process of the e-mails allowed many ideas to be shared and the four themes that emerged represented clusters of shared meanings. The research process also helped to uncover the taken-for-granted meanings in other words such as parental love, education and teaching, cultural identity. These insights about the taken-for-granted allowed the relationship to develop further.

MODEL: 'THE KNOWLEDGE DREAMING'

As the research process progressed, the analysis of the material seemed to be lacking. It seemed that the work so far was answering some of the initial questions yet was unable to account for shared interests in theory issues. Somehow it did not seem to fully capture the richness of our lives in relation to one another. Ideas about teaching had been considered, but issues surrounding the formation of relations did not seem clear.

We decided to expand the ideas through the use of a model. Cynthia drew boxes and circles. Denise took these ideas and removed the boxes and extended the circles. The knowledge dreaming was an idea of the flowing nature of knowledge that cannot be contained in written words. It required pictorial flowing symbols (see Figure 9.1).

THEORY AND KNOWLEDGE

The research process encouraged a consideration of the relation between theory and knowledge. These issues may seem to be remote from daily practices and yet these are the very paths that can inspire whole new sets of practices that can in turn create new knowledges.

The work of Game and Metcalfe (1996) is helpful, as they state:

Knowledge doesn't spring fully formed from genius or revelation. Nor does it exist abstractly, in 'thought' before being expressed in one or another form. Right from the start, knowledge is produced through intimate and tempestuous relationships with these organized forms, which are the constraints necessary for cultural production. (p. 6)

Game and Metcalfe (1996) identify the lived nature of knowledge and how it unfolds through daily life, through writing, through reading, through mutual connections. This work encouraged us to examine our material more carefully and seek extensions for our ideas. These extensions enabled us to draw out links between our findings and by various theoretical positions. The theoretical aspects of our work were supported by various sources but particularly by the writings of Game and Metcalfe (1996), Serres (1993), and Buber (1958).

The theoretical positions and visual images from Serres (1993, pp. 168, 169) opened up ideas for the research. Two images that Serres places side by were of particular significance. These images captured the millions of connections that happen both within our bodies and around us. One image is of a network showing rectangular shapes and integrated circuit

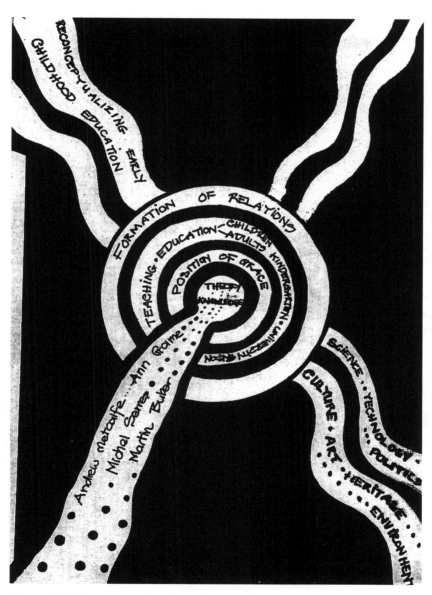

Figure 9.1. The knowledge dreaming model.

boards; the other image is billions of synapses at the ends of the brain's neurones' captured through 'micrography of a section of spinal cord'. Both systems are acting to create the daily life of connections, to transport millions of messages. Somehow it is the link between each message point that was exciting for us. The link between points involves possibilities about what might happen. In our research we had identified four clusters of ideas, but we knew that we had experienced far more. Serres' (1993) work reminded us of the rich interconnected networks of our lives and the extension of this through our shared positions of mutuality.

DOES THIS WORK HAVE IMPLICATIONS FOR TEACHING?

From this research we were reminded that teaching is a creative dialogue in which anything is possible. We have a multiplicity of lives and positions that we each hold and this became more evident to each of us as the work progressed. We found solace in sharing with one another without fear. We both consider that we remain teachers and, in particular, early childhood teachers and yet we work with adults.

We wanted more than the current connectedness had provided. The research process was a possible way to open and extend our feelings. Through this extension it seemed that our teaching would also be extended, as would our efforts to decolonize our work and research spaces. It is about trusting connections about respect and empathy. These qualities have much to offer teaching and they are addressed in one of the final e-mails in the research.

> By sharing . . . we have been connected in spirit . . . there has been mutual respect for each other, beauty and wisdom, strengths and empathy and compassion for each other's abilities on equal terms. I feel this is all a part of our understanding of each other. This is another face of grace. I feel we never fall from grace. (Denise, e-mail 14c)

REFERENCES

Buber, M. (1958). *I and Thou*. 2d ed. Edinburgh: T & T Clark.

Game, A. and A. Metcalfe. (1996). *Passionate sociology*. London: Sage.

Serres, M. (1993). *Angels: A modern myth*. Paris: Flammarion.

CHAPTER TEN

Listening to Voices in the Village: Collaborating through Data Chains

JOHN PRYOR, JOSEPH GHARTEY AMPIAH

BACKGROUND

The context for this chapter is educational research conducted in Ghana, and the context for educational research is an education system that is, apparently universally, found wanting. Its decline, from being considered one of the best in Africa at the start of the 1970s, to partial collapse by the mid-1980s, has been well documented and analyzed (UNESCO, 1997; World Bank, 1993, Yeboah, 1990). Since then, increased political stability has brought concerted attempts at improvement. The context for current initiatives is that the main players in development aid have accepted Ghana as a good example. In the 1990s, Ghana successfully embraced multiparty democracy, and has since accomplished a smooth changeover in its governing party. In 1987, a policy of Free Compulsory Universal Basic Education (FCUBE) by the year 2005 (originally 2000) aligned well with the worldwide agenda of the Jomtien Declaration asserting Education For All (Lockheed and Verspoor, 1991).

All this has led to a willingness by outside donors to contribute to education in Ghana. Nevertheless, the performance of schools has remained very modest (ODA/MOE, 1995; Quansah, 1997; USAID, 1996). A recurrent analysis identifies as a problem the widespread demotivation of pupils and teachers, due at least in part to lack of community involvement. This has led to the adoption of a policy of educational decentralization, which at the moment is mostly an aspiration rather than something that is being fully implemented, and to educational development programs, which emphasize community participation. Nonetheless as Condy (1998, section 5) has noted, "if we look for examples of how community participation . . . has helped to increase access to education in Ghana, the evidence is weak."

As well as raising issues about the potential meanings of community and the uses and values of education, this description of the situation begs a number of rather large epistemological questions, the most central being 'How do we know about the state of education in Ghana?' The short answer is that we have access to educational research, which is largely quantitative, positivist, and sponsored by government agencies and especially donors. This is largely framed within the discourses of development, where, although other disciplines such as sociology, anthropology, and psychology may be co-opted, the dominant discipline is economics and indeed the version of economics propagated by the main player, the World Bank. This type of educational research enjoys a position of almost complete domination within Ghanaian universities.

In this chapter we present our approach to doing educational research in Ghana, for which we make no more claim than that it is an attempt at decolonization. It takes place within a research project[1] investigating students', teachers' and parents'[2] understandings of schooling in a rural village in Ghana. Within this chapter the substantive ideas are less important than the methodological reflections; however, after directly addressing issues of methodology we give an example of the way that we have worked and follow this through by showing the impact of our research on one substantive issue, thus illustrating our approach and suggesting ways in which such research might be useful.

The project is a case study centered on one village. An initial source of data is photographic images and digital video authored by local people. Our aim is not only to explore what people think about education and to describe the educational practices observed, but also to suggest some explanations for our findings. However, rather than seeking to make cause-effect statements based on the data, we instead suggest a network of influences between the views and opinions of the participants, the practices observed, and the educational and social outcomes apparent both within our data and in the literature. Within this our own practices as researchers are deeply implicated.

Broadly then, the questions we are addressing are:

- How do people in a Ghanaian rural community choose to represent their lives and educational opportunities?
- How do they view the actual and potential contribution of schooling?
- How might these insights account for the practices that make up schooling in the village?

The project involves collaboration between researchers from Africa and Europe using participatory and ethnographic methods. In order to give a sufficiently problematic account of this, we appropriate three different voices. The majority of the text is written in the collective voice of the two main authors. Much of this is adapted from a conference paper (Pryor and Ampiah, 2002) that was written in Ghana to a tight deadline at a time when John was able to devote himself fully to the research, but Ghartey had pressing parallel duties. As a result, the majority of the text was initiated by John, but was then subject to a process of picking over, addition, subtraction, and editing from Ghartey. Inevitably, the words of the other co-researchers also crept in. The second and third voices, our own individual ones, are used to say things that cannot be said collectively. These passages are italicized.

CONCEPTUALIZING METHODOLOGY

Whatever stance one adopts, methodology can be thought of as the intersection of the three main areas of concern as shown in Figure 10.1. Briefly, what the researcher counts as reality and truth, the choice of methods, and the constraints on these provided by the social context, as well as the ideological or ethical beliefs and motivations of the researcher are all strongly implicated in the methodological stance. Thus, this diagram can act as a heuristic for researchers in describing and explaining their approach. It can also assist in accounting for the influence of the identity of both researcher and researched on the outcomes. The concept of intersection is important; a good example of this might be in feminist methodology whereby the embracing of feminist views, though most obviously within the ethical and macropolitical circle, interacts with both the other sets to produce distinctive and varying approaches (Weiner, 1994).

However, the image of the intersecting sets is only useful up to a point. Our own experiences of research suggest that in practice methodology is not so easy to map. As active researchers, we may have clear ideas, but especially when working in a participatory way, we find that it is very difficult to take up fixed positions. The research process is a dynamic one and involves a constant shifting. Under these circumstances, Figure 10.2 better represents methodology. Here, the image is of a rubber sheet, which is constantly being stretched and shaped by pulling from the three directions. What we wish to emphasize here is that methodology is dynamic, contingent, and dialogic. If this is true when there is a single researcher, it is even more so when there are several working in collaboration. This is because the pulls, though coming from similar sets of issues, may well be of different strengths and from different directions.

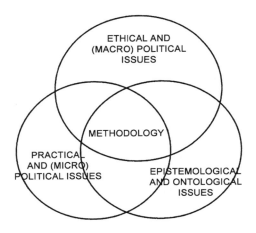

Figure 10.1. Methodology as intersecting sets

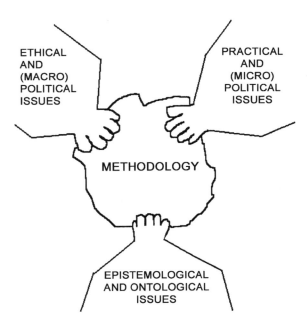

Figure 10.2. Methodology as rubber sheet

John writes:

I come to this research as a British educationalist with a background in qualitative research. My doctoral thesis was an ethnography of a class taught by a colleague in an English school, focusing on gender relations (Pryor, 1993; 1995). Since then I have worked extensively in the field of classroom assessment, applying a microsociological perspective (Pryor and Torrance, 1998; Torrance and Pryor, 1998) and more recently researching in collaboration with school teachers (Pryor and Torrance, 1999). I have had a connection with Africa and especially Ghana since 1977. Originally, I had intended to work there, but my initial study visit led me to conclude that the best way I could contribute to Africa's struggle was in my own country, through development and antiracist educational initiatives.

It was only much later that I returned to Ghana and found that there was interest there in my work as a researcher. Paradoxically, what seemed to be attractive to Ghanaians was that, in describing my research, I was advocating practices that appeared to offer an alternative to the positivist discourse binding researchers to 'those unequal and uneven processes of representation by which the historical processes experience of the once-colonized Third World comes to be framed in the West' (Bhabha, 1991, p. 63). It seemed that within Ghanaian universities, certainly in the field of education, all research was positivist and very little was qualitative. I therefore became actively drawn into research in Africa, collaborating especially on investigating continuous assessment (Pryor and Akwesi, 1998; Pryor and Lubisi, 2002).

However, there were always dilemmas about representation and authorship. As a lecturer in a UK university, research is a central part of my job with time allocated to it and, because of high stakes attached to the completion of research outputs, it is an imperative that I publish.[3] This was especially important when I was untenured (before 1999). However, for my African colleagues, the unfunded research we were attempting had to be fitted in with many other pressing duties. Thus, although I was anxious from an ethical standpoint not to dominate the research and reproduce traditional North-South relations, in practice it was I who had to take most responsibility for producing texts. Moreover, from the epistemological perspective I was anxious here, as in the rest of my research, not to edit myself out of the text and so give a false patina of objectivity to the outcomes. Despite the format of this chapter, I agree with Clough (1992) that 'experiments in writing' are not enough to solve this dilemma. Thus, my methodological uneasiness in Africa parallels my hybrid position, both as a member of a society that grew (and grows) rich on exploitation of the continent and as someone who has aligned himself politically and practically with counterhegemonic movements (Pryor, 1998).[4]

When the opportunity came to bid for the grant that supports our present research, it seemed that despite his different methodological background, the good human relations that I enjoyed with Ghartey and the fun that we had had learning together on previous research both in Ghana and in UK (Ampiah, 1999; Akyeampong et al., 1999) made him an obvious person to approach as joint proposer and lead researcher in Ghana.

In the research report on which this chapter is based (Pryor and Ampiah, 2002), most of the text originated with me, W. R. Ghartey assuming in most parts a mainly editorial role. My position as cultural outsider meant that there were inevitably parts where we disagreed about interpretation and meaning. When this happened I found that I had to explain and justify what I was trying to say. If I could make a satisfactory case, the text was altered to make it clear. If, after a short discussion, Ghartey was still in disagreement, the point was erased. What was hard for me, and also most instructive, was that these were inevitably the parts that I felt most attracted to, and which involved a strong element of cultural interpretation or theorization. This goes against the grain, since my constant imprecation as a teacher of research methods is for the researcher to take responsibility and interpret. The rubber sheet was being tugged at, not just by the issues that arose in the research, but by the different sensibilities and dispositions of the researchers. In order to develop a methodology that from one angle I feel comfortable with (the ethical) I have to adjust the strength of my tugging from the others.

Kwame Anthony Appiah (1991) describes an exhibition of African Art co-curated by a number of people from the United States, from Africa, and from the diaspora. He takes issue with the colonial attitude of many of these curators and indeed with the self-consciously but shallowly postcolonial attitude of others. He expresses distaste at the mélange of romanticism and condescension that characterizes much of the labelling of the images. However, the one that most attracts him is a Yoruba sculpture of a man on a bicycle, chosen and described by James Baldwin. He concludes his article by saying:

> It matters little whom the work was made for; what we should learn from is the imagination that produced it. Man with a bicycle is produced by someone who does not care that the bicycle is the white man's invention: it is not here to be other to the Yoruba self; it is there because someone cared for its solidity; it is there because it will take us further than our feet will take us; it is there because machines are now as African as novelists. (pp. 69–70)

There is very possibly a measure of self-delusion in my image of myself and my practices with respect to the research that I do in Africa and the extent to which I can participate in its decolonization. However, my aspiration is to be someone who thinks hard with African colleagues about how the bicycle might be serviced while getting my hands greasy along with them.

THE APPROACH OF THE PROJECT

Although the problems and shortcomings of Ghanaian education, particularly in the rural areas, have generated much comment, the most prevalent form of published analysis consists of evaluation studies associated with development projects, or quantitative work for post-graduate accreditation by local universities. These usually depend on surveys, observation studies, and scrutiny of documents, where the perspective of the professional evaluator is to the fore. Our work moves into the largely unfilled gap for qualitative work at the local level, seeking to provide an account that represents the perspective of village communities, of teachers and learners.[5] Our aim is that this might provide a vital input into policy making, since educational reform in Ghana has been frustrated not so much by conceptual shortcomings at the policy level, as by the way policy interacts with local understandings (Pryor & Akwesi, 1998).

We would claim that in the most common approaches to educational research in Ghana, surveys and one-shot interviews in contexts where there is a great power differential and/or a cultural distance between researcher and researched, the voice of the villager is at best very weakly heard. We have used more participatory research methods, where people are more active in generating data (Chambers, 1997; UNDP, 1998). The work is located within a tradition of qualitative educational research, drawing on a number of ethnographic models (Atkinson and Hammersley, 1998). It also accesses the more general ethnography of Ghana (e.g., Ansu-Kyeremeh, 1997). Its use of video generated by participants and other participatory approaches aligns it with Participatory Rural Appraisal (PRA) (Chambers, 1997; Gaventa and Lewis, 1991). Analytical frameworks are derived from the literature on international education.

The data set was collected over the period January to July 2001, including two intensive periods of data collection in March/April and July. It consists of:

- Uncut digital video footage created by young people and teachers and other community members in the village

- Informal interviews and discussions collected alongside the video sequences
- Informal interviews centered on the reactions to media produced from villagers' work
- Field notes and researchers' reflections
- Team discussions
- Notes taken during participant and nonparticipant observation of activities such as lessons and PTA meetings, some videotaped
- Group interviews and discussions
- Informal unstructured and semistructured interviews

Ghartey writes:

My original training was in chemistry and education and then in science education. As a lecturer and researcher at the University of Cape Coast I started by working mostly as an assistant researcher on large projects. Subsequently I have done a few projects as Ghanaian lead researcher. These projects have involved mostly structured interviewing and the application of questionnaires. Research training in Ghana is, however, almost entirely quantitative. Recently through links with the University of Sussex, I have been able to get more of a grip on qualitative research, including the analysis and writing-up stages.

Anyone researching (whether a foreigner outsider or an indigenous researcher) in a developing country like Ghana and particularly in a village like Akurase[1] is bound to face many challenges, which could constrain the effective conduct of any research. The most obvious ones are language, acceptance by the villagers, and how to avoid one's presence being of more interest than the issues being researched. In this respect even an indigenous researcher is liable to be caught in the same web of challenges as a foreign outsider. What made me an indigenous insider in research in this study were my familiarity with the Akan language (having been born in the Ashanti Region where the research was being conducted), and the culture of the people where the research took place.

Even though in a way I was an outsider from the city, the fact that I was a Ghanaian and more important could speak the local dialect of Akurase enabled me to have a better rapport and verbal exchange with the villagers (even among those who were literate). Just making sense of the language gives potential problems. In the Akan language spoken at Akurase, for example, if a negative question such as "Didn't you go to school?" is asked, it will be answered 'Yes' if indeed the person didn't go to school. Responses to questions, which involve negatives, therefore have great potential for ambiguities for any researcher not familiar with them. Also, some people are likely to answer 'Yes' to questions they do not understand. Unfamiliarity with this could easily lead a foreign outside researcher astray. But for the Ghanaians in the team it was not just about acting as interpreter, but being able to pursue the inquiry rather than just use interviews in which a schedule is prepared in English with accompanying explanations. The interviews used in the study were mostly unstructured and open-ended, thereby allowing people to talk about and around a range of issues broadly defined to be of interest to the study. In this way the discussions could be better structured as a social interaction by the indigenous researchers and the village people.

The advantage of a foreign outsider working in collaboration with indigenous insiders like myself in this research was the benefit of sharing some of these ideas during and after interview sessions. Added to this is the fact that I had general ideas about the issues being researched, though the extent and the magnitude of the dimensions were unknown to me. So I had a fair idea of what to expect generally in a village like Akurase even though there were specific issues that came to me as a surprise. Doing the research brought them out into the open. Familiarity with village life enabled the appropriate probing questions on issues to be asked in order to understand better the context in which the people in Akurase found themselves. There were therefore some check on people telling lies in order to please or deceive Oboroni (white man). Familiarity coupled with an open mind and the preparedness to learn new things was crucial in this research.

Generally, Ghanaian society attaches great importance to education. People from educational institutions, especially the universities, are therefore seen as having reached the pinnacle of knowledge and are accorded a great deal of respect. This gave us access to the people and hence to the kind of information we needed. I also believe that because there were Ghanaians from the university among the group of researchers this helped us to gain more insight and acquired more trust from the people than could have been the case if there were no indigenous researchers.

However, this also brought problems. In a small village like Akurase, any visitor to the village is conspicuously noticed particularly if he or she is a foreigner. Initially the presence of many outside researchers, some of whom also happened to be foreigners, raised skepticism about the presence of foreigners and their mission in a village like Akurase. However, my involvement as an indigenous inside researcher as well as that of the other Ghanaians in the research team helped to tone down this skepticism and allayed the fears of the villagers.

There is also the expectation in most places like Akurase that research in their village will lead directly to development projects being initiated. Many villagers are therefore prepared to cooperate and volunteer information if that would lead to development projects and subsequent alleviation of poverty in the village. Even though the research we were undertaking was not going to result directly in development projects in Akurase—and this had to be made clear to the people in order not to give them false hopes—the starting of a small project in the junior secondary school by another research team we were working with and the interest we showed in a Parent Teacher Association meeting raised the morale of informants.

Even though this research was initiated from the University of Sussex in the UK, my involvement as a lead researcher was crucial. It enabled us to maintain a sense of involvement within the team and gave John the opportunity to experience the content of our informants firsthand as this enabled us to understand issues and events as and when they occurred.

Moving from data to text was extremely important in this study because interpretation of data concerning the villagers' understanding of education had to be done in the context of the cultural settings of Akurase. Familiarity with the context of the research enabled realistic claims, assertions, and conclusions to be made. In some cases there was the need to go beyond the surface impressions provided by the informants at Akurase and here familiarity with the context in which the interview took place became important. Again I felt that an important part of my job was to minimize exaggerations and false claims. Since the quality of any study and judgment about its validity hinges on how it is reported, in moving from data to text therefore, meanings, interpretations, assertions, and conclusions had to be negotiated between myself and John, the foreign outside researcher. This to me was one of the most important aspects of the research process, which I found to be very useful. As an indigenous inside researcher familiar with the village settings it was easy for me to take for granted everyday issues and practices that require analysis from a more objective or disinterested standpoint. The differential experiences of John, a foreign outside researcher and me, an indigenous insider, in my opinion enable us to produce a more credible text than would have been the case if only one person (outsider or insider) was involved in the study. Our different opinions and perspectives helped to enrich the text as judgmental issues had to be carefully weighed and properly negotiated before acceptance. This research in a way also served as training for me in qualitative research since I was working in collaboration with a more experienced qualitative researcher from Europe.

DATA CHAINS

The original impulse for the project came from a project run by the Video Educational Trust, which was working in Akurase. Its aims were to promote cultural exchange and international understanding among children in the UK and Ghana by facilitating accounts of their lives using digital media. These accounts seemed to offer a particularly rich source of data for representing rural people's views of education. In fact, the video data did not prove as useful as anticipated. Even after three months, the camera was still such a novelty in the village that it attracted too much attention. The priority of the filming schedule was to get footage that would be useful for the development education project, so there was a need for staged filming. However, in the event, this was not such a problem, since it acted as an impulse toward the theorization of the methods of the research, which were designed to make the most of the skills and experience of the different members of the research team.

Central to our approach was the notion of data chains, a device used to make more explicit the way that we moved from our field experience to the textual outcomes of the research. The visual material was used not just in its own right as the first link in the data chain, but also to prompt reflection on the issues that concerned us and the people we were working with. This involves *Stimulated Video Recall* (Cowan, 1994), a less specific form of the *Interpersonal Process Recall* developed by Kagan (1976). Similar techniques are described by Collier (2001) as indirect analysis in visual anthropology, though in contrast to us he does not see the researched as the authors of the images. The visual material acts as a stimulus for dialogue, in the shape of informal interviews, which then generate another link in the chain. Alongside Ghartey, the researchers conducting these informal interviews were mature postgraduate students in a Ghanaian faculty of education and a rural development worker for a Ghanaian NGO. However, they were chosen because they had also spent much of their lives living and working in similar villages. The chain is therefore continued by their discussions of the previous links with the lead researchers. These aimed not only to interpret what had been gathered already, but also to generate further data in the form of narratives derived from the wide experience and understandings of the associate researchers. This then, in turn, was used to link with, make sense of, and extend other data already collected and guide further lines of inquiry (Figure 10.3).

We were, therefore, using at the data in a similar way to narrative researchers' use of stories, by seeking resonances with the personal experience of the researchers, though not so much to generate data about other places as to guide reflection on what was happening within the context discussed (c.f. Lenzo, 1995).

The data chain therefore links those who are completely within the cultural setting with those who are outside it and generates data from the dialogues into which they enter. This is building on a long tradition of exploring insider and outsider roles in anthropology and more recently within other traditions of cross-cultural educational research. The associate researchers occupy a position, which has much in common with the people whom Melanie Walker (1995) (after Spivak) describes as subaltern professionals, in that not only was their relationship to the academy shaped by their position as graduate students, but also in this context by their identity

A child has produced a photographic day-in-the-life account

Show still photographs as part of a focus group interview with schoolchildren:
Running to school—issues about attendance
What makes you late?
When do you not come at all?
Have you been away for a long period of time ever?
Why do people drop out?

Issues emerge concerning the number of household chores that children are required to do by their families.

Rural Ghanaian researchers' own experience was that their own parents were serious about schooling so chores were lessened in term time to enable them to attend well. Question therefore about how important it was to the majority of parents that the children in their care succeeded at school.

Link to suggestion by JSS teacher who notes that many of the children are living with foster parents.

Talk about family structure of Ashantis and the gradual demise of the matrilineal system (c.f. Palme, 1999, in Mozambique).

Link to data provided by senior secondary school graduate who says that both daily traveling and boarding are too much so he had to stay throughout his SS years with acquaintances of his parents in Kuro and they treated him very badly.

Figure 10.3. Example of a data chain

as members of the culture under study. The collaboration within the data chain seeks to address the ethnographic paradox that while seeking to present events and practices from the point of view of participants for whom they are familiar, normal, and taken-for-granted, we are also wishing to make them sufficiently strange to make them stand out and be perceived.

In practice, this is what research teams in this kind of research have always done. However, by using the device of the data chain we are seeking to make more apparent the blurred boundaries between data and interpretation and to problematize our collective practice. We are also acknowledging and making explicit through this what Brown and Dowling (1998) call the epistemological paradox—namely, that the process of recontextualization (selection, re-presentation, even before subjecting data to analysis) necessarily entails its transformation. Our approach is in no way discordant with ideas that have emerged in ethnography since Geertz's (1973; 1988) books and Marcus and Clifford's (1986) edited collection. However, these ideas have remained outside the educational mainstream and have certainly had no impact within Ghanaian education faculties. The data chains approach makes concrete the processes that one might go through: it pulls from the practical angle, and has profound influence on the epistemological. It leads on the one hand to what Measor (1985) describes as a feeling of knowing that what is emerging from your data is justified, having gone through a dialogic process of skeptical analysis, while on the other hand having to agree with Geertz's (1988) assertion that cultural analysis is always incomplete and that the further you get with the issues you are studying the more the suspicion grows on you that there is yet another side to the story and somehow you are not getting it quite right. The chain is never complete and a link is always left hanging in midair. Nevertheless, we are more confident in our findings as a result of what Stake (1995, p. 85) calls naturalistic generalizations, that is, "conclusions arrived at through personal engagement in life's affairs or by vicarious experience so well constructed that the person feels as if it happened to themselves." Yet throughout the process these conclusions have been challenged in our discussions.

Most of the rest of this chapter is devoted to following through on the issues raised in the exemplar data chain. However, we will end by briefly bring the text back to the methodological issues and in particular the rubber sheet image that we used earlier.

FOLLOWING THE CHAIN—COMMUNITY AND EDUCATION

The data chain that we summarized in Figure 10.3 was in fact very central to the way that we as a group of researchers developed a part of the text that we will report back to the funders of the project and within our dissemination process. It drew on the perspectives of children, teachers, and adult members of the village and gave us access to a key idea about 'community' within the village.

The chain started with a photograph taken by a schoolchild, in which the photographer had chosen to show a group of classmates running to school. The next link came from children discussing the photo and confirming that lateness was an issue for them:

> All of us often come to school late. . . .

They went on to explain why they were late:

> In the morning I prepare a fire, sweep the house, cook food and dispose of the refuse at a faraway place and this makes me come to school late.
>
> I am the only child in the house and I do all the chores in the morning, fetching water, sweeping, washing the dishes before I realize I am late for school. I walk along the track to school about four kilometers, I set off around 6.30 a.m. Most of us reach the school about 7.00 a.m. by 8.35 a.m.

They continued by suggesting that for many of the parents their labor was more important than their success at school:

> During the cocoa season some of us are asked by our parents to go for the cocoa grains from the farm before coming to school. This makes us come late.[7]

This led to reflection of the Ghanaian researchers on their own circumstances. Here, their parents moderated the chores and put schooling as a high priority, since education was seen as an investment. When considering the data that we collected around the village, there were several directions in which we followed this idea. However, the next link in this particular chain came from what teachers said about children's home circumstances:

> Most JSS pupils live with foster parents and therefore do a lot of house chores so that they don't have much time for schoolwork.

This was confirmed by what others said. Many of the pupils in the school live with either single parents (mostly mothers), and others, especially those in the junior secondary school do not live with their parents at all, but instead stay with relatives. Some have also moved from the settlements around Akurase to stay with foster parents in order to attend the JSS there. Others have come from much farther afield. This is by no means unusual in Ghana, and is indeed the experience of our research team; it is especially the case with ethnic groups (like the Ashanti) who follow a matrilineal system of inheritance. Under this system children belong to their mothers' family and therefore look for support from a maternal grandfather or uncle. These relationships are often obscured by the use of terms such as brother or sister, mother or father, son or daughter to denote any family member in the same, previous, or next generation, respectively. With stable populations, this system can work well in that it extends the responsibility as sense of belonging beyond the immediate relations. Despite this, matrilineal practices began to break down under the colonial regime and managing a nation that incorporates both patrilineal and matrilineal systems has always added complications to making state policy. However, government policy has always been that it is the responsibility of the biological father to provide for a child's education. This has all served to blur the position and, while conscientious adults take responsibility for a wide range of children, others are able to shrug off their obligations. In traditional society relations lived close by and children were liable to be visible to both sides of the family. However, with the move toward cash crops, the development of settler communities for agricultural purposes like Akurase, along with the effects of urban migration, families are widely dispersed.[8] Palme (1999) has noted similar problems in Mozambique when a matrilineal culture begins to break down. For poor rural people having children staying with them, especially when they have not bonded emotionally with them, feels like quite a burden. Educating them is an expensive business and one that may not provide any return for the investment. Children are expected to work to contribute toward the household to an extent that in some cases they consider to be exploitation.

The data chain has connected different parts of an ethnographic data set, the reflections of researchers on their own insider knowledge but from outside the specific context, and outsider knowledge derived from the literature. It could be seen that this chain stops at this point. However, our interpretation in this particular instance is that people's orientation to schooling in Akruase is affected by their being caught between traditional social structures that are being gradually eroded and the more universal globalized expectations of a modern state. This has resonances with other aspects of our analysis and so links with other chains of data. It therefore makes a small contribution to one of the main conclusions of the project that, as far as Akurase is concerned, government policy about community involvement in education is based on a romantic and unsustainable view of community. Community involvement as currently configured appears to satisfy the desires of all the most important drivers of policy: for economists it is cost effective, for educationalists it is theoretically sound, and for nationalist politicians it is ideologically attractive. It offers the dream of an effective form of indigenous schooling. However, our experiences in Akurase and elsewhere suggest that this is what it is—a dream, because like many dreams it is based on a romantic precolonial view of community rather than the postcolonial conditions that shape Akurase.[9] If education does not work in Akurase and places like it, even when policy is one of 'best practice' community involvement, once again the victims of the situation, the ill-educated rural school graduates will be blamed for their plight.

CONCLUSIONS

The situation we have described illustrates very clearly a postcolonial condition, which is embedded both in the specific history of Ghana and in the current world order. Any solution to the situation would therefore have to involve fundamental changes to the way in which the world is regulated. However, in the meantime, there are ways in which well-meaning policy might be changed so that the damage, particularly to the confidence and self-esteem of rural people, can be mitigated. Although one might be very skeptical about the power of research to influence policy, without this sort of knowledge there is no way that policy will be able to shift.

As Ghartey notes, the people in Akurase were concerned most of all about what research can do for them. They may have been thinking mainly about it attracting specific investment to their village, but, we would claim, ultimately it is knowledge, which likely to have more effect on the forces that shape their lives. Here it is not just a question of more research getting better results, but the nature and the approach of the research, its methodology, which drives the kind of knowledge that is produced. The 'findings' of our research are not startling or great departures from what is already known, but they derive from the village itself and represent an attempt through dialogue to listen to many voices. Smith (1999) outlines twenty-five projects as being at the center of decolonizing research. Our research team is working on some and groping toward others. Akurase is remote, but not sealed from the rest of the world. This research is local yet within a global discourse that seeks to take account of different perspectives. We believe it yields important understandings that may be developed into recommendations for local policy-makers. However, it makes a wider contribution for, as Stake (1995) points out, single cases may not be a strong base for generalizing about a wider population of cases, but when they provide new insights they offer general knowledge by enabling people to modify old generalizations. Similarly, the description of our research practices and the use of data chains are not revolutionary, but we are confident that they represent a useful way of conceptualizing how insider and outsider researchers might collaborate. Through reporting the research in this way we also hope that it makes more explicit some of the forces that are tugging at our methodology.

ACKNOWLEDGMENTS

The substantive analysis in this chapter derives from discussions of the whole research team including Elizabeth Opoku-Darku (independent researcher), Frank Aidoo, Kankam Boadu (University of Cape Coast), Louise Brett, and Sarah Lee (Video Educational Trust) and the authors. Everyone mentioned was involved in data collection in the field. Sarah and Louise facilitated the collection of visual data and authored film themselves; Frank and Kankam spent two periods and Elizabeth one period of time in the village interacting with people making notes and audiorecordings; Ghartey also did this as well as taking a main role in negotiating participation and coordinating group discussions; John collected documentary data, interacted especially with English speakers and collated the data. More formal analysis of concrete data was performed mostly by John and Ghartey, who also wrote the text. Others involved include Jo Barron, who transcribed much of the audio-based material, Francis Coffie, production assistant for the filming, Efia Gyaponaa Menu-Antwi, interpreter for the development education project, Afra, interpreter for the development education project, Alan Cawson, who also did some filming, and Alice Taylor, who commented on some of the ideas.

NOTES

1. The project Understandings of Education in an African Village: the Impact of Information and Communication Technologies is funded by the British Government's Department for International Development (Grant ED 2000-88). The views expressed here are purely those of the authors and do not represent in any way those of the government of the UK. The project is also concerned with the impact of technological change on these understandings and the implications that this might have for development initiatives.

2. The term parent is misleading within a Ghanaian context. Many children do not live with their biological parents and the different forms of matrilineal and patrilineal families further complicate the matter—this is discussed in more detail. Within this chapter, the term parent is used generically, as it is the usage of the school, to denote those adults with whom children are staying and who are considered to have guardianship of them.

3. UK universities receive government funding based on a review (the Research Assessment Exercise) every five years of the publications of faculty on a subject-by-subject basis.

4. The tensions described here are also evident in the writing of this text. Indeed, issues are further complicated by the technological advantages I hold in the completion of the text and in the communication with editors, which again steer me toward a dominant role.

5. Peil's (1995) article is an example in which more ethnographic work has been attempted in an urban setting.

6. In our research alternative Ghanaian names have been chosen for individuals. Place names have been reduced to generic Twi words. Thus, Akurase = 'village'.

7. Much of the data presented here has been translated from Twi by members of the research team.

8. Juliet is a typical case having lived in three different households and attended school in three different places Sometimes this can work to the benefit of children's education in that they might go and live with relations who are able to give them access to better schools, especially in the bigger towns and cities. However, children who have been sent to Akurase have almost certainly not come in order to benefit their education.

9. Romantic views of African collectivism are not without their critics (see, e.g., Gyekye, 1988, cited in Ansu-Kyeremeh, 1997, who maintains that communality was always balanced by a strong sense of individuality).

REFERENCES

Akyeampong, K., J. Pryor, and J. Ghartey-Ampiah. (1999). Purposes and consequences: Ghanaian teachers' understandings of learning, teaching and assessment. Paper presented to the Annual Conference of the *British Educational Research Association*, Brighton.

Ampiah, J. G. (1999). *Teacher instruction and assessment: Scenario of two contrasting set-ups*. Paper presented at a Link Seminar, Centre for International Education, University of Sussex, July.

Ansu-Kyeremeh, K. (1997). *Communication, education and development: Exploring an African cultural setting*. Accra: Ghana Universities Press.

Appiah, K. A. (1991). Is the post in postmodernism the post in postcolonial? *Critical Inquiry* 17, 336–357. (Reprinted in P. Mongia, *Contemporary postcolonial theory*. London: Arnold.)

Atkinson, P. and M. Hammersley. (1998). Ethnography and participant observation. In N. Denzin and Y. Lincoln (Eds.), *Strategies of qualitative inquiry*. Thousand Oaks, CA: Sage.

Bhabha, H. (1991). "Caliban speaks to Prospero": Cultural identity and the crisis of representation. In P. Mariani (Ed.), *Critical fictions: The politics of imaginative writing*. Seattle: Bay Press.

Brown, A. and P. Dowling. (1998). *Doing research/reading research: A mode of interrogation for education*. New York: Falmer Press.

Chambers, R. (1997). *Whose reality counts? Putting the first last*. London: Intermediate Technology Publications.

Clough, P. (1992). *The end(s) of ethnography: From realism to social criticism*. Newbury Park, CA: Sage.

Collier M. (2001). Approaches to analysis in visual anthropology. In T. Van Leewen and C. Jewitt (Eds.), *Handbook of visual analysis*. London: Sage.

Condy, A. (1998). *Improving the quality of teaching and learning through community participation: achievements, limitations and risks. Early lessons from the schooling improvement fund in Ghana*. Social Development Working Paper No. 2. London: Department for International Development.

Cowan, J. (1994). Stimulated video-recall. *Educational Action Research* 2(1), 141–142.

Gaventa, J. and H. Lewis. (1991). *Participatory education and grassroots development: The case of rural Appalachia*. Gatekeeper Series No. 25, London: IIED.

Geertz, C. (1973). *The interpretation of cultures*. New York: Basic Books.

Geertz, C. (1988). *Works and lives: The anthropologist as author*. Cambridge: Polity Press.

Gyekye, K. (1988). *The status of the individual in African social thought*. Paper presented to the *18th World Congress of Philosophy*, Brighton.

Kagan, N. (1976). *Interpersonal process recall—A method of influencing human interaction*. Instructors' Manual. Houston: Mason Media.

Lenzo, K. (1995). Validity and self-reflexivity meet poststructuralism: Scientific ethos and the transgressive self. *Educational Researcher*, 24,4.

Lockheed, M. and A. Verspoor. (1991). *Improving primary education in developing countries*. Washington, DC: World Bank.

Marcus, G. and J. Clifford. (1986). *Writing culture*. Berkeley: University of California Press.

Measor, L. (1985). Interviewing: A strategy in qualitative research. In R Burgess, *Strategies of educational research: Qualitative methods*. New York: Falmer Press.

Overseas Development Administration/Ghana Education Service. (1994). *Junior Secondary School Teacher Education Project (JUSSTEP). 1989–1993 Impact Study*. Accra: Ministry of Education.

Palme, M. (1999). Cultural ambiguity and the primary school teacher: Lessons from rural Mozambique. In F. Leach and A. Little (Eds.), *Education, cultures, and economics: Dilemmas for development*. New York: Falmer Press.

Peil, M. (1995). Ghanaian education as seen from an Accra suburb. *International Journal of Educational Development*, 15(3), 289–305.

Pryor, J. (1993). *He, she and it: A case study of groupwork in a gender-sensitive area*. Unpublished doctoral thesis, University of Sussex.

Pryor, J. (1995). Gender issues in groupwork: A case study involving work with computers. *British Educational Research Journal*, 29, 277–288.

Pryor, J. (1998). Action research in west African schools: Problems and prospects. *International Journal of Educational Development*, 18(3), 219–228.

Pryor, J. and C. Akwesi. (1998). Assessment in Ghana and England: Putting reform to the test of practice. *Compare* 28(3), 263–275.

Pryor, J., J. G. Ampiah, E. Opoku-Darku, F. Aidoo, K. Boadu, L. Brett, and S. Lee. (2002). *The value of schooling in Africa: Listening to voices at village level*. Paper presented to the Annual Meeting of American Education Research Association, New Orleans, April.

Pryor, J. & C. Lubisi. (2002). Reconceptualising educational assessment in South Africa—Testing times for teachers. *International Journal of Educational Development*, 22(60), 673–686.

Pryor, J. & H. Torrance. (1998) The interaction of teachers and pupils in formative assessment: Where psychological theory meets social practice. *Social Psychology of Education*, 2(2),151–176.

Pryor, J. & H. Torrance. (1999). *A framework for classroom assessment*. Paper presented at the Annual Meeting of the American Educational Research Association, Montreal, April.

Quansah, K. (1997). Report on the administration of P6 Criterion Referenced Test. Accra: Ministry of Education/Primary Education Project (USAID).

Smith L. T. (1999). *Decolonizing methodologies: Research and indigenous peoples*. Dunedin: University of New Zealand Press.

Spivak, G. (1988). *In other worlds: Essays in cultural politics*. New York: Routledge.

Stake R. (1995). *The art of case study research*. Thousand Oaks: Sage.

Torrance, H. and J. Pryor. (1998). *Investigating formative assessment: Teaching, learning and assessment in the classroom*. Philadelphia: Open University Press.

UNDP. (1998). *Empowering people: A guide to participation*. New York: United Nations.

UNESCO. (1997). *Country profile: Ghana*. IBE website: www.ibe.org.ch.

United States Agency for International Development. (1996). Ghana Strategy Survey (Draft). Accra: USAID.

Walker, M. (1996). Subaltern professionals: Acting in pursuit of social justice. *Educational Action Research* 4(3), 407–425.

Weiner, G. (1994). *Feminisms in education: An introduction*. Philadelphia: Open University Press.

World Bank. (1993). *Republic of Ghana: Primary school development project*. Report No. C12 2508—GH. Washington, DC: The World Bank.

Yeboah, V. (1990). *Educational reform in Ghana*. Address for USAID Conference on Educational Reform in Africa, September 9–15 in Lome, Togo.

CHAPTER ELEVEN

Ripple Effects: Fostering Genuine International Collaboration

VILMA SEEBERG, HAIYAN QIANG

This is the remarkable story of second-generation, international collaborations initiated by scholars in China on their return from studies in North America. Rather than increasing the brain drain from China to the West, the participants in this project instead created an international network of educator-activists. This story is characterized by a continual flow across cultural and political boundaries, including a very strong and more atypical reverse flow of knowledge and scholars.[1]

In this chapter, we focus on collaborations initiated by scholars at a Chinese national-level university specializing in education that is located in central-northwestern China[2] and several institutions of higher education in North America. We make no claims of scientific representativeness; rather we will describe the richness of the extraordinary extensions that emerged out of a development program. The story is far from over. At the time of this writing, the collaborations continue to evolve transcontinental projects. This story shows that projects that are conceived by democratically minded, energetic, and accomplished scholars can yield international collaborations of unexpected substance, magnitude, and long-term impact.

Reflecting on the extraordinary collaborations and networks, the authors and the principal participants concluded that what contributed most to their success was threefold. First, the leading scholars were truly committed to mutuality rather than self-interest or hidden career agendas. None of the key participants publicized their own contributions or sought career advancement over or at the cost of their collaborators. Second, participating scholars held their own culture and that of their partners in high regard and practiced respectful communication. North American scholars did not seek to shed their habits of individual freedom, nor did the Chinese scholars seek to imitate the Western educational management models or other unrelated cultural phenomena, such as professional writing style. For example, two conferences were convened, one on each continent, with the same topic but formulated differently to reflect culturally relevant perspectives. And third, due to this commitment to multiculturalism, the key participants were able to negotiate diverse strategies to address common problems and goals within the different cultural, regional, political, and economic contexts. In sum, the main themes that emerged from the participants' reflections on why these collaborations were and remain so fruitful were that a commitment to multiculturalism and collaboration laid the foundation of the work. Further, this commitment was deeply held and of enduring importance to the key participants. Hence, regardless of local political conditions, the key participants remained committed to the relationships and continued to foster formal and successful linkage projects. Participants defined success as a transfer of knowledge in both directions, and the establishment of enduring collaborative networks of partners, which can be interpreted as a form of decolonizing methodology through sustained, reciprocal collaboration.

Arguably *the* most painful issue of twentieth-century civilization has been and remains ethno-racial-social class strife—issues of personal-collective identity and social power relations. These issues enter the field of education in its various settings in China and in North America in the forms of unequal access to schooling, gaps in achievement, and other outcomes. To the key participants these were the most salient issues in education—this formed their shared sustained interest and line of scholarly inquiry.

We will briefly list some of the outcomes of joint efforts that have taken place: scholar and student exchanges, international conferences held on both sides of the Pacific, cooperative research projects carried out comparatively or both in China and North America and Europe, and staff training conducted in China. The Chinese returned scholars developed new courses and curricula and authored two book series with North American contributors. Perhaps most exciting, however, were the many "sideline" activities that individual scholars initiated. These include an extensive bilingual immersion school project in three provinces of China, a network of poor rural schools receiving coordinated capital and soft development funding from allied donor agencies partnered with teacher education universities in China, several scholarship funds for poor rural elementary school girls, and trans-Pacific K–12 teacher exchanges.

These are vital educational programs originating and operating in civic society, not just in the academy, that support equality of access to quality public education. Let us emphasize that the affiliated projects have been knit together by the actions of individuals. From this we have learned that private efforts and public, nongovernmental organizations, in the day of the Internet, can provide locally controlled, appropriate projects that have far-reaching and beneficial effect both locally and internationally.

This chapter is presented by two of the key participants in this project. In order not to privilege any one of the participants, we the authors have tried to place ourselves-as-observers outside of ourselves-as-participants. We hoped to foreground our role as participants. We also wanted to emphasize the value of the work and the ways that it was done, rather than the individuals themselves, in order to emphasize the possibility of cross-cultural, international, and democratic scholarly work. This creates a somewhat stilted style in which we refer to all participants in the third person.

In the first part of the chapter, we will describe in narrative fashion the multiple pathways of collaboration that were initiated by Chinese scholars who had returned from studies in North America that had been sponsored by a Western government development assistance project. The text traces how the collegial circles of three women scholars intersected and produced more extensive international networks of activist and scholarly collaborations—rather than a brain drain. Each section closes with the key participant's contribution of her understanding regarding what made the collaboration work cross-culturally and be sustainable.

Subsequently, the reasons for the successful construction of the collaborations are explored analytically and theoretically.

CRITIQUE OF AND RECONCEPTUALIZED CROSS-CULTURAL SCHOLARSHIP

A subtext can be gleaned in just the opening description of our projects and process, dialectic between the global and the local. As in the economy, globalization is reframing the work in many academic fields. Scholars in comparative international education initiated the collaboration described in this chapter. Bob Arnove (1999) introduces the most recent core text in the field, proposing that "the workings of a global economy and the increasing interconnectedness of societies pose common problems for educational systems around the world." Yet, he continues, "regional, national, and local responses also vary. . . . A dialectic is at work between the global and the local" (p. 1). The scholars involved in these collaborations shared the approach that a focus on common issues and locally diverse responses would contribute to greater understanding of global and local concerns on the part of all participants.

More traditionally, motivated by post–World War II hopes for the beneficial effect of education on world peace, comparative educators have attempted to find relationships between educational and societal factors in order to construct general theories but also to explore variations across cultures. A second tradition emerged, often sponsored by uni- or multilateral governmental institutions, wherein comparativists studied other countries' education systems to improve policy and practice at home.[3] This approach in practice often simulated power relations between countries, differentiating the international community into borrowers and lenders, or developing and developed countries.

This chapter explores how one international educational assistance project conceived as part of the borrower-lender model evolved through the action of participants who reconceptualized this basic framework. These scholars fundamentally understood the dialectic between issues that are global and responses or institutions that are local. These scholars were steeped in the local context of the educational institutions while recognizing this contextualization as a general principle. At the same time the scholars were not only somewhat familiar with the context of their collaborators' educational institutions, but also remained cognizant of the general principle that education anywhere can only be understood within its societal and historical context. They respected each other's worldview while attempting to construct a mutually understandable concept of the issues confronting them all in the context of globalization.

Despite the forces supporting the unidirectional transplanting of Western higher education, the participants reconstructed the relationships over time. They became actors in constructing international collaborations rather than subjects of a developed country to developing country aid-project. Many of these educational aid-projects have contributed to the unidirectional brain drain from the developing to the developed country.

For example, the *stay rates*[4] of foreign scholars recruited to higher education degree programs in the United States remain staggeringly high. The latest, post-1985 wave of China-origin scholars, who are concentrated in science and engineering studies, represents the highest stay rate of all foreign-origin scholars. In 1997, 92% of Chinese science and engineering students had remained in the United States five years after receipt of their U.S. doctoral degrees (Finn, 2000, cited in Johnson, 2000; Johnson and Regets, 1998). In the social sciences and humanities, including education, the brain drain is much smaller due to the embeddedness of these fields in their country's cultural and social context and its institutional system. Abundant anecdotal evidence suggests, however, that as many as one-third of these scholars from China also have stayed in North America. No detailed country statistics were available at the time of this writing; however, in 2001, the Chinese government (*Education Weekly*, January 31, 2001) stated that 320,000 young scholars had been sent out for overseas study during the past twenty years. By the end of 2000, 110,000 of these overseas students had come back and served the nation. Negative experiences on home visits to China made by U.S.-resident social science scholars in early 2001 were expected to have a dampening effect on return flows of social science scholars and knowledge.

Whereas many higher education assistance projects to China and other developing world nations were called scholarly exchanges, the directional flow was largely toward North America, as the above discussion shows. Bilateral education development programs such as the original point of contact that initiated the international collaborations described in this study, as well as multilateral ones, have long been critiqued by developing nations (see, e.g., *The Group of 77* and the *New Economic Order,* most recently analyzed in Mundy, 1998) and Western left educators for profiting the donor nations (Altbach, 1977; Arnove, 1980; Carnoy, 1980). Widely lamented and of particular concern in higher education development projects is the exportation of intellectual capital from the developing world to the core economies, the *brain drain* (Cao, 1996).

We do not dispute the validity of the critiques or their basis in fact. Instead, with this chapter we hope to extend the discourse on international mobility of knowledge and to emphasize a counterhegemonic trend. We hope to encourage scholars to collect data and write their stories of mutually beneficial international collaboration, new infrastructure development, and so-called ancillary, new, and indigenous programs generated within the home countries and regions of returning or expatriate scholars.

Civic space appears to offer flexibility for stakeholders to define their interest collaboratively and negotiate mutually beneficial projects that the formal processes of bi- and multilateral governmental development funds often do not allow. The advocacy of issues and projects of mutual benefit and procedural emphasis on mutuality are not typically possible in governmental development aid projects. The latter relationship presumes the expertise to be on one side and the need for it on the other.

Mutually beneficial international collaboration is an area ripe for exploration and theory building. Too little hard and soft evidence is available in the literature. Ramirez and Boli maintained that "the use of educational reform is an important solution to challenges to national power and prestige in the interstate system" (1987, p. 14). They continued, "The European model of a national society (and its public educational system) has become so deeply institutionalized as a world model . . . that in late-developing countries . . . it is . . . [simply] imposed" (1987, p. 15). Choi (1995) proposed a new picture of an international scientific community that shows that expatriate Chinese scientists and engineers in the United States participating in extensive networks that advise, disseminate, and assist in developing a Chinese high-tech commercial and academic infrastructure. Chinese-born U.S. faculty have played an important role in

initiating and carrying out the collaborations. Though collaboration initiated by returned scholars was still minimal, it "is facilitated by Chinese
scientists and engineers who have kept in touch with their U.S. advisor "
(Johnson, 2000).

Other than the statistics kept on international flows of scholars in science and engineering, very little systematic information exists about other
international collaborations in education. This chapter was written out of
a concern that truly collaborative international projects be given attention
and that their possibility not be sidelined in the face of the hegemony of
the European model of scholarship and education. The story we tell in this
chapter is the most successful, mutually beneficial international collaboration in which we have participated.

THE STORY OF THREE CIRCLES

Before going further, it might be good to give some background to allow
the reader to put this process into perspective. We believe that the success
of the collaborations described in this chapter can be credited to the independent, yet intersecting circles of like-minded scholars. Circles of people continually intersected and generated ideas, activities, events, and
resources much beyond the scope of the original development project,
the outcome of which was and remains an international community of
scholars and activists. For three scholars, H. Cheng, V. Teich, and R.
Hollins, professors at three different universities, their respective circles of
colleagues were about to intersect—as they continue to do at the time of
this writing.

ORIGINS

The original cross-cultural, intergovernmental contact instituted a fairly
typical international aid project that fits more neatly into the postcolonial
world system supporting the transplanting of formal Western education.
The development project was initiated in the mid-1980s at the ministerial
level of the governments of the PRC and a North American country.
Three years later, a North American central government international development assistance office approved a project proposed by R. Hollins
(personal communication, 2001) of a prestigious North American institution of higher education, which became the first IEDA project. The project was to do joint doctoral training between the North American
institution and six major higher teacher education institutions, known as
key normal universities, in China. A second linkage program (IEDA-2) that

trained young women and national minority scholars in multicultural education followed the first.

The First Circle

H. Cheng, on the faculty of an education university in northwestern China (SU), is at the vortex of the first circle and she told her story as follows. Her university had been involved in a few university-level academic exchanges with North American universities. With the help of R. Hollins, who was then a top official at a North American embassy in Beijing, SU established a center for the study of North American education. F. Zhun, a well-known scholar at SU, who had returned from one of the first university-level exchanges with R. Hollins' university, and had been appointed Dean of the Faculty of Education, was able to provide very strong support for the linkage projects. Thus, SU became one of the original universities brought into the first international educational development assistance project (IEDA) project, a joint doctoral program in education. Finally, SU and five other normal universities in China sent advanced scholars, including H. Cheng and some younger doctoral students, as visiting scholars to R. Hollins' North American university in 1992.

In 1992, R. Hollins with the Chinese scholars organized the conference *Knowledge Across Cultures: Universities East and West*, which brought together multicultural scholars from throughout North America with Chinese educators. The conference produced a book with that same title. V. Teich was invited to present on her independent Chinese university research. The first, second, and third circle intersected here for the first time.

Still under the first IEDA grant, several professors from the original North American university and other educational institutions visited SU the following year to conduct training and participate in joint conferences in areas of educational specialization, such as special education, psycholinguistics, and administration. R. Hollins commented that these were the "best scholars in North America and they got excited about what they could learn from Chinese colleagues" (personal communication, March 2001). For their part the Chinese colleagues apparently were excited about second-generation collaboration as well. For example, H. Cheng worked with R. Hollins on an investigation into education in northwest China, which was published as a chapter in a book on Chinese universities. In 1994, SU held the seventh annual conference in North American studies. Only a year later, H. Cheng and eight other Chinese scholars returned to the original North American university for a conference on future cooperation in education for women and minorities in China. Out of this conference came an application for a follow-up the first IEDA project, Special University Linkage Consolidation Program (IEDA-2).

Among the twelve returned Chinese scholars from the first IEDA project, seven were named project directors for IEDA-2. Most of the first IEDA project returnees have been given important positions in their home university on their return. For example, G. Tin was appointed to the dean of the faculty of education at a premier university in East China specializing in education. G. Wen became a director in the National Research Center in the Ministry of Education. H. Cheng was appointed associate dean of the faculty of education at SU and later associate director of the Center for Women's Studies at a prestigious national university.[5] (More of the outcomes of the first IEDA project will be discussed in the context of the second circle centered on R. Hollins.)

H. Cheng directed one project called *Women and Minorities as Education Change Agents* under IEDA-2. Through this project many young Chinese scholars received an international and intercultural perspective on education, and assisted H. Cheng in editing two volumes of a textbook on women in education to be used in the education colleges originally involved in the international linkage project. A study of school management models was the first ancillary comparative research project conducted both in China and the United Kingdom, and supported by both the British Council and the Ministry of Education of China. Scholars from both countries worked together as research teams to do case studies in schools in both countries. Five young Chinese scholars returned after significant academic experience abroad. Ancillary to IEDA-2, H. Cheng initiated a project funded by an ecumenical international educational assistance foundation, called the *University Curriculum Development for Gender Equity Education*. Under this project H. Cheng edited a further two volumes on gender equity, and organized an international conference by the same name at SU in 2000. At the conference the exchange on the state of research on women in education and China and North America greatly affected participants from both sides of the Pacific and Hong Kong. One of the goals of this conference was the publication of a series of curriculum guides for gender equity education to be used in the normal universities of the expanded IEDA network. In both book series the three circles intersected again.

The research in minority knowledge and bilingualism under IEDA-2 led to another ancillary creation, an active bilingual immersion project. H. Cheng calls this the most successful case demonstrating educational adaptation. We make a clear distinction here between *transpose* and *adapt*. *Transpose* belongs to the borrower-lender dynamic whereas *adapt* is a process of learning and transformation. The Early English Immersion Program (EEIP) is an experimental project conducted in approximately thirty kindergartens and primary schools in three Chinese provinces including Beijing. It is a continuing China-North American educational collaboration scheduled for an eight-year term for each cohort of kindergarten enrollees. Now in its fourth year, it thrives on its own momentum without any outside funding. H. Cheng expects the research to make important contributions to educational modernization in China by preparing a new Chinese generation for participation in a global information society.

In sum, under the auspices of the two IEDA projects, about thirty North American scholars and doctoral students paid academic visits to SU and other normal universities in the network. More than fifteen Chinese scholars visited North American universities, all but two of whom returned to China. The network of Chinese normal universities continues to be strong and spin off many projects. Returned scholars have produced the following independent ancillary output in China: eight small joint projects, two books on Canadian education, four textbooks on gender and women's education, four new courses, and five international conferences all held in China and relevant to the Chinese context.

H. Cheng reflected on why such prolific educational exchange activities developed in such a short period of time (personal communications, e-mail, 2001). She found that (1) a commitment to a mutually beneficial academic network was shared among the key participants. (2) The key participants' shared a commitment to explore multicultural issues in the partner societies and education. (3) The key participants were senior educational scholars and had a deep understanding of the other culture. Key participants had had previous experience in the universities of the other country and spoke each other's languages. Whereas the former three points were essential, she wrote, the previous experience and language familiarity facilitated the work logistically.

THE SECOND CIRCLE

In 1986, R. Hollins, then a newly appointed professor the original North American university, received a call from her director that the a PRC education official at the ministerial rank had asked at the original North American university to help Chinese normal universities establish doctoral programs in education. After several years of mastering the art of proposal writing, the first IEDA project was approved. The project was detained further by official governmental negotiations until 1990, but "by 1991 it was going more smoothly and began to take off in many directions" (R. Hollins personal communication, 2001). One of the project elements was the *Knowledge Across Cultures* Conference of 1992, which was so successful that the Chinese partners agreed to organize a follow-up conference at an ancient Chinese classical academy in China in 1994. The first conference had produced a book published in the United States, and the second produced another one, awaiting publication, *East-West Dialogue in Knowledge and Higher Education*. Needless to say, the impact these works have go well beyond the intention of the original development project. As mentioned earlier, the three circles had crossed paths by 1992.

The IEDA-2 started in 1996 and ran through 2001. Under the direction of the seven Chinese returned scholars, it was extended into many different and overlapping areas at the institutions in the network. Of particular interest here is the work of H. Cheng in the area of women's education in China. This is where the three circles intersected a third time with further worthwhile unanticipated outcomes.

In the process of the first IEDA project and her independent research into Chinese higher education, R. Hollins had visited poor rural schools in northwest China. Through returned scholar J. Huang and his wife, both professors at a provincial college of education located in northwest China, R. Hollins and her husband arranged for four very poor rural schools in southern Gansu, in Northwest China, to be given libraries. Then in the summer of 1998 when they visited these schools, they noted the declining number of girl students in each class. To assist girls in returning to school, they established a scholarship fund. The fund has produced about ten to twelve scholarships each year at the poorest of the primary schools given to girls to finish their primary education.

By 1998, R. Hollins had taken a position at a college in Hong Kong and the board of the Save the Children's Fund (SCF-HK) had asked her to chair its China Committee. SCF-HK had funded many rural school building projects and they wanted R. Hollins to link these schools in the "hinterland" with the teacher's colleges in the IEDA network. Normal university graduate students and young scholars were funded to supervise teacher training, develop libraries and other education activities in this network of primary schools. The R. Hollins scholarship schools became a part of this network. Over time more rural schools were included in Hubei, Qinghai, Xinjiang, Guangxi, all remote border provinces with large minority nationality populations. Also, SCF-HK has supported several purely "soft" projects in Gansu, Sichuan, and Shaanxi. H. Cheng and a colleague at SU managed one of the projects. This is where the first, second, and third circles finally intersected again. SCF-HK, a private nongovernmental organization, was able to maximize the impact of its contribution to education in China by linking with the network created under the original governmental development project. Again the second-generation impact surpasses the original intent substantially.

R. Hollins accounts for the success and diversification of international cooperation thus, by stating that there was a genuine commitment to mutuality from the beginning, even though the North American government officials of the IEDA office may not have understood or cared about this. Young and older participating Chinese scholars genuinely respected their own culture and heritage and were committed to taking up leadership in their own institutions. On the North American side all those involved were equally committed and got enticed into various sideline activities as they worked with Chinese colleagues. This, for example, is how the bilingual immersion project came about. Just recently, one of the founders and primary facilitators of the immersion project who is a professor at a North American university took a group of local teachers, all paying their own way, to the final IEDA-2 conference. R. Hollins emphasized that participants did not see themselves as experts or teachers and students, but as colleagues, and that they were experts in their field who were eager to extend their knowledge.

THE THIRD CIRCLE

This circle started with V. Teich's independent research into the social background of university students since the reforms in China. When preparing the follow-up study in 1995, V. Teich connected with the IEDA network through R. Hollins. Hollins referred her to two "promising returned scholars" at SU and another teacher's college, NU, two of the IEDA institutions. V. Teich had been working with a scholar, J. Xue, at another teacher's college, BU, who had been a master's degree student at Teich's university. On a previous project in 1990, V. Teich had introduced J. Xue to R. Hollins, when the latter held the appointment at the embassy in Beijing. This was the precursor of yet another intersection of the three circles.

When V. Teich conducted her research at SU and NU in 1996, returned IEDA scholars H. Cheng and J. Huang extended exceptionally useful help. Through their efforts at their respective universities, colleagues had become familiar with analytical research processes and were eager to participate collaboratively, whereas similar dispositions were not as common at most other sites in her work at Chinese universities. The returned scholars had been successful in promoting an orientation toward research that welcomed international collaboration.

H. Cheng, as perviously noted, had begun editing a series of textbooks for teacher educators on gender issues. J. Xue at BU had been active in the area of women's education in China. For example, she was a member of the Chinese organizing committee for the Fourth World Conference on Women in Beijing in 1995. Due to this intersection of expertise, H. Cheng invited her along with R. Hollins, V. Teich, and others to serve on the advisory editorial board for the gender in education textbook series. In 2000, the intersection of the work of the four women professors took shape in the publication of H. Cheng's first two volumes. As part of this work, H. Cheng organized the *University Curriculum Development for Gender Equity Education* conference at SU in April 2000. She invited V. Teich to give the keynote address. The circles drawn by R. Hollins, V. Teich, and J. Xue converged at this conference. According to V. Teich, the Chinese returned scholars' at the conference were extremely knowledgeable in the area of gender equity issues and authors, most of which work had been published abroad and in English. The conference also reinvigorated the connection between V. Teich and H. Cheng who continue working together both on research and writing projects.

While at the conference over lunch one day, L. Zhang, the colleague of H. Cheng who had been involved with R. Hollins' scholarship project, happened to talk about the encouraging effects of the scholarship fund for poor rural schoolgirls. She recounted that the girls were enjoying a newfound respect in their villages. They had gained tremendously in status due to the recognition given them by scholarships. This had not been a particularly expected outcome. But, more than that, a new outlook on the value of girls per se and on schooling for girls was spreading in the villages. The scholarship founders had hoped that perhaps these particular girls armed with a primary education would be able to make a life beyond the servitude and deprivation they often encountered as a poor female in a poor, backward village or, perhaps worse, on the rough streets of the cities (conference notes, 2000). The ameliorative effect of the scholarship apparently had touched families and girls who had not been recipients.

This story moved V. Teich and her family to establish a new scholarship fund in the name of their adopted Chinese daughter, Guanlan. L. Zhang of SU and her colleague, head of the Women's Association in a remote mountainous county of Shaanxi Province, have been administering the Guanlan scholarship. Every year ten more girls have received a three-year scholarship to finish primary school. On the other side of the ocean, V. Teich's family and friends have celebrated Guanlan's major life passages and holidays by donating to the scholarship. In the next generation a small meaningful bridge will connect a daughter of China in North America with girls in the country of her birth.

Reflecting on the enormously fruitful and successfully egalitarian nature of the cross-cultural collaborations recounted above, V. Teich pointed to shared interests and mutual respect based on professional knowledge and cultural awareness as the main fundamental elements. She had sensed from the beginning of her connection with various scholars in the circles of collaboration a shared commitment to social justice issues in education. The scholars already had held a disposition to engage in shared efforts to discover the processes that deselect youth from socially marginalized groups out of schools. The scholars recognized this as an issue of grave concern, though made of different dimensions and aspects, on both sides of the ocean. Along with this shared engagement, they were specifically interested in creating educational opportunity for girls. Another important aspect of the commitment, according to V. Teich, was every participant's willingness to put the larger goals of social justice before personal career advancement. They demonstrated that they would put forth individual private effort to promote social justice in their country and in that of their partner in collaboration, connecting a personal commitment and effort with the larger global social goals. V. Teich reiterated that it was this disposition of the activist scholar that led the participants to work creatively and effectively together.

CONCLUSION

The many intersections of the three circles have only begun to yield additional undertakings, which will generate more circles, more ripples across many generations. Each circle of scholars intersected with another at what were seemingly serendipitous points, which, on closer inspection, show themselves to be the necessary outcomes of each individual scholar's genuine and enduring interest in furthering scholarship in her field of interest. This sharing of interest revealed itself in continually sharper relief as the intersections of the scholars' circles of colleagues multiplied. The network of scholars strengthened itself in that fashion. With added persons and resources, it became more and more sustainable.

The nature of the shared interest, multiculturalism in education, also was of substantive support to the building of a cross-cultural network. However, evidence from international collaborations in natural sciences shows that the nature of the shared research is not necessarily crucial. In the collaborations discussed here, the key participants were aware, multiculturally aware. Through consistent cross-cultural contacts, work, and study, they were practiced in the art of personal-collective identity awareness, cross-cultural and ethnic self-respect. Not only was their own cultural identity salient to all the scholars involved, but it was expected to be salient for the collaborating partner of another culture as well. As is often the case, an awareness of one's collective identity with which one affiliates or is affiliated allows an individual to understand other dimensions of personal identity, gender, social class, and so on. Further, in the case of this network of collaborators, personal-collective identity was salient and formed to the point at which an understanding of social hierarchies and power distribution had been integrated with an affective awareness. The key participants were also aware of the sociohistoric positions of their respective countries in the global research community and global economy in general, but did not allow the social hierarchies to affect their egalitarian collaborations.

The theoretical foundation for the above argument is in the literature *of collective identity formation or development* (Carter, 2000; Cross, 1999; Helms, 1997; Hollins, 1999). The models of collective identity formation posit that the more a person becomes confident and secure about his or her own ethnic identity, for example, the more able she or he will be to resolve tensions and move through successive turning points and stages/phases. Extensive international or cross-cultural life experience, particularly where there are marked physical differences between the self and others, challenges individuals to address the cognitive dissonance between individual and social identity. This engagement moves the individual from a position of unexamined collective identity and social status. Hence, collective identity becomes a salient part of personal identity. Individuals tend to move through phases of *immersion/emersion*, examinations and rejection of ones own and others' collective identity.

This process evokes an examination of personal identity with that of socially assigned status. Through successive phases of immersion/emersion, individuals learn to resolve the personal-social dissonance in favor of an appreciation for the concept of social justice. Through this engagement, the individual moves into a phase or stage of *autonomy* from the socially assigned status order to taking a position in favor of social justice. In this the maturest phase of identity formation, considerations of social status have inextricably intertwined with a sense of identity and justice. The commitment to social justice in the case of the participants in this international collaboration flowed directly from their examination and expressive level of personal-collective identity awareness.

Our chapter described a case of multiple international collaborations wherein the borrower-lender model is transformed. The case study counterposes new ways of relating cross-culturally to mutual benefit. The case illustrates that a brain drain that is often associated with development aid projects in higher education is not a necessary outcome.

The projects undertaken in the case under study here were vital educational programs originating and operating in civic society in and beyond academia. Let us emphasize that the collaborations were knit together by the actions of individuals in the pursuit of scholarship—rather than grants. From this we can deduce that collaborative private efforts and public, nongovernmental organizations can create locally controlled, appropriate projects that have far-reaching and beneficial effects both locally and internationally.

We propose that scholarly exchanges, when they are approached from a stance of genuine scholarly commitment and built on democratic relations, have the potential to establish a pattern of mutually beneficial scholarly projects. For such collaborations to become sustainable, the participants at some point will need to address cross-cultural issues. Hence, the democratic relations among participants need to become grounded in an awareness of personal-collective identity accompanied by a commitment to equality and equity, a part of social justice. Cultural and political dynamics are constantly a part of international collaborations, and those that are cross-culturally bidirectional and sustainable, the study of this project suggests, need to be based in a mature awareness of personal-collective identity and social justice. Such grounding then can foster long-term interconnections and ever-wider ripple effects.

On a personal note, we the authors and other key participants have remarked on how personally rewarding the collaborations have been and how certain we are that the relationships will continue to grow.

NOTES

1. *Reverse flow* is a term used in the study of international flows of scholars in the natural sciences conducted by such offices as the National Science Foundation in the United States (Johnson and Regets, 1998). It is based on a center-periphery model of international relations and recognizes the fact of the brain drain from the developing world to the post-industrial, technologically advanced countries of the *North*.

2. The names of the institutions and scholars, except those of the authors, in this study have been changed to respect confidentiality since they add no value to the meaning of the work explored here. In keeping with the naming conventions of the authors' cultures, the participants in this study will be called by their last names. The authors want to express their respect for the accomplishments of the participants by using the last name form.

3. This section is based on Arnove's (1999) outline of the history of comparative education.

4. *Stay rates* refers to the proportion of scholars from one country of origin who stay in the United States past the end of their studies and student visa for a designated period of time, such as five years in the case of the presently cited data.

5. F. Zhun, formerly of SU and currently full professor at a premier education university in East China, M. Huang of NU, and another North American professor later became initiators of the EEIP along with H. Cheng.

REFERENCES

Altbach, P. (1977). Servitude of the mind? Education, dependency and neo-colonialism. *Teachers College Record, 79*(2), 187–203.

Arnove, R. (1980). Comparative education and world systems analysis. *Comparative Education Review, 24*, February (1), 48–62.

Arnove, R. (1999). Introduction. In R. F. Arnove, and A. T. Torres, (Eds.), *Reframing comparative education: The dialectic of the global and the local* (pp. 2–23). Lanham, MD: Rowman and Littlefield.

Cao, X. (1996). Debating 'brain drain' in the context of globalization. *Compare, 26*, 3, 269–284.

Carnoy, M. (1980). International institutions and educational policy: A review of education-sector policy. *Prospects, 10*, 3, 265–283.

Carter, Robert T. (2000). Reimagining race in education: A new paradigm from psychology. *Teachers College Record, 102*(5), 864–897.

Cheng, H. (2001). Personal communications: e-mail. Available from the authors' files.

Choi, H. (1995). *An international scientific community—Asian scholars in the United States.* New York: Praeger.

Conference Notes. (2000). *University curriculum development for gender equity education conference*, S-University, Shaanxi, PRC, April.

Cross, W. E., L. Strauss, and P. Fhagen-Smith. (1999). African American identity development across the life span: Educational implications. In R. H. Sheets and E. R. Hollins, (Eds.), *Racial and ethnic identity in school practices: Aspects of human development* (pp. 183–194). Mahwah, NJ: Lawrence Erlbaum.

Hayhoe, R. (1989). *China's universities and the open door.* New York: M. E. Sharpe; Toronto: OISE Press.

Helms, J. E. (1997). Toward a model of white racial identity development. In K. D. Arnold and I. C. King, (Eds.), *College student development and academic life: Psychological, intellectual, social and moral issues* (pp. 49–66). New York: Garland Publishing.

Hollins, R. (2001). Personal communication: e-mail. Available from the authors' files.

Hollins, R. (1999). Relating ethnic and racial identity development to teaching In R. H. Sheets and E. R. Hollins (Eds.). *Racial and Ethnic identity in school practices: Aspects of human development* (pp. 183–184). Mahwah, NJ: Lawrence Earbaum Associates.

Johnson, J. M. (2000). *Collaboration in S and T information exchange between the United States and China.* Paper presentation at the annual conference of the Comparative and International Education Society, San Antonio, March.

Johnson, J. M. and M. C. Regets. (1998). International mobility of scientists and engineers to the United States: Brain drain or brain circulation? *Division of Science Studies Issue Brief* (National Science Foundation 98–316).

Mundy, K. (1998). Educational multilateralism and world (dis)order, *Comparative Education Review, 42*(4): 448–478.

Teich, V. (2001). Personal communication: e-mail. Available from the authors' files.

PART IV

Complicating "Decolonizing" Education and Research: Challenges and [Im]possibilities

[Re]Anglicizing the Kids: Contradictions of Classroom Discourse in Post-Apartheid South Africa

Bekisizwe S. Ndimande

It is summer of 2000; I am sitting in the living room in our small four-roomed township house with my nephew, Thuto. It was not uncommon for Thuto and I to hang out and chitchat about many things whenever I was at home. Thuto was born in 1991, after I had already left home for college, and the only time I got to see or play with him was during my summer or winter vacations at home. On this particular day, Thuto and I were engaged in our routine storytelling, joking, teasing, and so forth. Around lunchtime, when we had just gotten back from buying bread for our lunch munchies, Thuto quickly realized that the mailperson had delivered some envelopes to our mailbox. Among the bunch of mail received, mostly my sister's bills and banking statements, there was an envelope for me with a U.S. stamp on it. I quickly opened up the envelope. It was a card from my friend Steve, who had written a short but pleasant message.

At this point Thuto was curious and anxious to hear what the card had to say. However, instead of telling him, I decided to hand over the card for him to read out loud for me. Interestingly enough, the message on the card had two portions written in two different languages—English and IsiZulu. He read the English portion quite fluently and then made a sudden stop. I was puzzled by this sudden stop, but when I asked why he would not continue to read the IsiZulu portion, he responded in a soft and lilting voice: *"Uncle, I do not know how to read IsiZulu because we do not learn this language at school."* Ironically, he was conversing in IsiZulu, the very language he cannot read and presumably cannot write either. At this point I turned to my sister who was in the kitchen to verify if Thuto was telling the truth. As if my question did not startle her, she answered: "*Oh yeah, Thuto's school does not teach IsiZulu until kids reach sixth grade level.*" For a moment, I thought her response was just a joke, but soon realized it was not. To this end, I could not reconcile with the fact that some desegregated public schools do not offer IsiZulu as a language that ought to be taught early in schools—taking into account that IsiZulu is one of the indigenous languages widely spoken in South Africa.[1] How could this be true?

I may have told the story of my nephew Thuto, but this chapter is not only about him. It is also about the broader sociopolitical conditions in South African public schools. I move from the premise that if the South African school system is supposed to build a democratic nation, then it must reflect the democratic objectives of the nation. In the last five years, the new curriculum—Curriculum 2005—modeled on outcomes-based education (hereafter referred to as OBE) was implemented to "replace" apartheid education.[2] Thus far, the new curriculum has encountered significant limitations in terms of improving the educational deficit incurred by Africans previously from apartheid education in South Africa. Indeed, Jansen's (1999) claim that OBE does not have a single positive historical legacy was correct. However, let me hasten to state that while it is important to understand the problems surrounding OBE in South African public schools, the purpose of this chapter is not to examine OBE.[3] Rather, this chapter examines the intricacies, contradictions, and (im)possibilities in South African education in the wake of the increasing desegregation of public schools and in the implementation of new school reform policy. I seek to problematize the unrepresentative classroom curriculum that has led to the (re)colonization of the "Other." I particularly want to examine the (re)colonizing tendencies visible in many classrooms similar to Thuto's—tendencies, which are largely influenced by the dominant social discourse. I argue that interrupting these dominant tendencies can provide possibilities for a decolonizing educational policy and practice.

In many nations, classroom curriculum is ideologically controlled. As Apple (1996) argues, curriculum is never simply a neutral assemblage of knowledge. Rather, what is deemed legitimate knowledge is determined by some groups' vision of knowledge. Recent studies (Seepe, 2001; Vally and Dalamba, 1999) on South African desegregated public schools show that crucial issues that consider the curriculum content and classroom practice relevant to the indigenous people of South Africa have been pushed aside and decentered. Instead, classroom practice, in particular, has been immersed in the acculturation of African students into the dominant White upper-class school discourse in the name of "standards," "accountability," and "meritocracy." This practice of acculturation is mostly notice-able in desegregated public schools in the suburbs. As too often seen in other contexts, this is a neoliberal and neoconservative agenda at work, which merely perpetuates social inequalities (Apple, 2001).

This chapter has three purposes. First, it presents a brief historical background of education in South Africa under apartheid by explaining policy, curriculum, and practice in the Bantu education system. Second, the chapter addresses the curriculum and policy problems encountered in the post-apartheid school reform initiatives. As the vignette at the beginning shows, a significant example of this (re)colonization is the debacle of the language issue in desegregated public schools. All too many desegregated public schools are much too far from implementing a multicultural curriculum that represents the cultural experiences of all students. On the contrary, these schools are still imbued with curriculum prejudice, racism, and the marginalization of students of color. For example, most desegregated public schools have retained dominant and "acceptable" practices of behavior, appearance, and language. And these "acceptable" practices are the only dispositions considered "appropriate" in school. Third, drawing from postcolonial and other critical traditions, this chapter aims to interrupt the dominant ideologies, such as the Eurocentric perspectives of interpreting the world. Interrupting these ideologies also means condemning the colonial hegemony of exploitation that takes place not only in schools, but also in the broader society.

HISTORICAL BACKGROUND

The Bantu Education Act was passed in 1953 to enforce a separate educa-tion system for Africans in order to meet the development plans of apartheid in South Africa (Christie, 1985). Needless to say, this was a very inferior education system that was used to bring the majority of South Africans under the control of the apartheid state, which was committed to white supremacy. H. F. Verwoerd's parliamentary speech of 1953 was an official call for a total educational exclusion of black South Africans.[4] This policy also implied that African teachers and students were neither permit-ted to question nor criticize the state, the school curriculum, school pol-icy, or any school authority. In many ways, as Mandela (1994) recounts, it was a way of institutionalizing inferiority.

Not only were these practices prevalent in public schools, they were also prevalent in higher education. Universities and teacher training col-leges in particular were also separated by race. Although Black universities had academic autonomy to a certain degree, Black teacher training institu-tions were directly under the control of the state and their curriculum was based on Bantu education.[5] In short, the curriculum policy functioned, to use Louis Althusser's (1971) term, as an Ideological State Apparatus (ISA) whereby the state ideology was transmitted through the explicit and hidden curriculum to advance the ideology of racial inequalities.[6] However, I must hasten to add that while it was the intention of the state to use education in the form of ISA, it soon became apparent that teachers and students were able to create a space for resistance. For instance, teachers and students were the ones who participated in the political struggles for liberation in the height of apartheid in the 1970s when most of our liberation movements were banned and many political activists were imprisoned.[7] Simply put, despite the adverse conditions, teachers and students had agency to decipher, predict, and resist the state hegemony.

REFORMS AND CONTRADICTIONS IN
POST-APARTHEID EDUCATION

While many public schools have been desegregated, and school policy on curriculum has changed a great deal compared to the Bantu education era, there are no significant changes that reflect the diversity of the country. And while the new curriculum—Curriculum 2005—has been a "better" alternative compared to the Bantu education, it also has noticeable limitations in its policy and practice. For example, the emphasis on the new curriculum is mainly on procedures or pedagogy and outcomes more than it is on the content and form of the curriculum.

However, I do not mean to argue that pedagogy is less vital in the classroom, but I want to point out that engaging in curriculum reform requires asking questions about the nature of school knowledge and how that knowledge has been legitimized. As Apple (1996; 2001) reminds us, classroom curriculum is a political act that involves negotiations, contestation, and conflicts. Abundance of research (Apple, 1996; Bourdieu, 1985; Nieto, 2002; Seepe, 2001; Ngugi wa Thiong'o, 1986) has shown that dominant groups have power and privilege to determine the kind of knowledge taught in schools. In a country that is riven by racial, gender, and social class inequalities, it is imperative that the school curriculum serve all students in an egalitarian way, regardless of their race, class, religion, gender, culture, or sexuality. Therefore, following on Apple's (1996) scholarship, we need to raise questions about what counts as school knowledge and who decides on what has to be taught in schools.

Again, the vignette in the beginning of this chapter articulates the conflict in the "official knowledge" and the unequal representation and how these pose a potential threat to equal educational opportunities, particularly in desegregated public schools. As the vignette reveals, there is little or no multilingual/multicultural education in Thuto's classroom. The classroom discourse is by and large based on middle or upper-middle-class values. Perhaps it is germane to mention that in the South African context most people who speak English on a daily basis fall under the middle or upper-middle-class category and such people are deemed to hold "decent" or "civilized" social values, thus having a high social class status. By default, the "official knowledge" and values instituted through classrooms then tend to represent high-class status people who constitute the dominant group of the society. For example, the use of English only until sixth grade in some public schools, when actually the country's Constitution points that IsiZulu is one of the official languages, and when there is empirical evidence (Alexander, 1989) that IsiZulu is one of the widely spoken languages much more so than English, is a striking phenomenon. It, therefore, becomes apparent that despite the attempt to desegregate and democratize public schools, the dominant group's values remain the "official" school values. This tendency of entrenching dominant group values in public schools clearly puts on the periphery those students who are foreign to the dominant discourse and this leads to education inequalities.

Pierre Bourdieu's (1985) work provides a significant analysis of how culture relates to educational practice and outcomes. Bourdieu conducted a survey to determine how the cultural dispositions and cultural competence that are germane in the nature of cultural goods consumed, and the way they are consumed, vary according to the category of agents and the area to which they applied. One of Bourdieu's findings was the close relationship that links cultural practice and educational success. Given this particular finding, Bourdieu concluded that students from upper-class backgrounds bring to school their cultural capital, which puts them in advantage with school culture because both the school and their culture share more or less the same understanding, values, and artifacts.[8]

Obviously, when the school operates on White upper-middle-class values, without regard of students of color who come from the working-class background, there is a problem with the curriculum. My point here, however, is not to argue that students of color and those who have been marginalized should not have access to dominant knowledge. Dominant knowledge is vital for social mobility, especially for students who are on the margins. In this case, I am also mindful that parents of marginalized communities might choose to have their children emphasize English because of the material conditions in which they live.[9] However, social mobility becomes problematic if it is at the expense of some students' cultural experiences. I want to argue that the classroom discourse should also recognize even those students who are culturally and socially considered minorities by starting where these students are with their lived culture. That way the culture of the "Other" will not be pushed to the periphery.

Lisa Delpit (1995) helps us understand the importance of dominant school discourse for students who come from socioeconomically disadvantaged communities. She argues that offering working-class students access to the language and the culture of power does not necessarily become a disservice to those students. Given the competitive and capitalistic nature of our society, and how educational success can lead students to "better" lives, students are judged, as Delpit (1995) puts it, by the "product" regardless of the process they utilized to achieve that product. However, Delpit (1995) does not necessarily advocate for a change of culture of those who are poor and Black to follow the dominant culture. She warns: "That may indeed, be a form of cultural genocide" (p. 30). The dilemma that we are faced with is an epistemological dilemma. Therefore, it becomes crucial that the classroom discourse represents all students' cultures not only to celebrate diversity, but also to acknowledge the worthiness of all students.

However, what is happening in Thuto's school is a total refusal to accommodate or at least acknowledge the knowledge and culture of the Other. If the culture of students like Thuto was embraced, not only introduced at sixth grade level, Thuto would be able to read and write IsiZulu language at an early stage. My radar screen shows a sharp warning—if classroom learning continues to elevate the already elevated upper middle-class Western values, the Indigenous languages and cultures will soon become endangered species.

ENDANGERED CULTURES

The situation in Thuto's classroom should be situated within the larger context of neocolonial tendencies of cultural imperialism. In an attempt to analyze this situation, I will use, among others, a postcolonial discourse as one of the lenses for critical analysis. According to John McLeod (2000), postcolonialism is not the equivalent of "after" colonialism. In other words, it does not suggest that values and practices that were inherent during the colonial era are now gone. Nor does a postcolonial lens define a radical new historical era, where the ills of the past have been cured. A postcolonial discourse, "In part involves the challenge to colonial ways of knowing, 'writing back' in oppositions to such views" (McLeod, 2000, p. 32). In this age of conservative modernization (Apple, 1996; 2001) it becomes important to interrupt hegemonic tendencies, including those that manifest themselves through educational institutions.

In his compelling analysis, Ngugi wa Thiong'o (1986) laments a neocolonial situation that has opened up a door once more for European bourgeoisie to steal talents and geniuses from the cultures of the people they colonized and oppressed, just as they have stolen their economies.

This, he argues, has been done mostly through language. Language as a form of culture carries along cultural values and beliefs. On the relationship between language and culture, it is worth quoting Ngugi wa Thiong'o (1986) at length here:

> Communication between human beings is also the basis and process of evolving culture. In doing similar kinds of actions over and over again under similar circumstances, similar even in the mutability, certain patterns, moves, rhythms, habits, attitudes, experiences, and knowledge emerge. . . . Over time, this becomes a way of life distinguishable from other ways of life. They develop a distinctive culture and history. Culture embodies those moral, ethical, and aesthetic values, a set of eyeglasses, through which they come to view themselves and place in the universe. Values are basis of people's identity, their sense of particularity as members of the human race. All this is carried by language. Language as culture is the collective memory bank of people's experience and history (p. 14).

Further, argues Ngugi wa Thiong'o (1986), colonial alienation takes two interlinked forms: an active or passive form that distances oneself from the reality around and an active or passive identification that is external to one's environment. Simply put, this is a deliberate effort of disassociation of the language of conceptualization, a language of daily interaction in one's home and in one's community. As Ngugi wa Thiong'o (1986) puts it: "On a larger social scale, it is like producing a society of bodiless heads and headless bodies" (p. 28).

Salim Vally and Yolisa Dalamba's (1999) disquieting report in a study by the South African Human Rights Commission shows similar colonial tendencies in the desegregated South African public schools. According to Vally & Dalamba (1999), the commission found that in almost all the cases where the survey was conducted, schools were engaged in "integrating while simultaneously assimilating black learners into dominant ethos of the school" (Vally and Dalamba, 1999, p. 14). Vally and Dalamba further report that the commission found that in former white schools (which are now integrated) there is a tradition of using a single language of learning and instruction. Given the commission's findings, Vally and Dalamba argue that schools were not moving proactively enough toward multilingualism and did not see language diversity as a school or classroom resource, but rather as a deficiency. Hence, claim Vally and Dalamba, in a number of schools the home languages of the majority of students are (unconstitutionally) banned. One of the students interviewed observed that "There is no freedom of speech and language—i.e., only English is to be spoken or else if you are heard speaking some other language, e.g., Venda, you will be punished" [English and Afrikaans are the only languages that can be spoken]. (learner, school 701) (Vally and Dalamba, 1999, p. 43).

Not only is cultural imperialism prevalent in public schools, it is also prevalent in South African higher education as well. Given the current economic crisis, a phenomenon partly attributed to the increasing neoliberal influence, universities have begun to wrestle with the decline of resources in African languages, literature, humanities, and education.[10] Thus, in most universities there has been a decline in enrollment in those departments (Zwane, 2001). While it may be correct to argue that there has been a general decline of enrollment across university departments because of the lack of funding, the humanities and African languages departments suffer disproportionately because the limited resources go to technology, science, and engineering departments. In this age of conservative modernization, where markets, competition, and "standards" have superseded democracy, the latter departments are most likely to receive private donations from multinational corporations. Thus, Simon Zwane's (2001) commentary depicts the situation accurately:

> The number of students studying African languages at universities has declined sharply in the past five years, giving rise to concerns about their future development in South Africa. Universities report that enrollment in African languages has been declining by half year since 1996. The Department of Education has described the decline as "an extreme worrying trend." . . . Kwena Mashamaite, Dean of the Faculty of Arts at the University of the North, blamed the decline on the government's emphasis that students should acquire skills in technology, science and engineering.

Traditionally, Black universities played a major role in conscientizing students about the racial politics of South Africa. Part of these conscientization efforts ought to be attributed, though not exclusively, to the anti-apartheid atmosphere that existed in such departments as humanities, African languages, law, and education. Can we really afford to allow the emphasis on technology and markets to undercut those departments that contributed so immensely toward democracy in South Africa? Besides, these departments offer academic subjects that enhance critical thinking skills (educational philosophy) and cultural richness (African languages). I contend that while such areas as technology, natural sciences and engineering are important, their importance should not be at the expense of African languages, cultural studies, humanities, and education departments.

Prioritizing the former over the latter has two dangers. First, we assume that once we have achieved access to the former disciplines, social mobility and equal opportunity will automatically prevail. All too many people believe that technology and market-geared education will reward us all equally. Unfortunately this is not the case.[11] Market-oriented curriculum furthers the needs of marketized democracy that only rewards few individuals and marginalizes the "Other" (Apple, 2001; Lauder and Hughes, 1999). Second, we assume that the skills needed for social mobility do not include critical thinking and cultural politics. Delpit (1995) reminds us that while students need technical skills to open doors, they also need to be able to think critically and creatively in order to participate in meaningful and potential liberating work inside those doors. She asserts: "Let there be no doubt: a skilled minority person who is not also capable of critical analysis becomes the trainable, low-level functionary of the dominant society, simply the grease that keeps the institutions which orchestrate his or her oppression running smoothly" (Delpit, 1995, p. 19).

The language debacle in Thuto's classroom, the racial and cultural crisis in those schools visited by the South African Human Research Commission, and the worrying decline in African languages and humanities departments at Black universities are not the only concerns. Marginalization extends to other institutions, such as banking institutions, courts of law, and police departments. All too many of these institutions use English, a language foreign to many people in South Africa, particularly older people. Even with President Mbeki's persuasive African Renaissance philosophy, there remains insufficient effort to develop our resources while maintaining our language and culture.[12] I also want to put it into perspective here that my argument is not necessarily against the use of English in public schools and in other institutions, but rather I argue that English has been perceived, at least in the South African context, as the high-status language, and this is problematic and, more precisely, it is wrong. We need to ask who defines what is "low" or "high" status language, and what criterion is used to define it.

The dynamics of language instruction and practice is also related to the textbook content studied in schools. Given the Eurocentric education that existed in colonial and apartheid South Africa, the politics of textbooks becomes important to understand the racial, class, gender, religious, and cultural differences within different communities. In the next section, I turn to the politics of textbooks to examine how textbook content and structure is politically determined.

TEXTBOOKS AND THE POLITICS OF KNOWLEDGE

Language is not the only form of curriculum control. Textbook content is another form of curriculum control and it is indeed related to curriculum control since language is taught through textbooks. Apple's (1993)

analysis on the politics of textbooks helps us understand that the content
of school textbooks is surrounded by controversies over what is included
and excluded in texts:

> Texts are really messages to and about the future. As part of cur-
> riculum, they participate in no less than the organized knowledge
> system of society. They participate in creating what society has
> recognized as legitimate and truthful. They help set the canons of
> truthfulness and, as such, also help recreate a major reference
> point for what knowledge, culture, belief, and morality really are.
> Yet such statement . . . is basically misleading in many important
> ways. For it is not a "society" that has created such texts, but spe-
> cific groups of people. (Apple, 1993, p. 49)

Reflecting back to my own schooling experiences in the Bantu education system, I remember vividly the Eurocentric content of textbook
knowledge—how that was used as curriculum control in school subjects.
The history subject, especially the history of South Africa, was distorted,
misrepresented, and some parts were omitted. Given the legacy of Bantu
education, one would think that the textbook prejudice would be addressed immediately in the new curriculum. On the contrary, I found a different scenario when I visited Ematsheni High School in the fall of 2001.[13]
     Oddly, I found that the history textbook has not changed much from
what I had experienced as a student in the Bantu education system. To my
surprise, though perhaps I shouldn't have been, the textbook looked outdated and in many ways resembled the Bantu education history textbook.
The current textbook is divided into two sections—General and South
African history. The first section, which is the general history, constitutes
the "almighty" European/U.S. history—with focus including Lenin,
Stalin, Roosevelt's New Deal, Monroe Doctrine, International Relations,
Cold War, and so forth. Again, I do not mean to argue that such history is
unimportant, but I think it would make more sense if, for example, the
textbook would tell students how Lenin or Roosevelt might be related to
South African politics or how they shaped the political world. I also want
to help us think about the textbook structure when European/U.S. history gets allotted the first section in the textbook. This is suspicious for
two reasons. First, it assumes that European/U.S. history is better than
the local history. Second, it gives ample time for European/U.S. history to
be taught to the end of the syllabus, while the South African section is
rushed as the semester nears the end.
     As I continued to peruse the general section, I realized a new theme
called *Africa since World War II*. A question that promptly came to mind
as I looked at this theme was, why would a textbook begin African history

at this particular period? This was approximately the period of decolonization of Africa. How would students know about the struggles of the colonized countries during the colonial era if colonialism itself was mentioned
in a superficial way? As a compromise, the text mentions, superficially,
movements for independence in Africa and the rise of nationalism as a way
of introduction to the theme. This is nothing other than glossing over the
theme as if it were less important. The simple fact that a textbook begins
an important theme about Africa in the middle of that particular history is
in itself a distortion of historical events, thus constraining efforts toward a
truly representative curriculum.

Let me also add that whether or not the purpose of the theme was to
talk about *Africa since World War II*, a representative history textbook
needs to lay out a historical and political context on how African societies
were shaped by colonial powers and colonialism (before and after World
War II). Not to talk about or even allude to such events is tantamount to
a total misrepresentation of African thought and philosophy. Also striking
was the fact that while the textbook talks about the decolonization of
Africa, there was no language of colonial critique. The textbook language
gives a misleading impression that the decolonization of Africa was a free
gift. There is very little mention of the struggle of men and women who
put a gallant fight that exerted pressure against colonization. Further, the
textbook talks about the common challenges facing the independent
African states, yet does not mention the existing neocolonialism in those
former colonized states. Should students be barred from learning about
the effects of neocolonialism, which by the way has assumed a new form,
namely, global economy, privatization, and markets? I want to argue here
that unless history is taught critically students would find it hard to engage
in historical events critically. Educators can do this by presenting textbooks
with different historical perspectives, and by encouraging students to give
different opinions as they support their claims.

The second section, the South African history, was even more striking.
The first part covered the period 1924 to 1948. It concentrated on such
topics as white political parties and white-only elections, economic policies, recognition of Afrikaans, great depression, Hertzog's racial policies,
effects of the World War I on South African politics, labor unrest, and
1948 elections among other topics. With the African National Congress in
existence as early as 1912, and with the active anti-apartheid mobilization
of the Communist Party South Africa, and the Defiance Campaign of
1953 that exerted a lot of pressure against the racial policies of the National Party government, it was surprising that the political history of the
latter was omitted.[14]

Perhaps more alarming was how the period 1976 to 1994 was perceived and treated. This period appeared in the textbook as an "add-on."

Worse still, the instruction on the history syllabus read the following: "2.3 The period 1976 to 1994 (Not for examination purposes)," which meant students were not to be examined on this theme. Given the significance of this period in the history of South African politics, a period of worldwide campaign against apartheid, how could it be treated as an add-on? Once treated this way and not required for examination purposes, this implies that students will not be rigorously engaged in this particular history. Therefore, we can conclude that what is considered "serious" history, which students would be rigorously engaged in and examined on, was mainly based on the history of white political parties and the political struggles in the white-only elections of the now defunct apartheid state. Put simply, the textbook was divided into serious history and add-on history whereby the latter ignored and invalidated the ongoing struggle of the indigenous people to acquire and retain their sociopolitical and historical identity. Textbooks that are biased, that distort facts or omit crucial moments, reflect one of the tendencies of neocolonial tendencies that erase the collective memory of oppressed peoples. It needs also to be said that it is ironic when the events leading to 1994 democratic elections and beyond are treated as add-on history in South African classrooms, yet the national and international media is still imbued with these historical events. As I write this chapter, the local theater is showing a documentary on the Truth and Reconciliation Commission (TRC) of South Africa.[15]

Given the curriculum contradictions that exist in classrooms, we need to find mechanisms to help us change the curriculum so that all students, including those who have been on the margins, could benefit equally. Like the textbook problem that has recently caught the attention of the ministry, the language issue and the classroom discourse in general warrant similar attention. Educators, administrators, and researchers need to collaborate on and emphasize the importance of a decolonizing research as they create possibilities of a curriculum that tries to realize the dream of democracy in our public schools. Simply put, decolonizing research on education can help us address the curriculum bias and the general educational deficit incurred by students from marginalized communities, and this can create leverage for unfettered curriculum.

DECOLONIZING RESEARCH AS LANGUAGE OF POSSIBILITY

Decolonizing research in education can help us think about different perspectives in education policy that have the potential for educational equality. In fact, educational researchers have begun to look at curriculum and policy issues in a sophisticated way. Their work, progressive educators challenge any form of education that (re)produces racial, class, gender, and cultural oppression of one group over the "Other." Sonia Nieto (2002), one of the advocates of decolonizing research, condemns a curriculum that assimilates students to the mainstream Eurocentric school culture. Rather, she proposes a curriculum that connects the issues of language, literacy, and culture in a substantive way. Nieto (2002) argues that it is a wrong assumption that students for whom English is a second language must master English before they can think and reason. As Nieto observes:

> All children come to school as thinkers and learners, aptitudes usually recognized as important building blocks for further learning. But there seems to be a curious refusal on the part of many educators to accept as valid the *kinds* of knowledge and experiences with which some students come to school. For instance, speaking language other than English, especially those languages with low status, is often thought of by teachers as a potential detriment rather than a benefit to learning. (Nieto, 2002, p. 8)

These problematic assumptions on the part of educators do not stand alone. They are influenced and reinforced by the neocolonial tendencies of rendering the cultural identity and experiences of the Other invisible. Therefore, it becomes necessary for educators to realize the importance of decolonizing curriculum and teaching methods.

Similarly, Grant and Sleeter (1996) argued that one of the things that schools could do to accomplish democratic education is to develop learning and thinking processes that reward all students equally. One way of accomplishing this goal, they argue, is to take into account the intersectionality of race, gender, class, sexuality, and disability. They believe that when schools take into account this intersectionality, they begin to see these together and are able to address the problem of unequal education opportunities. Also as important, teachers should be able to examine themselves and should always ponder if their classroom practices are multicultural. Grant and Sleeter (1996) argue that it is not simply enough to be nice to students in face-to-face interaction, since one can be nice but still perceive others as inferior.

Decolonizing educational practice requires that teachers and students engage rigorously in classroom learning that critically examines real-life experiences, social institutions, race relations, and the political system. For a critical curriculum like this to be implemented, the content of the curriculum and classroom practice has to be democratically and collectively decided upon, not by individual groups who control political and economic power and/or by politically insensitive educators who consciously or unconsciously perpetuate racial, gender, and cultural stereotypes. The debate over what counts as "official knowledge" of the school and who decides it is very important in classroom practice and curriculum reform. The better way to achieve this is to get parents, teachers, students, community activists, and administrators to deliberate on equal grounds, thereby ending the neocolonial hegemony that has persisted in our public schools.

Decolonizing discourse is also important for societal development and social equality. Sipho Seepe (2001) argues that societal development would never be achieved without placing African languages and culture at the heart of development. In one of his compelling arguments, Seepe (2001) states:

> Significantly, the reliance on a second/foreign language as a medium of instruction is a unique heritage of colonialism. In countries that were not colonized, students use their mother tongue throughout their schooling and learning career. Studies indicate that the use of a second language is an objective disadvantage affecting not only the ease and comfort with which knowledge is acquired by students but also its extent and depth. . . . Another study in South Africa showed that pupils performed better when bilingual instruction was used. . . . Despite this evidence there is reluctance to promote the use of African languages. Arguments advanced have varied from 'English is an international language' to suggest that indigenous languages are deficient as they lack scientific vocabulary. But scientific words can be, and are often, invented or adapted from other languages.

Seepe's analysis supports and validates the importance of decolonizing scholarship, and it also urges researchers and our educational institutions to engage in decolonizing research not only for the purpose of acquiring equal education opportunities through representative education, but also for the broader societal development and social justice.

CONCLUSION

While there are contradictions in curriculum policy and practice in desegregated public schools of South Africa, it is also important to acknowledge possibilities in some of the schools. It is encouraging to realize that despite the troubling factors of curriculum practice, some schools have made an effort to implement a multicultural curriculum in their classrooms. Swadener and Goduka's (1998) findings on educational reforms in the post-apartheid South Africa bear witness to the improvements made in these schools. According to them, educational sites visited were seriously concerned about real educational empowerment that demonstrated cultural inclusion: "Several teacher educators encouraged teachers to draw out indigenous perspectives from their learners 'by making students reflect on their own experiences, and integrating them with that of a particular topic' . . . [and] one teacher summed up the need for culturally relevant curriculum" (Swadener and Goduka, 1998, p. 13). This kind of empowerment is very important in classrooms because it not only acknowledges student diversity, but also motivates them to learn more.

Decolonizing educational research in schools and colleges of education is a challenging undertaking for us all. For researchers to initiate decolonizing strategies, they need to treat communities as equal partners in research projects rather than treating communities as "data plantations." It is indeed not an easy task, even in a situation when a researcher is considered both "insider" and "outsider" at the same time. For example, as I continue with my own research on curriculum, I need to be careful how my educational status positions me in my own community—a community that has relatively few people with higher education diplomas. I need to constantly guard against prejudices and shortsightedness embedded in the Western education curriculum that has dominated my schooling. Similarly, I need to bring communities closer to my research, ask suggestions from community leaders about what they need in their own schools. School curriculum is not a black box. As a researcher, I want the community I work with not to see my research as an elite knowledge, or a thing that belongs to education experts, who may or may not be able to know the pressing problems that exist in the community. In addition, it will certainly explain the need for communities to retain ownership of their own schools by implementing a relevant curriculum that advocates the welfare of the community for social mobility and societal development. This is one of the efforts that could help us as researchers to enhance a decolonizing research.

Indeed, through the decolonizing theory and practice, our desegregated public schools can be afforded a chance to transcend colonial and apartheid education. Teachers and students alike can openly engage in enabling educational discourse that reflects on the day-to-day sociopolitical and economic realities, as opposed to the repressive (re)colonizing discourse, which exists in Thuto's classroom. Decolonizing education is when educators and curriculum developers begin to evaluate and examine the nature of the curriculum and the textbook content to determine if it is indeed liberatory. In short, decolonizing research is a democratic collaboration of not only providing representative curriculum, but also inviting voices of different communities to the curriculum decision-making processes.

The effort to implement curriculum diversity in those schools visited by Swadener and Goduka (1998) and the ministry's recently initiated project to oversee the process of transformation in history textbooks and history teaching in schools brings a sense of hope for the future of South African public schools. However, what about schools like Thuto's? This is a cause for concern for the future of those students. What would Thuto's future look like if the school denies him a chance to learn to read and/or write IsiZulu at an early age? What would his future look like if the school affords him that chance? Perhaps these questions tell us something about the relations between education and power.

NOTES

I would like to acknowledge the intellectual support I received from Professor Michael Apple's Friday Group at the University of Wisconsin–Madison where I first presented the argument in this chapter. I would also like to thank Beth Swadener, Kagendo Mutua, Bob Regan, Grace Livingston, Marcus Weaver-Hightower, Denise Oen, Andaluna Borcila, and Rita Verma for their thoughtful comments at various stages of this chapter.

1. Neville Alexander correctly documents that in South Africa IsiZulu is one of the widely spoken languages compared to English for the simple fact that there are fewer English speakers compared to speakers of IsiZulu. For further inquiry on language position in South Africa, see Alexander (1989).

2. I must hasten to mention here that while OBE is an alternative to the brutal Bantu education, it does not necessarily offer liberatory education. For example, Chris Dali reminds us that in other countries where OBE was first instituted it did not replace political, social, and economic forms of discrimination against oppressed people: thus, the claim that OBE was introduced to replace apartheid education is a dubious one. See Chris Dali (2001).

3. Jonathan Jansen (1999) provides an insightful analysis on outcomes-based education in South Africa.

4. H. F. Verwoerd was the minister of education who introduced the Bantu education bill to Parliament in 1953. For his parliamentary speech quotes on Bantu education, see Pam Christie (1985).

5. I would like to clarify that the term "training" has a negative connotation in this context. It suggests that under apartheid, prospective teachers were not supposed to be "educated," but to be "trained." This was to achieve the apartheid plan of (re) producing a docile teacher.

6. For detailed argument on ISA, see Louis Althusser (1971), especially the section on "Ideology and Ideological State Apparatuses." It is also important to mention that while Althusser's argument on ISA was partly correct, his analysis is also essentializing and reductive. Repressed people have a profound way of creating agency.

7. The 1976 Soweto uprisings and the continuation of school boycotts throughout the 1980s, the formation of alliances with workers unions, and the participation in national strikes attest to the teacher/student agency that created a space to interrupt the hegemonic state.

8. According to Bourdieu (1985), cultural capital is the production of class privilege in which power is transmitted largely within families through economic

property. Further, it involves ways of understanding and acting on the world that acts as forms of cultural capital that can be and are employed to protect and enhance one's status in a social field of power.

9. With the increasing neoliberal and neoconservative influence in South African institutions, for example, the privatization of public utilities such as water, electricity, and the telecommunication system (see Garson, 2002), and the persisting capital flight, most parents, especially those from the townships, have a legitimate concern for the future of their children. They might prefer their kids to learn mainstream culture with the hope of improving their material conditions. In fact, most people will assume this perspective.

10. Devan Pillay's (2002) provocative argument on the African National Congress' policies on markets and privatization is helpful in understanding the neoliberal tendencies as manifested in the post-apartheid economy.

11. The insightful scholarship of Lauder and Hughes (1999) is particularly helpful in this argument.

12. See, for example, President Mbeki's "I am an African" speech (then Deputy President) at the adoption by the Constitutional Assembly of the Republic of South Africa Constitution Bill on May 8, 1996. http://www.anc.org.za/ancdocs/history/mbeki/1996/sp960508.html.

13. The name of the school is fictitious. Also, this was not a full-scale research, but given the fact that I was in South Africa when schools began in the fall for the 2001 academic year, I made an effort to visit a local high school to interact with teachers and students. Indeed, this was the same public school where I did my student teaching few years ago.

14. For a detailed history of anti-apartheid mobilization in the early and mid-twentieth century, see Motlhabi (1985).

15. It needs to be mentioned here that the appalling textbook situation has finally caught the attention of the Minister of Education, who just recently has set a two-year deadline for a new set of history textbooks, including one on apartheid. In addition to this two-year deadline, Minister Asmal has launched the South African History Project to oversee the process of transforming history teaching in all schools (see Thokozani Mtshali's (2002) commentary on this subject).

REFERENCES

Alexander, N. (1989). *Language policy and national unity in South Africa/Azania.* Cape Town: Buchu Books.

Althusser, L. (1971). *Lenin and philosophy and other essays.* New York: Monthly Review Press.

Apple, M. W. (1996). *Cultural politics and education.* New York: Routledge.

Apple, M. W. (1993). *Official knowledge: Democratic education in a conservative age.* New York: Routledge.

Apple, M. W. (2001). *Educating the "right" way: Markets, standards, God, and inequalities.* New York: Routledge.

Bourdieu, P. (1985). *Distinction: A social critique of the judgment of taste.* Cambridge: Harvard University Press.

Christie, P. (1985). *The right to learn.* Braamfontein, South Africa: Ravan Press.

Dali, C. (2001). "Responses to W. Morrow's 'Scripture and Practices' 1. Is yesterday brighter than today to morrow?" *Perspectives in education* (19) 2, 159–162.

Delpit, L. (1995). *Other people's children.* New York: New Press.

Garson, B. (2002). Znet commentary. http://www.nyevirolaw.org/PDF/Guison-NewJerseyAndJoannesburgWater.pdf

Grant, C. A. and C. E. Sleeter. (1996). After the school bell rings. Washington, DC: Falmer Press.

History Syllabus (Higher Grade), Standard 8–10. Ministry of Education, South Africa.

Jansen, J. D. (1999). Why outcomes-based education will fail: An elaboration. In J. D. Jansen and P. Christie (Eds.), *Changing curriculum.* Kenwyn, South Africa: Juta & Co. Lauder, H. and D. Hughes (1999). *Trading in futures: Why markets in education don't work.* Buckingham: Open University Press.

Mandela, N. (1994). *Long walk to freedom.* Boston: Little, Brown.

McLeod, J. (2000). *Beginning post-colonialism.* New York: St. Martin's.

Motlhabi, M. (1985). *The theory and practice of black resistance to apartheid.* Johannesburg: Skotaville Publishers.

Mtshali, T. South Africa is losing its memory: Revisiting apartheid throws up the challenges of teaching history in a new way. *Sunday Times,* October 13, 2002, p. 17.

Ngugi wa Thiong'o. (1986). *Decolonizing the mind: The politics of language in African literature.* Portsmouth, NH: Heinemann.

Nieto, S. (2002). *Language, culture, and teaching: Critical perspectives for a new century.* Mahwah, NJ: Lawrence Erlbaum.

Pillay, D. Between the market and a hard place. *Sunday Times,* October 6, 2002, p. 24.

Seepe, S. We should talk the talk of Africa: Nature's laws are not written in English. *Daily Mail & Guardian,* August 10, 2001.

Swadener, B. B. and I. N. Goduka. (1998, April). *Healing with Ubuntu: Educational reform in post-apartheid South Africa.* Paper presented at the annual meeting of the American Education of Research Association, San Diego.

Vally, S. and Y. Dalamba. (1999). Racism, 'racial integration' and desegregation in South African public secondary schools. A report on a study by the South Africa Human Rights Commission, Pretoria, South Africa.

Zwane, S. Students shun African languages. *Sunday Times,* March 4, 2001.

CHAPTER THIRTEEN

(Re)conceptualizing Language Advocacy: Weaving a Postmodern *Mestizaje* Image of Language

Ellen Demas, Cinthya M. Saavedra

Deslenguadas. Somos los del español deficiente. We are your linguistic night-mare, your linguistic aberration, your linguistic mestizaje, the subject of your burla. Because we speak with tongues of fire we are culturally crucified. Racially, culturally and linguistically somos huérfanos—we speak an orphan tongue.

—Gloria Anzaldúa

WHY CRITIQUE LANGUAGE ADVOCACY?

As language advocates in the United States, *creemos que estamos* standing up for/with language minorities—*los deslenguados*, we make decision regarding the lives, *vidas*, of young children and we think we know what is best for them. We place great emphasis on language research in order to find the best language acquisition/learning theories. We believe that we know when children have had enough first language experience to acquire a second or third language. We espouse language minorities' learning styles. We have constructed assessments for language minorities that have been labeled as appropriate. We speak the rhetoric of bilingualism and multilingualism in the development of cognitive, social, and emotional skills. We think we know the importance of language in cultural and personal identity development. We have created a plethora of culturally, linguistically, and developmentally sensitive curriculum. In the name of our children, we work diligently with language minority parents to assist them in improving home environments.

These efforts reflect a strong commitment to provide language minorities with an equitable education. However, as language advocates, we need to examine the knowledge base used to ground our pedagogy and research as it has the potential to serve as a colonizing tool. By not problematizing our knowledge base, we run the risk of eradicating the subject with our own discourse—committing "epistemic violence" (Branson and Miller, 2000).

Our discourse/knowledge of language advocacy has become so dominant that it has been accepted as truth. Taking refuge in a modernist discourse of science, we blindly have believed/engaged in its search for truth, order, and progress. Stemming from Enlightenment concepts of natural law, we have accepted the notion of "human nature" as an axiom (Cannella, 1997), that is, humans as natural beings whose lives can be explained through truth-oriented scientific inquiry.

Thus, we assume that our understandings of language minority children are universal and applicable to *all*. We have cast our scientific gaze on language minorities to categorize and order their language learning/acquisition. As a result, we have established that language learning/acquisition is natural, linear, and predictable (Cummins, 1981; Krashen and Terrell, 1983; Ovando and Collier, 1998). We have not problematized or called into question our concepts of language learning and research as rooted in positivistic science and imperialistic project (Burman, 1994).

As language advocates, we question (rightly so) the dominant educational discourses/structures that have excluded language minorities from an equitable education. Yet, we do so using what Audre Lorde calls the "master's tools"—in this instance scientific thought/inquiry. We must rupture the scientific shackles that chain us to the broken promises of Enlightenment/modernist discourse (Giroux, 1991). As Smith (1999, p. 58) points out, knowledge was "as much part of imperialism as raw materials and military strength." In fact, Smith (1999) argues that European Enlightenment ideas and knowledges continue to colonize indigenous people. The Enlightenment project, also referred to as modernism, adheres to the belief that humans progress via a linear, universal, predetermined process (Cannella, 1997). Constructed as a "truth," Western knowledge has been legitimized as the standard for "normalcy." Thus, other understandings of human relations become marginalized and in need of control, surveillance, and colonization. (Viruru and Cannella, 2000).

Our purpose is to problematize the knowledge/discourse espoused by language advocates, including U.S. English, bilingual education, and multilingual/linguistic rights groups. In this chapter, we will explore how language advocacy groups have shaped the way we view language diversity and language minorities. Perhaps we should consider the possibility that language advocacy groups, in attempt to "protect" language, have rigidly defined and categorized language and the language minority. Thus, we believe that it is crucial for those interested in language advocacy for/with language minority students to create new *teorías mestizas*. And as Anzaldúa (1990) posits,

> *Necesitamos teorías* that will rewrite history using race, class, gender and ethnicity as categories of analysis, theories that cross borders, that blur boundaries—new kinds of theories with new theorizing methods. We need theories that will point out ways to maneuver between our particular experiences and the necessity of forming our own categories and theoretical models for the patterns we uncover . . . [w]e need to de-academize theory and to connect the community to the academy. 'High' theory does not translate well when one's intention is to communicate to the masses of people made up different audiences. We need to give up the notion that there is a 'correct' way to write theory. (pp. xxv–xxvi)

WEAVING A POSTMODERN MESTIZAJE IMAGE OF LANGUAGE

We must consider the possibility that knowledge is a social construction embedded in power relations in which some are privileged over others (Foucault, 1980). In order to uncover whose knowledge is privileged, we engage in the act of deconstructing what we "think" we know (Derrida, 1981). Deconstruction offers a venue for revealing the multiple locations of power, as well as inconsistencies in dominant discourses (Cannella, 1997; Kincheloe, 1993). Therefore, we employ a critical postmodern/Chicana feminist lens to our analysis. Critical postmodern theory "involves an interplay between the praxis of the critical and the radical uncertainty of the postmodern" (Kincheloe and McLaren, 1994, p. 144). It allows us to (1) analyze the history of enlightenment and modernist thought; (2) reject Western constructions of truth, dualisms, reason, progress, and universals; (3) defy definitions and welcome ambiguity; (4) blur the boundaries of disciplines, theory, and ways of existing in the world; and (5) challenge the construction of the Other (Cannella and Bailey, 1999; Kincheloe and McLaren, 1994).

We believe that the *metodologías* of our *hermanas* on the borders contribute to such liberatory projects (Anzaldúa, 1987, 1990; Keating, 2000; Moraga, 1983; Saldivar-Hull, 2000; Sandoval, 2000). *Mestizaje*, that mode of Chicana feminism often referred to as "borderlands" feminism, describes theorizing and methodology that transverse boundaries, resist hierarchies, and transform social relations. The "borderlands," a metaphor grounded in but not limited to geographic space, was used by Anzaldúa (1987) to illustrate the positionality of Chicanas living in and crossing multiple cultures, multiple worlds. When these women, *la mestiza*, "dare examine and question the restrictions placed on them in the borderlands," a "New Mestiza" emerges (Saldívar-Hull, 2000, p. 59). *La conciencia de la mestiza* facilitates borders crossings—from marginalized Other to social change agent. As described by Anzaldúa (1987), *la mestiza* deconstructs oppressive colonizing traditions and constructs new metaphors; she unlearns patriarchal assumptions and engages in a transnational feminist struggle; she reinterprets history and writes new myths; she tears down categories and invites ambiguity.

Intrinsic to *mestizaje* is an analysis of power differentials, domination, and social injustices. *La conciencia de la mestiza*, "woven with anti-imperialist and decolonizing lenses, illuminates pedagogical tools and theorizing strategies that challenge Euro-centric thought and notions of western objectivity" (Elenes, González, Delgado Bernal, and Villenas, 2001, p. 598). We believe Chicana *mestizaje* can expose the underlying assumptions in language advocacy that serve to hide and perpetuate the domination of language minorities.

U.S ENGLISH: UNA LENGUA, UNA MENTE

Over the past several decades, to counter the browning of the United States and bilingual education efforts, the U.S. English group has relentlessly crusaded for an official language—using English as an *arma,* the weapon of choice. In 1981, fearing that the English language was under siege, Republican Senator S. I. Hayakawa of California proposed a constitutional amendment that would declare English the official language of the United States. In failing at this attempt, he founded U.S English in 1983 to continue to advocate the "unity" of America under "one" common language and heritage.

Veiled, *enmascarado* under the discourse of "commonality" and "national identity," U.S English has devised an agenda to ensure that the *mestizaje* of the world will not change the dominant white face—the innocent *cara* of the *gringo.* For U.S English advocates, respecting diverse languages and cultures is strictly a private endeavor with no government sanction. As a result, public institutions, including schools, are not responsible for infusing *respeto* for diverse languages and cultures. Schools, then, become a colonizing space where the English language and the culture of power are imposed, regulated and protected. As bell hooks reminds us, "it is not the English language that hurts me, but what the oppressors do with it, how they shape it to become a territory that limits and defines, how they make it a weapon that can shame, humiliate, colonize" (1994, p. 168).

Further stipulated in their agenda is the notion that "foreign" languages are reserved for academic fancies and economic/foreign policy whims. Questionable, however, is their criteria for what constitutes a "foreign" language. As a *kind* gesture, U.S. English only supports the protection of Native-American languages. Their argument is that "these languages were spoken by Native Americans before Europeans arrived in this continent . . . [and] are not spoken anywhere else in the world, and if they are not preserved, they will disappear completely" (U.S. English, 2001). But we are disturbed by their historical amnesia and hypocrisy. For instance, Gloria Anzaldúa (1987, pp. 5,6) reminds us that historically,

> [o]ur Spanish, Indian, and *mestizo* ancestors explored and settled parts of the U.S. Southwest as early as the sixteenth century. . . .
> In the 1800s, Anglos migrated illegally into Texas, which was then part of Mexico, in greater and greater numbers and gradually drove the *tejanos* (native Texans of Mexican descent) from their lands, committing all manner of atrocities against them . . .
> *Tejanos* lost their land and overnight became the foreigners.

Linguistically, Chicano Spanish *nació de* two centuries of oppression and colonization at the iron hands of the Spaniards and Anglos in the U.S. Southwest (Anzaldúa, 1987), thus making Chicano Spanish unique to the United States. Interestingly, however, U.S English has not extended that *kind* gesture to the Chicano people. Their hypocritical and narrow interpretation of linguistic rights perpetuates the annihilation of Chicano culture and language.

Thus, U.S English's efforts are legitimated by using the rhetoric of the "melting pot." "*Somos iguales,*" they claim, as they try to tame our "savage" minds, behaviors, and tongues. "*Necesitamos una identidad,*" they insist, as they strip us naked of the one we already posses in order to whitewash *nuestros lenguas y mentes.*

BILINGUALISM: A MONOLINGUAL CONSTRUCTION

In 2001, we were asked to co-chair a committee formed for the purpose of examining and disseminating information regarding "language advocacy." As bilingual education educators and advocates, we visualized this effort to include a discussion of the dominant educational discourses/structures that have excluded language minorities from an equitable education, as well as the ways in which bilingual education is a liberatory, progressive practice. Initially, our intent was to contrast the assumptions underlying both English-only and bilingual education in attempt to demonstrate the benefits of bilingual education. While, like any bilingual education advocate, we found the efforts and motivations of the English-only movement to be shameful, humiliating, and colonizing, we were not expecting to be disturbed by what was revealed in our examination of bilingual education. That is, we realized that the assumptions and issues underlying bilingual education remained mostly unquestioned.

While it may be tempting to treat this critical analysis as just a *commentario* on, rather than a *contribución* to bilingual education, this examination should be considered integral to the field. A deconstruction of bilingual education advocacy is a part of bilingual education (Burman, 1994). Bilingual education has been the spoiled child of critical theory— *un niño mal criado. Sin crítica anda por las calles* constructing the language learner. Those who challenge the intent and outcomes of educational discourse dare not venture into a critical analysis with bilingual education for fear of handing over ammunition to bilingual education adversaries. But, as bilingual educators/advocates, *creemos que es importante* to examine the hidden assumptions and imperialist dominant ideologies that lurk at the core of bilingual education. In fact, as Popkewitz (1997) contends (referring to the "child" but quite applicable to the "language minority child"), " the [language minority] child as [language] learner has become so natural in the late twentieth century, that is difficult to think of [language minority] children as anything but [language] learners; yet in a sociological sense, the 'making' of the [language minority] child-as-[language] learner involve particular transformation in the social reasoning that we now associate with modernity" (p. 134). *Somos identificados solo por nuestras lenguas—sin cuerpos.*

Further, it is assumed that the category "bilingual" is true and universal—that there are distinct, real, and identifiable characteristics that apply to *all* "bilinguals." We impose a predetermined knowledge about bilinguals that assumes that they are proficient in two languages, and that we know the truth about those languages and how they are learned. However, this predetermined category may oversimplify the knowledges of those we call bilingual. The creation of a "universalized, domain-partitioned" human being limits our capacity to see the complexity in language learning, as well as the lives of those we call bilingual.

Moreover, we fail to recognize the possibility that the category of bilingual is a monolingual construction. Experts, such as psychologists and educators, have taken the right to define and construct the category of bilingual based on their assumptions of language and language learning. Their understandings are limited by these fabricated, domain-specific categories that they assume are true. Thus, the category of bilingual represents a monolingual, Eurocentric, middle-class understanding of what is means to engage in the act of learning and living multiple language, multiple worlds. The monolingual takes the right to decide what is a normal bilingual—the construction of bilingual as a true, universal category creates a power position for experts, monolinguals, that allows for the constant control and regulation of those deemed bilingual.

Birthing Bilingual Education

Until the 1960s, state and federal legislation and policy generally sought to restrict bilingual education. Children who were not proficient in English might have been ignored, left to "sink or swim," or segregated into distinct schools (Kibbee, 1996; Ovando & Collier, 1998). However, over the past several decades, language rights advocates have struggled to protect the educational rights of language minority students. Fueled by a belief that freedom to speak one's native language is a fundamental human right, advocates press for the adoption and support of bilingual education in U.S. schools (Roberts, 1995).

Over time, federal legislation and court decisions led to federal policy that extended the basic rights provided in the U.S. Constitution to include language rights. For instance, the first federal legislation for bilingual education was passed by Congress in 1968 under Title VII of the Elementary and Secondary Education Act (Jiménez, 1992). Instigated by the 1960s climate of social change and the civil rights movement, the Bilingual Education Act of 1968 represented the first national acknowledgment that the prevalent sink-or-swim approach to teaching English "was both an educational failure and a denial of equal opportunity for language minority students" (Ovando and Collier, 1998).

In addition, the allegation that the basic rights of language minority students were violated spawned numerous lawsuits. The foundation for these lawsuits were the three federal laws that established "basic rights"; the Fourteenth Amendment of the U.S. Constitution, which guarantees equal protection for all persons under the laws of the United States; the Civil Rights Act of 1964, which prohibits discrimination on the basis of "race, color, or national origin" in any federally funded program; and the Equal Educational Opportunity Act of 1974, which states that

> No state shall deny equal educational opportunity to an individual
> on account of his or her race, color, sex, or national origin, by . . .

the failure of an educational agency to take appropriate action to overcome language barriers that impede equal participation by its students in its instructional programs. (Cited in Ovando and Collier, 1998, p. 45)

While several cases demonstrated that language advocates would not tolerate halfhearted attempts at compliance with bilingual education legislation, it was the U.S. Supreme Court decision *Lau v. Nichols* (1974) that has had the most significant impact in defining legal responsibilities of schools serving language minority students (Kibbee, 1996). This decision proclaimed that Chinese children in San Francisco who would not speak English were denied an equal oportunity without education in their language. This landmark case set in motion an awareness for providing language minorities an equal educational opportunity.

While these federal mandates and legislation forced U.S. school systems to reexamine their educational practices regarding language minority students, they did not specify exactly how bilingual education would work. In fact, neither the curriculum nor the purpose of bilingual education was stipulated. Although state and federal policies influenced school programs, the specifics of bilingual program implementation were decided at the local level (Ricento, 1996). To this day, there is no "one" bilingual education model across the United States. However, bilingual education adheres to certain principles of second language learning and acquisition. These second language principles stem from studies conducted during the 1960s, 1970s, and 1980s that examine how a second language is acquired and developed (Cummins, 1978, 1979; Hakuta and Diaz, 1985; Krashen, 1988; Peal and Lambert, 1962).

LANGUAGE ACQUISITION AND DEVELOPMENT:
CONSTRUCTING LOS DESLENGUADOS

As with dominant notions of early childhood education, bilingual education is deeply embedded in developmental psychology. Critically examining the sociohistorical roots of developmental psychology, Burman (1994) reveals that

developmental psychology participated in social movements explicitly concerned with the comparison, regulation, and control of groups in societies, and is closely identified with the development of tools of mental measurement, classification of abilities and the establishment of norms. It is associated with the rise of science and modernity, subscribing to a specific, gendered model of scientific practice. (p. 9–10)

Governed by notions of progress, hierarchy, and universalism, developmental psychology has promoted growth and advancement as *the* human condition (Burman, 1994; Cannella, 1997). Emerging from scientific positivism, the field of developmental psychology claims to implement objective, neutral, apolitical measures for the purpose of discovering "truths" about human beings (Cannella, 1997).

In bilingual education, we assume that language acquisition is a natural, developmental process (Cummins, 1981; Gonzalez, 1999; Ovando and Collier, 1998) that reflects broader questions of human development (Burman, 1994). We look to our *investigaciones* on language development as the route to "discover" the "normal" language learner. The language *que usamos* speaks of progress and normalization—no room for *ambiguidad*. Failing to do justice to the complexity of what it means to "have language," language development research/theories have perpetuated notions of "normalcy" and created privilege for some over others. They legitimized the surveillance and social control of language minority children "in the name of normal growth and human change" (Cannella, 1997, p. 63).

Border Patrol, la Migra: The Surveillance of Language

Relying on language development research, bilingual education advocates claim that language acquisition is driven by the existence of predictable stages that most learners pass through (Gonzalez, 1999; Krashen, 1981; Ovando and Collier, 1998; Thomas and Collier, 1997). Adhering to the belief that there is a developmental sequence to language acquisition results in the creation of norms—truths applicable to all. These norms or expectations are developmental constructions that allow for the *regulación* of the language learner. *Por ejemplo*, those who do not fit the "norm" need to be guided toward developmental goals and standards.

Language development theories that support such notions of normalcy legitimize *el constante* surveillance of younger human beings. We cast our scientific gaze on the child to ensure they learn language in a "developmentally appropriate" way—a Western, Eurocentric, English-speaking, middle-class way. Recognizing that hierarchies are inherent in a developmental model suggests that these Western ways will always be privileged over "others." Thus, the "language minority" child will always be seen as *inferior*, underdeveloped, and in need of guidance-surveillance.

Taming Tongues: Privileging Language Standards

The creation of language norms has also resulted in the privileging of particular language styles. Believing that human truths can be discovered, ordered, and categorized, particular "types" or "styles" of language are assumed to be universal. For instance, social constructs such as "proficiency" and "balanced bilingualism" perpetuate the notion that "standard" language styles exist— *son una certeza*. While the popular current view among many bilingual education advocates *afirman* the importance of home "dialect" and its *uso* within the community, they often adhere to the idea that there is a "standard" version of language. Viewing particular language styles/forms as variations or departures of a "standard" reinforces dominant Western discourses that construct some humans as *inferior, abnormal*, and in need of remediation. Thus, the construction of "standards" serves to perpetuate the status quo and privilege those in power. As Anzaldúa (1987, p. 80) articulates, "Chicanas who grew up speaking Chicano Spanish have internalized the belief that we speak poor Spanish. It is illegitimate, a bastard language. And because we internalize how our language has been used against us by the dominant culture, we use our language differences against each other."

The field of bilingual education *no pueden ignorar* that developmental psychology has been the foundation of our advocacy efforts. We must critically challenge our assumptions regarding language, development, and human existence. We must recognize how the social construction of developmental notions of *progreso*, hierarchy, and universal truth have privileged some, while hurting others. Perhaps *debemos* generate *nueva y multiples posibilidades para aquellos que llamamos* younger human beings.

MULTILINGUAL JUSTICE FOR ALL: IN LINGUISTS WE TRUST?

The field of multilingual and language rights is a movement that promotes language diversity around the world. The multilingual/linguist rights group is composed of human rights lawyers, politicians, linguists, sociolinguists, and philosophers to name a few (Skutnabb-Kangas, 2000). This movement began with the peace treaties created after World War I that included rights for language minorities. Recently, language rights and human rights have been united as linguistic human rights—rights to which every individual is entitled (Skutnabb-Kangas, 2000).

According to this group, safeguarding language diversity is key to maintaining the physical and cultural diversity of the world (Phillipson, 2000; Skutnabb-Kangas, 2000). Multilingual and language rights research, based on Western conceptions of language and linguistics (Singh, 1996), has been and still is being conducted to help us understand language diversity and linguistic genocide. According to multilingual rights scholars, our biodiversity is dependent on the language diversity of the world (Skutnabb-Kangas, 2000). We must therefore preserve the languages of the world for the biological world to survive.

Although we believe we must respect and protect the diverse cultures and languages of the world, we find problematic, not the idea of respecting and protecting language diversity, but how multilingual and language rights advocates deify linguists and their Western concepts of language. *Son vistos como unos dioses*. It is assumed that they know the truth about language; that they can put an order to language; and that their vision of multilingualism is a utopia. Unquestioned are the Western assumptions of language that permeate their research. *Que nos se nos olvide que* language, in and of itself, is a Western modernist concept. Linguists dissect, order, and normalize language in an attempt to mold it to our Western understandings (Branson and Miller, 2000). As Anzaldúa argues, "*nos quieren poner candados en la boca.* They would hold us back with their bag of *reglas de academia*" (Anzaldúa, 1987, p. 54). And indeed, the duty of linguists is to make rules, *reglas*, and criteria about language that they impose on others. Thus, they hold people back (limit other ways of existing) in their search for the universal linguistic rules.

This does not mean that we do not believe that we should fight for linguistic rights. But as with any social justice issue, *debemos de tener cuidado*, that we do not create new standards that under the guise of social justice go unproblematized. For instance, privileging the right to protect a language may be a pressing issue for linguists who are trained in Western traditions. But is this a pressing issue for those they presume to be protecting, *los deslenguados?* Multilingual and linguist rights advocates assume that language minorities need rescuing from the grips of dominant languages (Kontra, 1996; Rassool, 2000; Voulab, 2000). However, as Edwards (1994) contends, "It is not only the 'large' languages of the world which have attempted to throw their way around in this jingoistic way" (p. 7). *Los del tercer mundo no pueden ni mantener sus propias lenguas*. This assumption constructs language minorities as void of any kind of human agency.

We contend that border languages around the world are an example of a kind of agency. For instance, Chicano English/Spanish, could potentially serve as spaces for *resistencia*, power, and liberation. It is a way to subvert language standardization of any kind. Chicano English/Spanish is a language *que ha nacido* naturally (Anzaldua, 1987). It is a result of the clash or *mestizaje* of two languages coming in contact. It is a way for a people to claim and name their own language for their own *propositos*.

The Truth about Language

In Western linguistic tradition it is assumed that language *es un concepto universal* understood by all. Branson and Miller (2000) offer an example how language as we know it—used to communicate and ruled governed—is contested. The Kata Kolok language in north Bali in Indonesia problematizes basic linguistic assumptions. For instance, the word and concept of 'language' did not even exist until it was imported from Western linguist research. The word that linguist believed to be the equivalent to language, *bahasa*, was found to mean culture. Further, much to everyone's surprise, linguists could not find any word "order" for them to dissect and analyze. In many instances there was no identifiable subject, verb, or object. *Este es un ejemplo*, of the indefinite ways of existing—an unthought of possibility.

THE LINGUIST'S SUEÑO—A MULTILINGUAL UTOPIA OR DIE

No es que estamos contra un mundo multilingual, however, we should be weary of advocating multilingualism as a new truth. Multilingual and linguistic rights advocates have visions that a multilingual society is a better society (Kibbee, 1996; Phillipson, 2000; Skutnabb-Kangas, 2000). *Creemos que este argumento* is in line with the Enlightenment/modernist project that seeks to improve the state of human beings through adequate understanding and application of Western reason/research.

Under the discourse of scientific inquiry, sociolinguists believe that languages can be examined in the same way biologists examine and classify species. Multilingual/linguistic rights advocates are working hard to draw parallels between language and species (Maffi, 2000; Phillipson, 1999; Skutnabb-Kangas, 2000). The need to classify organisms fits with the Western belief in an ordered world that is controllable and predictable. By striving for this parallel, multilingual and linguist rights advocates are inadvertently striving for a theories of multilingualsims that are ordered, predictable, and controllable. They argue that just like biological species can spread additively or subtractively, so can languages spread additively or subtractively. This addition or subtraction occurs when biological species come in contact with non-native species (Skutnabb-Kangas, 2000). This introduction of non-native species often leads to "hybridization, competition for resources, predation, disease, parasites, and the alteration of ecological relationships between species" (www.rbge.org.uk/data/wcmc/plants.by.taxon.html, quoted in Skutnabb-Kangas, p. 72). This could be seen *como un* fear of contamination, hybridity, and mutation of languages. It is also as if linguists want language to stay *pura*. When we engage in scientific "slice and dice," we run the risk of imposing and limiting definitions and possibilities for language. *Creemos* that we should have linguistic rights, however, using science, the master's tools, perhaps may limit language possibilities as opposed to expanding them.

Linguistic rights advocates see worldwide language education as the arena in which subjects could/should be multilingual (Garcia, 2000;

Skutnabb-Kangas, 2000). *No pensamos* that the teaching of multiple languages is a bad idea. It is the imposition to be multilingual or bilingual that we find problematic. Further, when the language being taught is dissected, classified, and ordered, then it becomes an object of scientific gaze and thus limited. *Por ejemplo,* younger human beings come to classrooms already equipped with rich language experiences (or multiple other kinds of experiences) only to find in the classroom that their language and the target language must be an object of study to be ordered, monitored, and altered. And that there is *una manera específica* to communicate (Heath, 1983). We do not allow humans, much less younger human beings, the opportunity to expand, *estirarse*—stretch their language experiences (or multiple other kinds of experiences). Thus, we ask the question, are linguists' *sueños* really eradicating the very ideal they advocate?

PLATICANDO AND THEORIZING

Chicana feminist work has ripped open a new space for theorizing about pedagogy *y los deslenguados.* Our Chicana feminist perspectives have helped us to deconstruct many of our traditional taken-for-granted assumptions about language advocacy. We hope to encourage other advocates, scholars, and educators to rethink our advocacy, research, and pedagogy. Perhaps *necesitamos teorías mestizas* that will enable us to (re)imagine new possibilities for language. Perhaps we could use border theorizing to incorporate "everyday cultural practices as a source for the construction of knowledge outside the officially sanctioned space for such a creation" (Elenes, 2001, p. 691). Theorizing can become an act of resistance and power—a space in which language can be flexible, not fixed. A space in which language minorities (all people) can renegotiate, decolonize, and reclaim (multiple) identities.

Sonia Saldívar-Hull (2000) urges Chicana feminists to look for theories in the "nontraditional places." Places like interviews, *pláticas y encuentros* (González, 2001), prefaces to anthologies, interstices of autobiographies and cultural artifacts serve as spaces for "meaning making." As Anzaldúa (1990) suggests, "(b)y bringing our own approaches and methodologies, we transform that theorizing space" (p. xxv). As an example, we believe that conversations become sites for theorizing. Conversations are a way to collect spontaneous meaning making about the world via communication of our identities, thoughts, ambiguities, and constructions (González, 2001). We hope that the following dialogue will expand and clarify the ideas *que hemos presentado* in this chapter. What follows are our thoughts and reactions to our own research. We invite further discussion and expansion on our ideas so that we can critically advocate with/for *los deslenguados* in hopes of creating a world of endless *posibilidades.*

CS: What we have done so far has put into question what and how we advocate for/with language minorities—*los deslenguados* and I say *deslenguados,* which translates into "people with no tongues," because that's how I see we treat language minorities, as if they have no language and we must provide for them all the right experiences so they can develop this language whether it is English or Spanish or whatever language.

ED: *Por eso* I think we have to constantly question what we do when we say it is "for/with" others.

CS: I guess my problem with advocacy and in particularly language advocacy is that the "advocacy" part begins to establish *nuevos* norms and standards for those we presume to be helping. I see it as *una manera* to impose on others a way to be, be it liberalism, conservatism, or postmodernism.

ED: So are we imposing a *nueva manera* "to be"?

CS: We sure could be. After all, I guess we are imposing being critical and questioning as a way to exists. However, I feel that our field, meaning bilingual education, needs to be questioned and examined to allow for other *posibilidades de ser.* What do you think?

ED: I agree with you. I think we can do it critically. I hope that what we are doing makes those working with "language minorities"—*los deslenguados*—to question taken-for-granted assumptions. However, this critique is not meant to be used as ammunition against bilingual or multilingual education. As we mentioned in the chapter, this critique *es parte de* language advocacy, not outside of it.

CS: I was really scared to present this at AERA. I know that we both thought *que la gente se iba a friquear*—you know, freak out. We are all so caught up in dichotomous thinking that I was afraid that people might see it as an all-or-nothing thing.

ED: Right, they might think we were saying "bilingual ed. or no bilingual ed."

CS: Yes, and that is not all what we are saying. What we are try to bring to light is that bilingual education and multilingual education are deeply embedded in developmental psychology and positivistic research. And these two camps are particular views of the world coming from the Enlightenment—thus white and male. Although the two groups might be afraid of the "disappearance" of minority languages, as maybe·they should be, they don't recognize how hybrid languages like Chicano Spanish/English are a way to resist and be an emancipation or decolonizing tool for language minorities.

ED: Right. And while it seems that bilingual education is fighting against this Western domination—attempting to "empower" language minorities—are we really *si seguimos usando los* colonizing tools that have been constructed to exclude, and thus not allow us to recognize like you say, Chicano Spanish/English as a decolonizing tool?

CS: Yeah, and what I really don't understand is the need to measure langauge all the time. I think of when I was testing children in Dallas for language proficiency. It was interesting that I was testing the language proficiency of the brown children. If your home language is not English, than it is assumed that your home language, in this instance Spanish, must be assessed. Yet we do not measure the language proficiency of white children. Anyway, all this testing is done to sort, categorize, and eventually exclude.

ED: You mentioned AERA. I thought these ideas may be perceived as "out there," or undermining bilingual/multilingual ed.

CS: I hope that what got to them was the idea that we bring up in the chapter that bilingual education is the "spoiled child of critical theory." And that the early childhood reconceptualist movement hasn't really dialogued with bilingual education or vice versa.

ED: We have to realize that bilingual education *is* early childhood education. We, in bilingual ed., make major decisions about the lives of young children. This should definitely be a concern for early childhood educators.

CS: Mmm. I want to really work on taking these ideas and expanding on them. We have some good suggestions for action. One of my favorites that we came up with *es integrar una perspectiva* Chicana feminist *en nuestras* classrooms and in our work/scholarship in attempt to create more *posibilidades* with those we call younger human beings. What about you?

ED: I think it is important for the reconceptualists in early childhood education to share work with the field of bilingual education. *Podemos presentar nuestro* research at—or attend—the National Association for Bilingual Education (NABE) and/or local bilingual ed. conferences. Also, we could submit papers to journals that focus on language issues. And we shouldn't forget to communicate with the bilingual/ESL programs in our colleges.

CS: In the class that we both are taking this semester, it was stressed to advocate critically for/with families and children. I think that as a possibility we could create some kind of clearinghouse or think tank that encompass workshops, conferences, and training for the purpose of addressing issues of critical advocacy. So let me ask you after all this deconstruction business, how do you view a postmodern *mestizaje* image of language?

ED: I see this as a weaving of multiple *posibilidades* for language—for existing. There are no set boundaries, no set definitions. We would welcome *ambiguidad*. We could begin to blur the borders we have imposed on language.

CS: Mmm. I like that! I see language as an artistic expression and should be left alone to wonder, mutate, and decolonize itself. Perhaps we can begin weaving this *nueva imagen preguntandonos* questions like: Is the notion of language *un concepto universal?* Are linguists prescribing a certain way of being or existing—*de ser?* Can/should we apply linguistic *reglas* to all? How is the discourse of language advocacy a totalizing discourse? Who benefits/privileges from linguist research? How does our focus on language issues distract us from other issues that may also be pertinent to those whom we advocate for/with? How can we advocate for/with language minorities in ways that do not oppress them or reify new categories or truths?

REFERENCES

Anzaldúa, G. (1987). *Borderlands/La Frontera*. San Francisco: Aunt Lute Books.

Anzaldúa, G. (Ed.). (1990). *Making face, making soul: Haciendo caras*. San Francisco: Aunt Lute Books.

Branson, J. and D. Miller. (2000). Maintaining developing and sharing the knowledge and potential embedded in all our languages and cultures: On linguists as agents of epistemic violence. In R. Phillipson, *Rights to language: Equity, power and education*. London: Lawrence Earlbaum.

Burman, E. (1994). *Deconstructing developmental psychology*. London: Routledge.

Cannella, G. S. (1997). *Deconstructing early childhood education: Social justice and revolution*. New York: Peter Lang.

Cannella, G. S. and C. Bailey. (1999). Postmodern research in early childhood education. In Reifel, S. (Ed.), *Advances in early education and day care*. Vol. 10 (pp. 3–39). Greenwich, CT: Jai Press.

Cummins, J. (1978). Bilingualism and the development of metalinguistic awareness. *Journal of Cross Cultural Psychology*, 9(2), 131–149.

Cummins, J. (1979). Linguistic interdependence and the educational development of bilingual children. *Review of Educational Research*, 49(2), 222–251.

Cummins, J. (1981). *Bilingualism and minority-language children*. Toronto: Ontario Institute for Studies in Education Press.

Derrida, J. (1981). *Dissemination*. (B. Johnson, Trans.) Chicago: University of Chicago Press.

Edwards, J. (1994). *Multilingualism*. London: Routledge.

Elenes, C. A. (2001). *Transformando fronteras:* Chicana feminist transformative pedagogies. *Qualitative Studies in Education, 14*(5), 689–702.

Elenes, C. A., F. E. González, D. Delgado Bernal, and S. Villenas. (2001). Chicana/Mexicana feminist pedagogies: *Consejos, respecto, y educación* in everyday life. *Qualitative Studies in Education, 14*(5), 595–602.

Foucault, M. (1980). *Power and knowledge: Selected interviews and other writings 1972–1977.* New York: Pantheon.

Garcia, O. (2000). Language: A diversity category beyond all others. In R. Phillipson (Ed.), *Rights to language; Equity, power, and education.* London: Lawrence Erlbaum.

Giroux, H. (Ed.). (1991). *Postmodernism, feminism, and cultural politics: Redrawing educational boundaries.* Albany: State University of New York Press.

González, V. (1999). (Ed). *Language and cognitive development in second language learners.* Boston: Allyn & Bacon.

González, F. E. (2001). *Haciendo que hacer-*Cutivating a Mestiza worldview and academic achievement: Braiding cultural knowledge into educational research, policy and practice. *Qualitative Studies in Education,* 14(5), 641–656.

Hakuta, K. and R. Diaz. (1985). The relationship between degree of bilingualism and cognitive ability. In K. E. Nelson (Ed.), *Children's language.* Hillsdale, NJ: Lawrence Erlbaum.

Heath, S. B. (1983). *Ways with words: Language, life, and work in communities and classrooms.* New York: Cambridge University Press.

hooks, b. (1994). *Teaching to transgress.* London: Routledge.

Jiménez, M. (1992). The educational rights of language-minority children. In J. Crawford (ed.). *Language loyalties: A source book on the official English controversy.* Chicago: University of Chicago Press.

Keating, A. L. (2000). *Gloria E. Anzaldua: Interviews/entrevistas.* London: Routledge.

Kibbee, D. A. (1996). Legal and linguistic perspectives on language legislation. In D. Kibbee (Ed.), *Language legislation and linguistic rights.* Amsterdam: John Bejamins Publishing Co.

Kincheloe, J. L. (1993). *Towards a critical politics of teacher thinking.* Westport: Bergin & Garvey.

Kincheloe, J. L. and P. McLaren. (1994). Rethinking critical theory and qualitative research. In N. K. Denzin and Y. S. Lincoln (Eds.), *Handbook of qualitative research.* London: Sage.

Kontra, M. (1996). Language rights arguments in Central Europe and the U.S.A: How similar are they? In D. Kibbee (Ed.), *Language legislation and linguistic rights.* Amsterdam: John Bejamins Publishing Co.

Krashen, S. D. (1981). *Second language acquisition and second language learning.* Oxford: Permagon.

Krashen, S. D. (1988). *On course*. Sacramento: California Association for Bilingual Education.

Krashen, S. D. and T. D. Terrell. (1983). *The natural approach: Language acquisition in the classroom*. Oxford: Pergamon.

Lewelling, V. (1997). *Official English and English Plus: An update*. Washington, DC: ERIC,. ED 406849.

Maffi, L. (2000). Linguistic and biological diversity: The inextricable link. In Robert Phillipson, *Rights to language: equity, power and education*. London: Lawrence Erlbaum.

Moraga, C. (1983). *Loving in the war years: Lo que nunca paso por sus labios*. Boston: South End Press.

Ovando, C. J. and V. P. Collier. (1998). *Bilingual and ESL classrooms: Teaching in multicultural contexts*. Boston: McGraw-Hill.

Peal, E. and W. Lambert. (1962). The relation of bilingualism to intelligence. *Psychological Monographs: General and Applied, 76*(27, whole no. 546), 1–23.

Phillipson, R. (1999). International languages and international human rights. In M. Kontra, R. Phillopson, T. Skutnabb-Kangas, and T. Varady (Eds.), *Language: A right and a resource*. Budapest: CEU Press.

Phillipson, R. (2000). (Ed.), *Rights to language: Equity, power and education*. Mahwah, NJ: L. Erlbaum.

Popkewitz, T. S. (1997). The production of reason and power: Curriculum history and intellectual traditions. *Journal of Curriculum Studies, 29*, n2, 131–164.

Rassool, N. (2000). Language maintenance as an arena of cultural and political struggles in a changing world. In R. Phillipson (Ed.), *Rights to language; Equity, power, and education*. London: Lawrence Erlbaum.

Roberts, C. A. (1995). Bilingual education program models: A framework for understanding. *The Bilingual Research Journal, 19* (3 & 4), 369–378.

Salvídar-Hull, S. (2000). *Feminism on the border: Chicana gender politics and literature*. Los Angeles: University of California Press.

Sandoval, C. (2000). *Methodology of the oppressed*. Minneapolis: University of Minnesota Press.

Singh, R. (Ed). (1996). Towards a critical sociolinguistics. Amsterdam: John Benjamins Publishing Co.

Skutnabb-kangas, T. (2000). Linguistic genocide in education-or worldwide diversity and human rights? Mahwah, NJ: Lawrence Erlbaum.

Smith, L. T. (1999). *Decolonizing methodologies: Research and indigenous peoples*. London: Zed Books.

Thomas, W. P. and V. P. Collier. (1997). *School effectiveness for language minority students*. Washington, DC: National Clearinghouse for Bilingual Education.

U.S. English. (1992). In defense of our common language. In James Crawford, *Language loyalties: A source book on the official English controversy*. Chicago: University of Chicago Press.

U.S. English, (2001). www.us-english.org/inc/official/native.asp. Washington, DC.

Viruru, R. and G. S. Cannella. (2000, October). *Postcolonial thoughts on education: Or lifestyles of the rich and famous.* Paper presented at the annual meeting of the *Journal of Curriculum Theorizing.* Bergamo, OH.

Vuolab, K. (2000). Such a treasure of knowledge for human survival. In R. Phillipson (Ed.), *Rights to language; Equity, power, and education.* London: Lawrence Erlbaum.

CHAPTER FOURTEEN

An Indigenous Perspective on Self-Determination

KATHRYN MANUELITO

Throughout the world indigenous communities are at work to gain and establish recognition in societies that have colonized them for centuries. Indigenous people seek a role in societies that have marginalized them because of their small numbers, culture, language, and physical differences. They want to determine their own destiny, whether it is in the realm of education or economic development. Some indigenous people such as the Hawaiians (Wilson, 1999), Maori of New Zealand (Durie, 1999), Sami of Norway (Todal, 1999), Quechua (Hornberger and King, 1999), and American Indians (McCarty and Watahomigie, 1999) in the United States are enacting self-determination through community-based education. For American Indians, self-determination has been described as "an experiment of major significance. It is an effort to win for Indian communities the same rights of self-determination enjoyed by other American communities, while preserving a special, constitutionally sanctioned relationship with the federal government" (Gross, 1978, p. 1196). In this chapter, I will examine how one Indian tribal group, the Ramah Band of the Navajo Tribe, defines and practices self-determination.

The U.S. government encouraged self-governance for Indian people in the passage of the 1934 Indian Reorganization Act, also known as the Wheeler-Howard Act (Szasz, 1974). However, measures for self-governance through the Indian Reorganization Act were restrictive and did not include education and schooling of American Indian youth. With the passage of the 1975 Self-Determination and Education Assistance Act and the 1990 Native American Languages Act, the possibilities for appropriate culturally sensitive education for American Indian children have become greater than ever before. Even so, among the dominant Euro-Western society, most politicians and educators do not actively support these two acts, which was evident in the 2001 passage of English Only legislation in Arizona, as well as in other states including California and, most recently, Massachusetts. Even today, formal education of Indian children is provided (in part) by the Bureau of Indian Affairs, the most colonizing agency in the United States, where the priority is the development of citizenship in a Euro-Western, middle-class world, in a neoliberal world intolerant of differences and insensitive to the world of Indian communities.

Dialogue between indigenous people and the dominant society is essential for the implementation of self-determination by indigenous people and support of self-determination. Presently, prescriptions and descriptions of self-determination are one-sided from the dominant society. Assumptions that indigenous people agree with the dominant society's definitions of self-determination continue to prevent progress toward self-determination by indigenous people. Misunderstandings between the two groups abound without dialogue. Passage of legislation for self-determination in education is important, but even more important is communication between indigenous people and dominant society lawmakers and educators.

The operationalizing of self-determination is crucial for American Indians because it directly impacts the sovereignty of each tribal group as well as the appropriate education for American Indian youth. In 1975, the Self-Determination and Education Assistance Act granted American Indians governance of their schools. With the exception of a few nationally known community and tribally controlled schools, such as Rough Rock Demonstration School (known now as Rough Rock Community School), Rough Rock, Arizona, information about Indian controlled schools is scarce, even though there are presently 114 tribally controlled schools (Tippeconnic, 1999). Information on how Indian people themselves understand self-determination is even more scarce. I will describe a study that explored how the Ramah Band of the Navajo Tribe understands and has enacted self-determination. The study is important because it provides a Navajo voice and perspective on self-determination and appropriate education.

RAMAH NAVAJO COMMUNITY

The Ramah Navajo Community is located outside of the main Navajo reservation. It is seventy-five miles south of the main Navajo Reservation, borders the Zuni Indian Reservation to the west, borders federal Bureau of Land Management (BLM) land to the east, borders private ranches to the south, and is fifteen miles south of the village of Ramah, a predominately Euro-American Mormon settlement. Land of the Ramah Navajo Reservation covers 146,953 acres (Federal Appropriation Request of the Navajo Chapter, 2000). The Ramah Band of the Navajo Tribe is a satellite Navajo community in New Mexico with a population of 3000. Satellite communities are set apart by their great distance from the main Navajo Reservation, and are surrounded by non-Navajo and non-Indian lands.

Since the early 1900s children from the Ramah Navajo community have attended off-reservation government boarding schools in New Mexico and the neighboring states of Arizona, California, Nevada, Utah, and Oklahoma. In 1943, a government day school was built in the Ramah Navajo community in Mountain View. The school had one teacher for grades one to three. Enrollment was limited to thirty youth, and thus could not meet the needs of most of the children of the Ramah Navajo community.

By 1950, the White Mormon Ramah community had opened a public school, which some Ramah Navajo youth attended. The Ramah Public School was in the Gallup-McKinley County School District. This school, which was fifteen miles north of the Ramah Navajo community, had grades one through twelve. The Ramah Public School, like the Mountain View Day School, could not accommodate all the Ramah Navajo youth. Many Ramah Navajo children had to attend government boarding schools far from home. In 1968, the Gallup-McKinley County School Board condemned and closed the Ramah Public High School. Instead of enrolling to attend school elsewhere, many Ramah Navajo students simply dropped out. By 1968, formal education for most Ramah Navajo youth was neither accessible nor appropriate, and the outlook for the future of the Ramah Navajo Community was grim.

On February 10, 1970, the Ramah Navajo School Board was formally incorporated after two failed lawsuits by the Ramah Navajo Chapter to reopen the local Ramah Public High School. The newly formed school board, consisting of local Ramah Navajo people, requested funding for a new school from the Bureau of Indian Affairs (BIA) office in Washington, D.C. On March 25, 1970, funding was promised only after a frail but courageous elder, Bertha Lorenzo, blocked the entryway in the BIA building in Washington, D.C., and announced in the Navajo language "We have been waiting since 1920 [for a school]. We won't leave this building until we get a definite commitment of support from the BIA." Another school board member, Chavez Coho, also reminded the BIA about the Treaty of 1868, which promised a teacher for every thirty children (*Dine aa-Hani*, 1970, June-July). On April 21, 1970, funding was granted. Without outside support and guidance and only with sheer determination, Ramah Navajo people provided the opportunity for formal education in their community.

On June 4, 1970, the Ramah Navajo High School began its first session in brown army tents on the grounds of the aging Ramah Public High School in the non-Navajo community of Ramah. Unlike other Indian community-controlled schools that were supported and established by outside agencies, the Ramah Navajo High School was established exclusively through grassroots efforts. The courageous community leaders experienced numerous obstacles, but they have forged ahead for thirty years with total Navajo leadership. In 1975, the Ramah Navajo High School moved fifteen miles south to the Ramah Navajo community and changed its name to the Pine Hill School. Since that humble beginning in 1970, the Ramah Navajo School Board has developed a total educational system for infants to higher education.

Today, the Pine Hill School Campus is a multimillion dollar establishment consisting of a high school, middle school, elementary school, library, media center, early childhood complex, computer lab, cafeteria, gymnasium, clinic, social service offices, a teen center, a radio station, a post office, a bilingual materials center, administration offices, higher education offices, maintenance and facilities building, football field, swimming pool, and individual homes and duplexes for school staff. The Pine Hill School Campus, located in the high mountainous plateaus surrounded by Navajo homes, grazing sheep, pinion trees, and tall pines, is credited with bringing in electricity, running water, a paved road, and telecommunication into this Navajo community for the first time. From brown army tents to a school campus providing not only formal educational services, but health, social services, electricity, water, telephone service, and roads to the community, the Ramah Navajo School Board and Pine Hill School have impacted the total community. Today, Pine Hill School as a catalyst for self-determination is only one aspect of total community development and empowerment.

In addition to the establishment of a total educational program, Pine Hill School is noted for many "firsts" in Indian country throughout the United States. In 1972, the Ramah Navajo School Board became the first Indian group to have their own FM radio station that still broadcasts from the Pine Hill School. The Ramah Navajo School Board is also the first Indian group in the United States to contract their own health clinic complete with dental, optometry, and emergency (EMT) services for the community. Being remote and even unknown to residents of the greater Navajo Reservation (as related in interviews of the study) and the world, the Ramah community put itself on the map and into the consciousness of the greater Navajo community as well as greater Indian communities of the United States.

Grounded in their cultural values and beliefs, the Ramah Navajo School Board and the Pine Hill School has enacted self-determination *as they understand it.* Thus, the question of how the Ramah Navajo School Board and community understand *self-determination* will be explored in this chapter. Before examining self-determination from the insider Navajo view, I will briefly reflect in the next section on the concept of self-determination as it applies to Indian communities both from outsider non-Indian views and by educators who are American Indian.

REFLECTIONS ON SELF-DETERMINATION

The 1968 Bilingual Act supported and became a catalyst to Indian education by promoting bilingual program development, curriculum development, bilingual materials development, and bilingual teacher education. Indian community-controlled schools benefited immensely by the support of this legislation to develop community-based education. As mentioned previously, information about the 116 Indian-controlled schools is scarce. Successes have been documented in a few schools such as Rough Rock Demonstration School, Rock Point School (McCarty, 2000; McCarty and Watahomigie, 1999) and the Peach Springs School on the Hualapai Reservation (McCarty and Watahomigie, 1999). These schools on record have had the good fortune to have university academics interested in them, and thus were written about in academic circles. However, the many other Indian-controlled schools whose Indian leadership was totally involved in the trenches of daily operation of schools could not readily publish their accomplishments even if they wanted to do so. In addition, at the Pine Hill School, outsiders were not welcomed to record or investigate the school and community because the Ramah Navajo people have felt that they had been previously exploited by outside researchers. Blanchard concurs with the perception that the Ramah Navajo people have been overly researched and stated that the Ramah Navajo "are the most studied people in the world" (Blanchard, 1971, p.3). The Navajo value of modesty was also a major factor, thus publicity and attention was shunned. Because little is actually known about the majority of Indian-controlled schools, self-determination and self-governance in education still appear to remain, as Gross has noted, "an experiment of major significance" (Gross, 1978, p. 1196).

Since the 1975 Self-Determination and Education Assistance Act was passed, Indian communities have separately defined and operationalized self-determination. Many definitions of self-determination have evolved as a result. In many contexts, self-determination has become synonymous with self-governance. Self-governance has various operational definitions: tribal control, local control, community control, and Indian parent involvement. According to Tippeconnic, "The terms Indian parent involvement, community control, local control, and tribal control are used interchangeably to denote aspects of Indian control of education. But these terms do not necessarily mean the same thing" (Tippeconnic, 1999, p. 39). Huff states, "The models of Indian-controlled schools are as diverse as Indian Country" (Huff, 1997, p. 174).

Among members of Indian communities, perspectives on the 1975 Self-Determination and Educational Assistance Act are varied. Many distrust the implications and intent of this legislation and feel that this is the beginning of termination of Indian tribal government. This view is based on the experience of over 100 tribes who were terminated as federally recognized tribes in the in the 1950s. On becoming self-sufficient and self-determined, their sovereignty status was severed. The federal government unjustly ended their entitlements to health and educational benefits.

Another important reason for Indian people not wholly trusting governmental mandates is the vacillating treatment, the characteristic pendulum swing, demonstrated by the U.S. government in creating and administering federal policies. Like other federal policies, the Self-Determination and Education Assistance Act can be annulled at any time with congressional action. Political climate can and does change in Congress.

In Indian education and in Indian communities, a critical problem exists because the concept of self-determination has not been defined. Deloria, a renowned American Indian educator and philosopher, comments, "Self-determination grew like topsy over the past three decades and it [self-determination] never was clearly defined at the onset of the era" (Deloria, 1994, p. 52). The question of what we, as Indian people, are supposed to determine has not been specified. As a result, many types of Indian-controlled schools have been established under the umbrella of self-determination. But we must ask ourselves: What is self-determination? What is it that we as selves and communities are determining? (Deloria, 1994, p. 56).

Thus, twenty-eight years after the self-determination legislation was passed, the question remains: What is self-determination and how do Indian people understand it?

A STUDY OF SELF-DETERMINATION IN THE RAMAH NAVAJO COMMUNITY

A study that I conducted examined the questions: What is self-determination? How is self-determination enacted in the Pine Hill School and the Ramah Navajo community? The qualitative study followed the inductive naturalistic paradigm. The study design was emergent and theory was thoroughly grounded in the data. The study was grounded and constructed around a Navajo context and with a view of other naturalistic methods. The study incorporated ethnographic techniques. Up until the present research, studies about American Indians have been conducted mainly by outsiders. In this study, I, a Native researcher, was the main instrument in conducting research in a Navajo community. In qualitative studies, the main instrument of research is the researcher (Wolcott, 1975, p. 115).

I am Navajo and am both bilingual and biliterate in Navajo. I grew up in and around Navajo communities in the checkerboard area near Gallup, New Mexico. After receiving my Bachelors Degree, I taught in Ganado, Arizona, and later at the Ramah Navajo High School when it first opened in the 1970s. Not only was I a teacher and director of a Title VII Teacher Training Program on site, but my husband, a Navajo, was an executive director of the school in the 1970s. Since my employment with the Ramah Navajo School Board, I have worked in other Indian communities at both the local and national level. In my employment with Pine Hill School, I first became aware of community-based education and participated in the first efforts at Navajo curriculum and materials development in the early 1970s.

During my research, I had established rapport with the Ramah Navajo community and, as a Navajo, was related through my matriarchal and patriarchal clans to members in the Ramah Navajo Community. In Navajo communities, clan associations are most important for establishing relationships and developing trust. Throughout the study, I maintained Navajo values and respect, known as "K'e" in the Navajo language. I upheld and practiced Navajo protocol at all times. I was continually aware of the context of the study, which was constructed around a Navajo framework and explicated in Euro-Western ideology.

DATA COLLECTION METHODS

I used three data collection methods: participant observation, document collection, and interviews. Activities for participant observation were many and diverse. I attended school board meetings, chapter meetings, staff workshops, special events such as the Veteran's Day Celebration at the Ramah Navajo Chapter House, the 30th Anniversary Celebration, Staff Awards Banquet, and General Election Day Voting at the Ramah Navajo Chapter House. An important aspect in participation observation was tuning into KTDB-FM, the Pine Hill School Radio Station, for an update of community events, school announcements, commentaries, airing of the taping of actual events, and reports from health, education, and legal services in the community. I visited classrooms at the school, ate at the school cafeteria and at staff potluck luncheons, as well as visited other programs on campus such as the Family and Child Education (FACE) Program, Higher Education, Ramah Rug Weavers Program, Pine Hill Clinic, and the KTDB Radio Station. Since my focus was on perspectives from Navajo community members, I spent the majority of my time in Navajo settings such as the Pine Hill Market, Chapter House, a sheep camp, and homes in the Ramah Navajo community.

Document collection included historical, demographic, and personal information from the Ramah Navajo perspective. I collected information from various sources. One source was written and recorded interviews and oral histories from the Ramah Navajo people recorded by Ramah Navajo high school students in a Foxfire Project in the 1970s, 1980s, 1990s, and 2000. I found many of these interviews in the *Tsa' Aszi'* magazine, a publication from the Pine Hill High School students. Many of the elders who were interviewed by the high school students are now deceased.

The earliest documented interview was by Many Beads's Son. (Many Bead's Son is the individual's real name in Navajo and is translated literally from the Navajo language.) Many Beads was the headman of the Ramah Navajo after *Hweeldi*/Long Walk, 1864–1868. This interview was recorded in 1930 and written in the Navajo language in 1954 by linguists Young and Morgan; it is included in the *Navajo Historical Publications, Historical Series #14.*

I collected written documents and reports from the Ramah Navajo School Board either as position statements, brochures, or required reports for private and /or federal funding. Newspapers, both local and national, and journal articles provided additional information. I found information about Pine Hill School's curriculum concerning Navajo language courses and Navajo culture classes in the Navajo Tribe's *Statistics on Navajo (Dine)* Education for the school years: 1992–1993–1994, 1994–1995, and 1998–1999. The school archivist shared materials so that I was able to review original documents from the school's early years and some monographs from the early Harvard Values Study.

I collected information from a non-Navajo perspective in Harvard University's "Harvard Values Study" and the Bureau of Indian Affairs' "Personality and Government Study." The Harvard Values Study, led by Clyde Kluckhohn, and the Ramah Project Study occurred during the 1930s, 1940s, and 1950s. These studies focused on various topics about the Ramah Navajo people such as families, religion, veterans, sexuality, witchcraft, schoolchildren, and ethno-herbology, to name a few. Many of the studies were dissertations, and others became important monographs such as *The Navajo* (Kluckhohn and Leighton, 1947) and *Navajo Witchcraft* (Kluckhohn, 1944).

Another study that I reviewed was conducted in the 1930s and 1940s about the Ramah Navajo community and two other Navajo communities. This study, *Personality and Government Study*, was funded by the Bureau of Indian Affairs. It was conducted jointly by the Committee on Human Development of the University of Chicago and the United States Office of

Indian Affairs (Thompson, 1951). Some of the noted members of the research team included Clyde Kluckhohn, Margaret Mead, Erick Erickson, Robert Havighurst, Dorothea Leighton, and others. *Children of the People* (Kluckhohn and Leighton, 1947) resulted from the study.

Other studies about the Ramah Navajo Community from non-Navajo perspectives were *The People of Rimrock* (Vogt and Alber, 1966) and *The Economics of Sainthood*, (Blanchard, 1977). I also reviewed *Ernst Albert Tietjen* (Tientjen, 1992), a book written by a descendant of the first Mormon settler to Ramah.

The historical, anthropological, and ethnographical perspectives from previous publications on the Ramah Navajo were written about colonized people by colonizers from their frame of reference (Fixico, 1998; Sheridan, 1988; Smith, 1999; Spicer, 1962). The numerous studies about the Ramah Navajo from outsider perspectives were not congruent with the Ramah Navajo people's perspectives. Yet, these Euro-Western based documents are regarded as facts, while indigenous accounts are disregarded.

Biased reports from outsiders have created prejudice and hardships for the Ramah Navajo. For example, several outsider accounts strongly imply that the Ramah Navajos were a marginal, drifting people. Kluckhohn and Leighton in *Children of the People* (1947) stated: "After release from captivity, a few related families drifted into this region instead of settling on the Reservation" (Kluckhohn and Leighton, 1947, p. 131). Vogt and Alber in *People of Rimrock* (1966) stated that the Ramah Navajo people like other settlers in the area: "are local manifestations of cultures whose centers of power and influence are elsewhere . . . are geographically and in some respects culturally at some distance from the main body of Navajo society" (Vogt and Alder, 1966, pp. 24–25). Outsiders and Euro-Western researchers seem to believe that the arbitrary boundary designating the Navajo Reservation, which changed several times according to Presidential Executive Orders, was the absolute designation of land for the Navajos. Navajo opinion on land ownership did not seem to matter.

With the sacred mountain, *Tsoodzil* or Mount Taylor to the east of them, Ramah Navajos have always known that they were in the boundaries of Navajo land as prescribed in Navajo Creation Stories. They did not drift into this region after the Long Walk, but, indeed, returned to their homeland. They lived their culturally rich lives like other Navajos across the great expanse of Arizona, Utah, and New Mexico. Regional differences exist due to historical, social, and economical influences, but certainly Ramah Navajos were not "in some respects culturally at some distance from the main body of Navajo society," as stated by Vogt and Alber (1966).

Throughout the history of the Ramah Navajo people, they have had to struggle for survival on their own apart from the greater Navajo Nation and mostly without the support of the Navajo Nation. Representing similar sentiments from other Navajos from the greater Navajo Reservation, one individual stated, "I guess . . . when you're distantly located from Window Rock or the bigger Navajo Reservation, and you're like in your own turf . . . you try harder to fend for yourselves, to think, plan, how you're going to survive. I think they see that and they strive harder . . . at least I see them [Ramah Navajo] that way. (Participant N)

Comments about their identity differ greatly from outsider Euro-Western researchers. The Ramah Navajo identify themselves as a separate Navajo people, the Ramah Navajo Band of the Navajo Nation. One Ramah Navajo stated: "I'm proud and glad that I belong to the Ramah Navajo Community, because we're so unique and . . . the Navajo Nation, they look at us as a role model. We might have been isolated from the Navajo Nation and they might not have really wanted to provide us much assistance, but a lot of the things that we've done, we've done with our uneducated people (Participant Q). The Ramah Navajo people identity is defined by their collective experiences since *Hweeldi*/Long Walk, and their survival was assured by their sheer efforts of self-determination as they understand it.

The third method that I utilized for data collection was interviews. Most of the participants of the study were Navajo, who gave interviews in both Navajo and English, often code-switching. Of the thirty-nine participants, four were non-Navajo. The four outsider non-Navajo participants spent ten years or more working in the Ramah Navajo community. As I started interviewing participants, I found the two research questions being given explanations from a historical perspective. In order to comprehend, translate, and interpret the experiences of the Ramah Navajo community I included historical research of the Ramah Navajo community as part of the research design.

Ramah Navajo history became an important aspect of the study because "To understand a phenomenon, you need to know its history" (Glesne and Peshkin, 1992, p. 53). I divided historical information into four periods: (1) Pre and Post *Hweeldi*/The Long Walk, 1860–1899, (2) Boarding School Days, 1900–1967, (3) Ramah Navajo School Board, 1968–1970, and (4) Community Building, 1971–2001. I examined political, social, and economic forces in each of the time periods. Unlike most history written about American Indians, the historical view in this study was presented from an American Indian perspective. From this historical analysis, I discovered that self-determination is not just a Euro-Western political and/or economical concept. Self-determination is a Navajo concept that was enacted throughout the four periods of history of the Ramah Navajo people.

In addition to the historical perspective, I included the development of a conceptual framework of self-determination. The development of the framework was based on the Navajo paradigm of the building of a Hogan from the Beauty Way Prayer. I selected the building of the Hogan as a metaphor to represent the construction of self-determination. The Hogan metaphor was chosen because an elder stated that the founding school board members had insisted the new Pine Hill School be built on the principals of the Hogan from the Beauty Way Prayer.

Translation and interpretation of social experiences within a culture are clearly difficult, but the difficulty is much greater when translation and interpretation occur between a Western culture and non-Western culture. Translation and interpretation of social experiences and concepts between the Navajo worldview and the Euro-Western worldview are facilitated by the metaphor of the construction of the Navajo Hogan. The Navajo Hogan is truly significant in the Navajo worldview and is loaded with concepts both social and religious.

For Navajo people, the Hogan has far greater significance beyond being simply a structural dwelling. The Hogan is first mentioned in Navajo Creation Stories where the construction is directed by the Holy People. The Hogan mentioned in the Beauty Way Prayer has sacred and mystical characteristics. "The description of the *hooghans* [hogans] in the Underworld gives mystical images and power to an ordinary *hooghan* [Hogan] and knowing these stories provides the very meaning of what a *hooghan* [Hogan] is" (Beck, Walters, and Francisco, 1977). This traditional dwelling has sacred significance with teachings, songs, and prayers. The male and female Hogan have their own functions. The Hogan is a sacred place and is a living entity. "The Navaho Hogan is not just a place to sleep and eat; it truly is a home and also a temple. It is a 'being', which must be fed and kept, strong and good" (Callaway, Witherspoon, et al., 1974, p. 56).

From topical and conceptual coding of data, I found four patterns that ultimately became the four posts of the metaphoric Hogan. The patterns and their relationship became clear from the historical view and from interviews. The patterns are themes, which I decided to refer to as processes, because processes connote living and non-static entities. These processes appear to be the basic elements of self-determination that are occurring in the Ramah Navajo community. The processes are: community-based planning, maintaining self-awareness, being proactive, and persevering. These processes construct a metaphoric Hogan, which is self-determination in the Pine Hill School.

FINDINGS

Findings are categorized according to (1) historical analysis and (2) conceptual framework of self-determination.

Historical Analysis. My historical analysis demonstrates that Pine Hill School and the Ramah Navajo community are similar to American Indian communities across the country. Two important similar aspects are: (1) a language shift is occurring in the Ramah Navajo community; and (2) self-determination from the Navajo worldview is in conflict with the goals of American schools.

Language shift is occurring in the Ramah Navajo community. According to Ramah Navajo educators at the Pine Hill School, in 2001 approximately 25% of elementary students could speak Navajo fluently. In 1970, 99% of Ramah Navajo High School students spoke Navajo fluently. A study conducted in 1993 among Head Start Navajo children in the main Navajo Reservation found that approximately 15% of Head Start five year olds spoke Navajo fluently (Platero, 1992). In a most recent study, House determined that language shift among the Navajo people was occurring at an alarming rate so that most if not all Navajo gatherings are mainly conducted in English (House, 2002). Thus, a similar type of language shift occurring on the main Navajo Reservation is occurring in the Ramah Navajo community, a satellite community of the Navajo Reservation.

The second finding is that self-determination from the Navajo worldview is in conflict with the goals of formal education in America. "The general tendency is for formal educational institutions to reflect the knowledge, values, and attitudes of the society's dominant groups" (Gutek, 1991, p. 25). American education (formal education) does not reflect the knowledge, values, and attitudes of the Indian communities such as the Ramah Navajo community. Education, as most Ramah Navajo people have traditionally understood it, is grounded in Navajo philosophy and promotes bilingualism and biculturalism.

Navajo education, as the Ramah Navajo people perceived it, is an important part of self-determination. I developed a framework of Navajo education from the responses of the Ramah Navajo participants to the interview question: What is an educated person? Navajo education included four areas: Ancestral Wisdom, Ancestral Teachings, Navajo Language, and Contemporary Knowledge. The categories and subcategories of Navajo education are different from Euro-Western curriculum categories of subject matter.

Navajo education for the Ramah Navajo participants emphasizes bilingualism and biculturalism to ensure survival, a force that permeates their history even today as a satellite community of the Navajo Nation. Unlike most existing Navajo teachings, the majority of Ramah Navajo responses deemphasized the sensitive issues of Creation Stories and/or information on Navajo religion.

CONCEPTUAL FRAMEWORK FINDINGS

The study examined the questions: What is self-determination? How is self-determination enacted in the Pine Hill School and the Ramah Navajo community? The three findings were:

1. There are many terms for self-determination from the Navajo perspective. Responses to the study questions from participants were similar. Some of the terms are: T'aa hwó'ájít'éego (progress comes from within), T'áá áwolíbee ánít'í (persevere), Biniyé ánít'įh (persevere with a goal in mind), Ání ádá'ánít'įh (do it for yourself), Ák'ih yazhjílt'i'(plan and talk for yourself), ha'átííshį́ í ádíílííłíígíí ádíílííł (whatever you plan to do, do it), Hazhǫ́ǫ́jí at'iin (Beauty Way), T'áádídíín biaat'iin (Pollen Road). The Beauty Way and Pollen Road are terms for the same philosophy. These terms are all part of the basic philosophy for leading a good and harmonious life by following the Beauty Way. From the Navajo perspective, living the Beauty Way and following the Pollen Road is living a self-determined life.

From the Navajo perspective, the Navajo concept of self-determination conflicts with the Euro-Western perspective. Elders provided insight into the difficulty that Indian communities have of identifying, defining, and operationalizing the Westernized concept of self-determination. While referring to "self-determination" as they keep hearing it in the media and at chapter meetings, elders repeatedly verbalized in English the word "self-determination" while all the time speaking only in Navajo. Self-determination, as verbalized in the English language and used relating to the Self-Determination Act, did not have any relevance to their world. The elders felt that "self-determination"(as spoken in English) creates chaos and consternation in Navajo communities because it promotes unfair competition among the Navajo chapter communities. One elder stated: "Self-determination causes selfishness. It creates the desire to obtain for oneself without regard for others."

Other responses were: Self-determination is not only being proactive, but it does not allow for bragging and personal conceit. Self-determination is a road, the Beauty Way and /or the Pollen Way. It is based on commitment to the community.

2. Self-determination in the Ramah Navajo community consists of the processes: community-based planning, maintaining self-awareness, being proactive, and persevering. These processes were reoccurring themes throughout the history of the Ramah Navajo since 1864 and are pronounced in the present Ramah Navajo society. The four processes are the four foundational posts of the metaphoric Hogan.

Figure 14.1 and 15 is drawing of the constructed metaphoric Hogan. In the construction of a Hogan, as prescribed in the Creation Stories

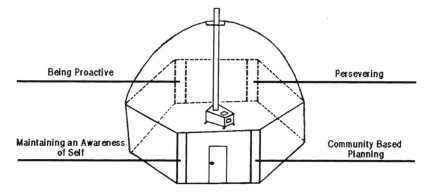

Figure 14.1. Self-Determination

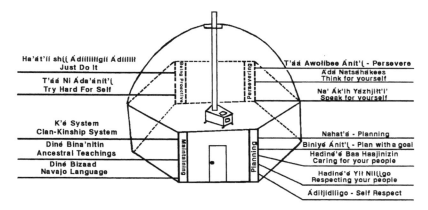

Figure 15. Self-Determination (with Navajo terms)

(Aronilth, 1994) and as found in the Beauty Way Prayer mentioned by a Ramah elder as the principles chosen by the founders of the Ramah High School, a precious gem or stone is placed under each of the four foundational posts of the Hogan. Like the precious stones placed under each of the foundation Hogan posts, each process is a precious or important part of what self-determination is in the Ramah Navajo community. Interpretation of self-determination, from the Navajo perception, is provided by the Hogan metaphor. The metaphor, the construction of a Hogan, provides a connection between the Navajo perspective and the Western perspective about the concept, self-determination.

3. The processes of self-determination do not specify formal education and American schools as foundational elements of self-determination. The processes represent the construction of empowerment of a Navajo individual and/or community. Formal education and schooling have always been foreign to the Navajo society. Historically, the federal government's Indian policy became "educate" and "civilization" (Kickingbird and Charleston, 1991, p. 6). Formal education was utilized through the Civilization Act of 1819 to transform the Indian child from his or her "Indianness"(De Jong,1993; Huff, 1997; Reyhner, 1992; Spring, 1996; Szasz, 1974).

In the Ramah Navajo community, formal education and schooling are *not* the focal point of self-determination but catalysts for community development. The multimillion-dollar school establishment is just as important as other aspects of the community, such as the clinic, radio station, social services, the Ramah Navajo Rug Weavers Association, and their Pine Hill Market. The Ramah Navajo people have demonstrated self-determination by their dynamic accomplishments seen not only in the school but also throughout the total community.

Self-determination, as the Ramah Navajo people have perceived it since 1864, is not dependent on economics and formal education, but on a holistic construction of an entity, an individual, or a community. The construction comes from within. It is based on the mystical and powerful construction of the metaphoric Hogan of the Beauty Way Prayer.

CONCLUSIONS

Self-determination is an important concept and an inherent attribute of Navajo society and life, defined and operationalized in its own context, and is unlike the Euro-Western concept of self-determination. Self-determination from the Navajo perspective is functional and rational in a Navajo framework. It is not based on a Euro-Western understanding or on federal guidelines and criteria. The concept of self-determination is embedded in the Beauty Way and Pollen Road, and accounts for the Ramah Navajos' strong sense of survival.

Self-determination from the Navajo perspective cannot be truly expressed in the non-Navajo institution of public American education, whose main goal is assimilation of all youth into the white, middle-class society. In 1868, after four years of incarceration, Manuelito, the famous Navajo leader, in his well-known entreaty to his people at the signing of the treaty between the United States and the Navajos stated, "My grandchild, the whites have many things we Navajos need but cannot get. . . . We can hear them talking, but we cannot get to them. My grandchild, school is the ladder. Tell our people this" (Acrey, 1979, p. 124). Manuelito's entreaty has been interpreted by historians, politicians, and educators to mean that formal education is the ladder to success. I don't profess to know what Manuelito meant but I do think that having been humiliated and made powerless by the U.S. Cavalry and government, but remaining proud, Manuelito would not have encouraged his people to become like their conquerors and be assimilated into their society through the assimilationist framework of formal education.

My own interpretation of Manuelito's entreaty to his people is that he wanted not only material goods for immediate survival but also the same rights of self-determination enjoyed by other American communities, mentioned in the introduction of this chapter. I also believe that the "ladder" was also meant to provide a two-way process. This "ladder" was to be a process of dialogue between the dominant society and the Navajo society. I believe formal education, which is sensitive to and based on Indian life ways, can promote dialogue, yet there are tremendous obstacles to surmount, insidious obstacles that come from within Indian communities.

Indian people obstruct dialogue through their own internalized colonization. Often formally educated Indian leaders and educators forget that their own Indian communities have perspectives on concepts such as self-determination, as portrayed in the definitions of self-determination by the Ramah Navajo people. The concepts from the Euro-Western worldview don't match the Navajo understanding of those concepts. In present day society, these Euro-Western definitions and criteria have become the evaluative guidelines for Indian people. Furthermore, Indian people usually give decision-making responsibilities to "outside experts" who don't understand the Indian culture and the community's history. As a result, tribal governments and even tribal schools, relying on outside expert opinion, have contributed to their subjugation and colonization.

Dialogue between indigenous people and the dominant society is the beginning of self-determination for Indian people. As long as Indian people do not share or are not permitted to share their understanding of concepts such as self-determination and education and as long as Indian people do not throw off their shackles of internalized colonization, they will continue to support the implementation of self-determination in the Euro-Western sense, which defies their own existence. Dialogue and the decolonizination of our own minds as Indian people are vital for equity and survival of not only the Ramah Navajo people, but also all American Indians.

REFERENCES

Acrey, B. P. (1979). *Navajo history, the land and the people*. Shiprock, NM: Rio Grande Press.

Aronilth, W. (1994). *Foundation of Navajo culture.* Tsaile, AZ: Dine College.

Beck, P. V., N. Fracisco, and A. L. Walters. (1977). *The scared, ways of knowledge, sources of life.* Tsaile, AZ: Navajo Community College.

Blanchard, K. (1971). The Ramah Navajos: A growing sense of community in historical perspective. *Navajo Historical Publications, Historical Series No. 1.,* Window Rock, AZ.: Navajo Parks and Recreation.

Blanchard, K. (1977). *The economics of sainthood.* London: Associated University Press.

Bruner, E. M. (1986). Ethnography as narrative. In W. Turner and E. M. Bruner (Eds.), *The anthropology of experience* (pp. 139–155). Urbana and Chicago: University of Illinois Press.

Calloway, S. M., G. Witherspoon, C. Badonie, M. Bluehouse, C. Burbank, F. Harvey, J. Honie, D. Jumbo, H. Kinsel, and P. R. Platero. (1974). *Grandfather stories of the Navajos.* Tsaile, AZ: Navajor Curriculum Center Press.

Champagne, D. (1998). American Indian studies is for everyone. In D. A. Mihesuah (Ed.), *Natives and academics, researching and writing about American Indians* (pp. 181–189). Lincoln and London: University of Nebraska Press.

De Jong, D. H. (1993). *Promises of the past, A history of Indian education.* Golden, CO: North American Press.

Deloria, V. (1994). *Indian education in America.* Boulder: American Indian Science & Engineering Society Publishing.

Durie, A. (1999). Emancipatory Maori education: Speaking from the heart. In S. May (Ed.), *Indigenous community-based education* (pp. 67–78). Great Britain: Short Run Press.

Fixico, D. L. (1998). Ethics and responsibilities in writing American Indian history. In D. A. Mihesuah (Ed.), *Natives and academics, researching and writing about American Indians* (pp. 84–99). Lincoln and London: University of Nebraska Press.

Glesne, C. and A. L. Peshkin. (1992). *Becoming qualitative researchers.* White Plains, NY: Longman.

Gross, M. (1978). Indian self-determination and tribal sovereignty: an analysis of recent federal Indian policy. In *Texas Law Review* (pp. 1195–1244). Austin, Texas.

Gutek, G. L. (1991). *Education in the United States: An historical perspective.* Boston: Allyn and Bacon.

Hornberger, N. H. and K. A. King. (1999). Authenticity and unification in Quechua language planning. In S. May (Ed.), *Indigenous community-based education* (pp. 160–180). Great Britain: Short Run Press.

House, D. (2002). *Language shift among the Navajos, identity politics and cultural continuity.* Tucson: University of Arizona Press.

Huff, P. (1997). *To live heroically, institutional racism and American Indian education*. Albany: State University of New York Press.

Kickingbird, K. and G. M. Charleston. (1991). Responsibilities and roles of governments and Native People in the education of American Indians and Alaska Natives. Commissioned paper. *Indian Nations at Risk Report*. Washington, DC: U.S. Department of Education. Eric/Cress.

Kluckhohn, C. and D. Leighton. (1947). *Children of the people*. Cambridge: Harvard University Press.

Kluckhohn, C. and D. Leighton. (1962). *Children of the people*. Rev. ed. New York: Doubleday.

McCarty, T. L. (2000). *Learning to be Navajo: Rough rock and the struggle for self-determination in indigenous schooling*. Mahwah, NJ: Lawrence Earlbaum.

McCarty, T. L. and L. J. Watahomigie. (1999). Indigenous community-based language education in the USA. In S. May (Ed.), *Indigenous community-based education* (pp. 79–94). Great Britain: Short Run Press.

Platero, P. R. (1992). *Navajo Head Start language study*. Abridged version. Window Rock, AZ: Navajo Curriculum Center.

Reyhner, J. (1992). *Teaching American Indian students*. Norman: University of Oklahoma Press.

Sheridan, T. E. (1988). How to tell the story of a "People Without History": Narrative versus ethnohistorical approaches to the study of the Yaqui Indian through time. *Journal of the Southwest*, 30, 168–189.

Smith, L. T.(1999). *Decolonizing methodologies: Research and indigenous peoples*. London & New York: Zed Books.

Spicer, E. H. (1962). *Cycles of conquest*. Tucson: University of Arizona Press.

Spring, J. (1996). *The cultural transformation of a Native American family and its tribe 1763–1995: A basket of apples*. Mahwah, NJ: Lawrence Erlbaum.

Szasz, M. (1974). *Education and the American Indian, the road to self-determination, 1928–1973*. Albuquerque: University of New Mexico Press.

Thompson, L. (1951). *Personality and government*. Mexico: Ediciones Del Instituto Indigenista Interamericano.

Tietjen, G. (1992). *Ernest Albert Tietjen, missionary and colonizer*. Bountiful, Utah: Family History Publishers.

Tippeconnic, J. (1999). Tribal control of American Indian education: Observations since the 1960's with implications for the future. In K. G. Swisher and J. Tippeconnic, III (Eds.), *Next steps, research and practice to advance Indian education* (pp. 33–52). Washington, DC: Appalachia Educational Laboratory, Inc. ERIC.

Todal, J. (1999). Minorities with a minority: Language and the school in the Sami areas of Norway. In S. May (Ed.), *Indigenous community-based education* (pp. 124–136). Great Britain: Short Run Press.

Vogt, E. Z. and E. M. Albert. (1966). *People of Rimrock*. Cambridge: Harvard University Press.

Wilson, W. H. (1999). The sociopolitical context of establishing Hawaiian-medium education. In S. May (Ed.), *Indigenous community-based education* (pp. 95–108). Great Britain: Short Run Press.

Wolcott, H. (1975). Criteria for ethnic research in schools. *Human Organization, 34*, 111–127.

Afterword

BETH BLUE SWADENER, KAGENDO MUTUA

Just as we began the introductory chapter by raising a number of questions, in part to frame issues addressed in the chapters to follow, we end with some brief reflections and raise additional questions about this collective decolonizing research project. Why "decolonizing research" and not "postcolonial research"? Post(-)colonialism (with or without the hyphen) is a discourse that is at once highly contested and enormously popular. Shohat (1992) and other scholars note that used loosely, postcolonialism collapses identities of individuals who lived in former colonies and whose experience of colonialism was qualitatively different, for example, the experiences of the white American settler and the Native American or the white Australian and indigenous people of Australia- both groups having been under British colonization. One of the chapters in this volume explores the inexplicable and inescapable positionality of being colonizer and colonized. Postcolonialism, in this case, suffers what Shohat (1992) calls a "suffocating neo-colonial hegemony" (p.105).

We would argue that any construction of the "postcolonial" still embodies much of what is termed "colonial," similar to ways in which post-modernity embodies modernity (Swadener and Wachira, 2003). In this book, in fact, we have adopted Quist's (2001) use of the term "postcolonial," rather than post-colonial, which can be read as "carrying the idea of a linearity and chronology, signifying one period followed by another" (p. 299). As McClintock (1992, p. 85) asserts, "the term post-colonial is haunted by the very figure of linear development . . . and marks history as a series of stages along an epochal road from pre-colonial, to colonial to the post-colonial." Quist's (2001, p. 299) use of the term postcolonial suggests that continuity, a back-and-forth relationship, a constant between the past and present-day cultural and sociopolitical relations with implications for the future. This affords the opportunity of engaging with the continuing complex interrelationships among factors and forces that simultaneously impact the postcolonial situation.

The term "decolonizing," on the other hand, implicitly carries within it recognition of the existence of neocolonialism, thereby acknowledging the regeneration of other forms/means of coloniality that support a geo-economic hegemony. This geo-economic hegemony then makes possible the "voluntary" immigration of postcolonial scholars to the Western metropoles that sustain and continue their oppression.

Also present in this volume are iterations of the uneasy relationship between the postcolonial scholar (postcolonial here used in a temporal sense) and the Western academy—to which many are beholden and dependent. The colonizing tendencies of the Western academy, paradoxically a place that many of the authors in this volume received their graduate degrees and continue to work in, are often evidenced in the ways in which structures of knowledge within the academy create conditions that exercise intellectual domination that balefully cripple and subjugate Othered knowledge forms. Within many of the critical personal narratives in this book is a resounding resistance to domination by the Western academy of their Othered knowledge forms, and also a rearticulation of indigenous scholars' ways of knowing.

Chapters in this book have also interrogated implicit assumptions of cross-cultural research. Where do research questions, problems, and methodological approaches come from? Whether researchers are indigenous or non-indigenous, the influence of the Western academy in restricting the frame of what counts for scholarship creates tensions and contradictions in attempts to "decolonize" research. Even with the best of intentions of indigenous researchers or "allied others" (Rogers and Swadener, 1999) working in collaboration with indigenous researchers, particularly those with Western education, it is very hard to break away from the colonizing/Western authority claims of what constitutes research, who frames the research questions, for whom the research is intended/will be consumed, and, therefore, in whose language the research shared, validated, and disseminated. Another, related issue alluded to in several chapters is the question of who benefits from research with indigenous people.

Further questions that emerge include: Who has the power to name, and how does naming reify existing power relations? Who defines and legitimizes what counts as "scholarship"? Where are some of the current "data plantations" in educational research? Is experience, particularly "indigenous insiders' experience," a necessary precursor for asking the right questions in pursuit of culturally legitimate scholarship—or can the privileging of "insider" experience be problematic? Are the tools for decolonization available only to indigenous researchers or can this be a shared process? If so, what are cautionary signs or limits of cross-cultural collaboration?

In terms of the roles of indigenous versus non-indigenous scholars and the cultural validity of research, questions raised by Angela Cavender Wilson (1998), in her essay "American Indian History or Non-Indian Perceptions of American Indian History?" are relevant. Her work relates to issues raised in this volume—particularly questions concerning who has the right to tell a group or culture's history. Wilson (1998) states,

> When the topic of writing about Indians comes up the first questions that come to mind are, who is doing the writing? why? and what do the subjects have to say about this? These are questions that rarely have been considered by those in American Indian history, but they are extremely important when addressing the ethical and moral considerations that arise when those outside the culture write about subjects who can speak for themselves. (p. 23)

These issues are reflected in both Julie Kaomea's and Kathryn Manuelito's chapters. Kaomea problematizes her role as an indigenous academic working in Native Hawaiian educational communities and describes her efforts to incorporate Native Hawaiian protocol and tradition and forge "hybrid indigenous/Western research methodologies that draw from and speak to both indigenous and Western ways of knowing and being." Manuelito problematizes Western discourses of "self-determination" and explores how members of a Navajo community enact self-determination as *they* understand it. Central to this chapter is not only the importance of better understanding how indigenous communities frame, resist, and reconstruct popular discourse, but the critical role of indigenous language to convey cultural meaning making.

Wilson (1998) further addresses the large body of historical scholarship on American Indians completed with virtually no contact with Native people or primary sources and asserts that

> The idea that scholars can "sift through" the biases of non-Indian written sources sufficiently to get at the Indian perspective is presumptuous and erroneous. These scholars should not discontinue their research in the field, but they should discontinue the pretense that what they are writing is American Indian history. This kind of scholarship remains, instead, American Indian history largely from the white perspective. (p. 26)

In terms of her advice to non-Indian researchers, Wilson (1998, p. 25) argues strongly against researchers "swarming to Native communities to record stories from our precious elders," and in favor of "slowly developing acquaintances with Indian people and giving Native people from the community they are studying the opportunity to comment on their work while it is being written."

Another strand that runs through several of the chapters in this volume is the authors' individual and collective struggles and resistance of the "subalternity," namely, the rejection of feelings of mental inferiority and habits of subservience and obedience that the Western academy often enacts upon them. The critical personal narratives in this volume speak of various attempts to resist appropriation of their Othered knowledge forms, while engaging in a cautious dance around issues of valorization, in which their work and voices are dangerously elevated to the level of being "representative" of a culture or spokespersons for a civilization. Several chapters in this final section explore the dangers of the English language as the language of research that, as the authors observe, is often the language through which indigenous knowledge forms are represented often without regard to what is lost in translation and transculturation. Many of the authors in this volume are constrained and caught up in the use of English as the language of research representation—a very colonizing endeavor—from which, though they are aware of the dangers of English, they cannot extricate themselves. The intellectual vagabondage of the postcolonial scholar in the Western academy and the production of the knowledge of Othered/indigenous knowledge for and within the academy are compelling dynamics, which several of the chapters have explored.

Indeed, for such postcolonial/indigenous scholars, the identity politics and professional experiences in the Western academy can perpetuate the oppressions of colonization and serve to render such scholars invisible and/or excessively visible—particularly if they, like the authors in this book, are engaged in "decolonizing" research and postcolonial critique. As Devon A. Mihesuah (1998) states, in reference to indigenous contributors to his book *Natives and Academics: Research and Writing about American Indians,*

> Some contributors have faced the reality that their stances are not accepted by many scholars, and they are accused by some as being "oppositional," "political," "radical," or "emotional." . . . Those of us who have been perceived as "not fitting in" with mainstream academia have continued our work, slightly bruised, perhaps, but undaunted. We still believe that our discussions are necessary. After all, the ideas we present are similar to those Indian scholars have expressed verbally to each other for years. None of us pretend that we have all the answers, but we do be-

lieve there are alternative ways of researching and writing about
Indians. (p. x)

Although Mihesuah's (1998) book focuses on American Indian experiences, it could be argued that a number of the issues raised have parallels
in the lives of indigenous people in other contexts.

Another question raised in the Introduction and addressed at least implicitly in several chapters related to ways in which hybridity theory might
inform the struggle to decolonize research—not serve as a "resolution,"
but complicate it in critical ways. Hybridity theory (e.g., Bhabha, 1994;
McCarthy, 1998; Spivak, 1999), which deconstructs cross-migratory patterns, relationships between colonizers and colonized, and hybrid forms of
information, policy, and shifting, mutually influenced, practices, would
seem to relate to contributors to this book who have been frequent bor-
der-crossers between traditional culture and heritage language(s) and the
colonizing/privileging world of Western higher education.

Walter Mignolo's (2000) book *Local Histories/Global Designs: Coloniality, Subaltern Knowledges, and Border Thinking* acknowledges the role
of hybridity and border thinking in the decolonization project, but cautions that discourses used for framing this endeavor often reflect mod-
ernist/postmodernist Western epistemologies and continue to silence
histories and metaphysics of the "colonized." As Mignolo (2000) states:

> I see decolonization imbedded in border thinking and transience
> epistemology as different ways of transcending the colonial differ-
> ence. I see deconstruction, instead, as a critique of and from modern
> epistemology more concerned with the Western hegemonic con-
> structions than with the colonial differences; and the colonial differ-
> ence from the perspective of subaltern knowledges . . . Thus,
> deconstruction within Western metaphysics needs to be decolonized
> from the silences of history. Decolonization needs to be decon-
> structed from the perspective of the coloniality of power. The logic
> of the conversation shall change, not just the terms. (pp. 323–324)

Mignolo (2000) further argues that "decolonization should be
thought of as complementary to deconstruction and border thinking complementary to the 'double séance' within the experience and sensibilities of
the coloniality of power" (p. 326). In this reading of the potentiality of hybridity theory, Mignolo (2000) asserts that

> Double consciousness, double critique, an other tongue, and other
> thinking, new mistiza consciousness, Creolization, transculturation,
> and culture of transience become the needed categories to undo the

subalternization of knowledge and to look for ways of thinking beyond the categories of Western through from metaphysics to philosophy to science. (p. 326)

Much has been written about and from a postcolonial and increasingly transcultural or hybrid perspective. Given the present context, in which knowledge is highly contested, disputed, and negotiated, postcolonial/indigenous (?) scholars working in the Western academy as "voluntary" immigrants find their voices as researchers muffled and often silenced in the cacophony of noises/voices that claim authenticity. Identities for this postcolonial scholarship are both ambiguously multiplied in this context and highly depoliticized. In this volume, we have chosen, instead, to focus on decolonizing research and at once several questions beg to be asked—particularly whether research itself is colonized/colonizing. Assuming, with Smith (1999) and others, that research is both colonized and colonizing, what are those dynamics? Who has/is colonized/colonizing research? Can it be decolonized? How can it be decolonized? Far from providing formulaic answers to these broad questions or roadmaps for postcolonial researchers, contributors to this book have actively grappled with these issues in an attempt to forge a pathway on which decolonizing researchers might gingerly tread.

REFERENCES

Bhabha, H. K. (1994). *The location of culture*. London: Routledge.

McCarthy, C. (1998). *The uses of culture: Education and the limits of ethnic affiliation*. New York: Routledge.

Mignolo, W. D. (2000). *Local histories/global designs: Coloniality, subaltern knowledges, and border thinking*. Princeton: Princeton University Press.

Mihesuah, D. A. (1998). *Natives and academics: Researching and writing about American Indians*. Lincoln: University of Nebraska Press.

Rogers, L. J. and B. B. Swadener. (1999). Reflections on the future work of anthropology and education: Reframing the "field." *Anthropology and Education Quarterly*, 30(4), 436–440.

Shohat, E. (1992). Notes on the "post-colonial," *Social Text*, 31/32, 99–112.

Smith, L. T. (1999). *Decolonizing methodologies: Research and indigenous peoples*. London: Zed Books.

Spivak, G. C. (1999). *A critique of postcolonial reason: Toward a history of the vanishing present*. Cambridge: Harvard University Press.

Swadener, B. B. and P. Wachira. (2003). Governing children and families in Kenya: Losing ground in neoliberal times. In M. N. Bloch, T. Popkewitz, I. Moqvist, and K. Holmlund (Eds.), *Restructuring the governing patterns of the child, education and welfare state* (pp. 231–258). New York: Palgrave-Macmillan.

Wilson, A. C. (1998). American Indian history or non-Indian perceptions of American Indian history? In Mihesvah, D. A. (Ed), *Natives and academics: Researching and writing about American Indians* (pp. 23–26). Lincoln, Nebraska: University of Nebraska Press.

Epilogue

CARLOS OVANDO

An ideal culture is one where there is a place for every human gift.
—Margaret Mead

Why have the notions of "otherness" and "borderlands" become so widely examined in academic circles in recent times? Why is it that many fellow Western researchers operating in comparative and international contexts tend to find it challenging to walk the egalitarian talk at the personal, institutional, group, and cultural levels? Why do some cultural processes and forms of knowledge appear to have greater stock value within research communities? And why are "borderlands" seen as the Promised Land for human growth, intellectual fermentation, cross-cultural challenges and possibilities, the deconstruction of Western intellectual privilege, and places for the affirmation of every human gift?

In *Decolonizing Research in Cross-Cultural Contexts*, Kagendo Mutua and Beth Blue Swadener have done a superb job of introducing a plurality of voices representing indigenous researchers who offer counternarratives to Western ideas about the benefits of the pursuit of knowledge and research practices. The reader will find of particular interest the various case studies that illuminate the struggles that many indigenous researchers— often socialized in Western universities—face, "situating the development of counter practices of research within both Western knowledge and global indigenous movements" (cf. Lather, 1999). Through compelling personal narratives, the book also provides fresh evidence that it is in indigenous contexts where researchers struggle with internal and external issues of trust and acceptance. Will culture brokers in indigenous communities accept, reject, or tolerate the researcher socialized in Western intellectual traditions?

Will the researcher trust herself or himself with the internalized Western ideas about the benefits of the pursuit of knowledge and research practices within traditional indigenous communities? Will the goal to decolonize research in cross-cultural contexts alienate indigenous researchers from their intellectually oriented Western peers? Despite the possibility of not coming up with easy answers to the latter questions, it is in these "borderlands" contexts where investigators can wrestle with tentative hypotheses related to complex variables related to "otherness." For "People and their cultures perish in isolation, but they are born or reborn in contact with other men and women of another culture, another creed, another race. If we do not recognize our humanity in others, we shall not recognize it in ourselves" (Fuentes, 1992, p. 353).

I believe that this volume will inspire and facilitate the development of research consciousness, policies, and school practices that will be more in tune with the multicultural and multilingual realities and dreams of our children in an increasingly interdependent global village—where the future of multiculturalism and a more just and equitable social order rests (see Ovando and McLaren, 2000).

REFERENCES

Dimitriadis, G. and C. McCarthy. (2001). *Reading & teaching the postcolonial: From Baldwin and beyond*. New York: Teachers College Press.

Fanon, F. (1967). *Black skin, white masks*. New York: Grove Press.

Fuentes, C. (1992). *The buried mirror*. Boston: Houghton Mifflin.

Gandhi, L. (1998). *Postcolonial theory: A critical introduction*. New York: Columbia University Press.

Lather, P. (1999). Backcover. In L. Thiwai Smith, *Decolonizing methodologies: Research and indigenous peoples*. London: Zed Books.

Ngugi wa Thiong'o. (1993). *Moving the centre: The struggle for cultural freedoms*. Nairobi: East African Educational Publishers.

Ovando, C. J., and P. McLaren. (2000). *The politics of multiculturalism and bilingual education: Students and teachers caught in the cross fire*. New York: McGraw-Hill.

Smith, L. T. (1999). *Decolonizing methodologies: Research and indigenous peoples*. London: Zed Books.

Contributors

Susan Matoba Adler is assistant professor in the Department Curriculum and Instruction at the University of Illinois at Urbana-Champaign. She has been on the Early Childhood Education faculty at the University of Michigan (Ann Arbor and Flint), the University of Wisconsin (Madison and Platteville), and Oakland University in Michigan. Her research is on Asian-American families and she has written, *Mothering, Education, and Ethnicity: The Transformation of Japanese American Culture.*

Joseph Ghartey Ampiah is a lecturer in the Institute of Education, University of Cape Coast, Ghana, where he teaches in a number of undergraduate and postgraduate programs. His research interests are science and technology education, teacher education, assessment, and teacher development. He has worked on a number of projects with researchers from other African countries as well as the United States, UK, and Japan.

Cynthia à Beckett is a senior lecturer and course cordinator for the Early Childhood Education Program at the University of New England in rural New South Wales in Australia. She is an experienced early childhood teacher who has worked with young children and families in a number of different early childhood settings. She has also worked as an advisor with early childhood teachers and for the past twenty years as an academic working in early childhood education programs. She is currently researching in the area of the sociology of young children and families.

Leodinito Y. Cañete has been a teacher and educational administrator in the Philippines. He completed a Ph.D. in elementary education at the University of Thessaloniki, Greece, and did research in Athens with Filipino immigrant communities concerning their relationships with the local education system. He also has worked with socially excluded minority groups in northern Greece, including Rom, Pontian, and immigrant communities.

He returned to the Philippines in 2001 and is currently Chief of Operations Division of the National Economic and Development Authority Regional Office based in Cebo City.

LISA J. CARY is an assistant professor of Curriculum and Instruction at University of Texas at Austin, focusing on curriculum studies. Her work revolves around how educational discourses exclude possibilities for equity in education and focuses on issues in educational reform, research, and cultural studies analyses. She has published in a number of qualitative research journals, including *Qualitative Inquiry* (1999) "Unexpected Stories: Life History and the Limits of Representation" and *Theory and Research in Education* (2001) "The Refusals of Citizenship."

ELLEN DEMAS is a doctoral candidate and lecturer in curriculum and instruction at Texas A&M University. Her research and teaching involve critical postmodern/Chicana feminist perspectives of early childhood education, language/literacy/cultural diversity, family/school/community dynamics, and critical advocacy. Recent publications include a critical examination of the dominant historical representations of childhood (with co-author Cinthya Saavedra) in the *Journal of Curriculum Theorizing*.

MIRYAM ESPINOSA-DULANTO is assistant professor in Curriculum and Instruction and professor-in-charge of the World Languages Teacher Education Program at the Pennsylvania State University. Her research explores social/cultural events in which language/power issues are at the core. She researches and writes using qualitative methods that respect diversity of identity/ies and social backgrounds.

HAOUA M. HAMZA is an Assistant Professor of Teacher Education at Niagara University, New York, where she teaches courses in foundations of education, motivation and learning, and multiculturalism in education. She has degrees from the national University Abdul Moumouni Dioffo of Niamey, Niger, and an M.Ed. and Ph.D. in Cultural Foundations of Education from Kent State University. She has done research on gender disparity in educational outcomes and policy impact analysis. Her other interests include multilingualism and the African child, collaborative research, and women's issues in sub-Saharan Africa. She has a great interest in creative writing, and is currently working on several short stories and a novel.

DUDU JANKIE is a lecturer at the University of Botswana in the Department of Languages and Social Sciences Education, Faculty of Education.

She completed her Ph.D. in Curriculum and Instruction at the University of Wisconsin–Madison, and currently teaches courses on Setswana education, multicultural literacy education, reader-response theories, educational research, and interdisciplinary approaches to literacy education. Her research interests include language, literacy and literature education, postcolonial theoretical perspectives, curriculum and policy issues, comparative education, culturally relevant/responsive pedagogy and teacher education.

JULIE KAOMEA is a native Hawaiian assistant professor in the College of Education at the University of Hawaii at Mânoa, where she specializes in indigenous education and decolonizing research methodologies. Her recent articles include "A Curriculum of Aloha? Colonialism and Tourism in Hawaii's Elementary Textbooks" (*Curriculum Inquiry*, 2000) and "Reading Erasures and Making the Familiar Strange: Defamiliarizing Methods for Research in Formerly Colonized and Historically Oppressed Communities" (*Educational Researcher*, 2002)

KATHRYN MANUELITO is an assistant professor in the Division of Curriculum and Instruction in the College of Education at Arizona State University. She is from the Dine Nation and is Naakai Dine'e and born for the Kinlichiinii clan. She received her undergraduate and master's degrees at the University of New Mexico in Albuquerque and her Ph.D. from Arizona State University. Dr. Manuelito grew up in Fort Wingate, New Mexico, and lived in Albuquerque, New Mexico, for over twenty years. She started out as a high school English teacher and later held various administrative positions as well as ran her own consulting firm. Dr. Manuelito has worked in Indian education for over twenty years at the local, regional, and national level and her work was recently recognized by the American Educational Research Association.

KAGENDO MUTUA is Assistant Professor of Special Education at the University of Alabama. Her primary research is in the area of transition and secondary programming for adolescents with severe/multiple disabilities, in which she struggles to find ways of creating ethical and decolonized representations of the Kenyan and American families of adolescents with severe/multiple disabilities about whom she researches and writes. Her work has appeared in several journals, including *Journal of Special Education, Education and Training in Mental Retardation, International Journal of Disability, Development and Education*, and *Educational Studies*. She is also a co-editor (with Cynthia Sunal) of a book series entitled *Research in Africa, Caribbean, and The Middle East* published by Info Age Press.

BEKISIZWE S. NDIMANDE is a Ph.D. candidate in the Department of Curriculum and Instruction at the University of Wisconsin–Madison. His research focus includes sociology of curriculum, critical theories, and educational policy, especially examining how current educational policies in South Africa and in the United States are influenced by neoliberal and neoconservative politics. He was the recipient of a Compton Fellowship for completion of his dissertation research in South Africa and an ATLAS (African Training for Leadership and Advanced Skills) fellowship for his master's degree work at University of Massachusetts, Amherst.

CARLOS OVANDO is associate dean for teacher education at Arizona State University. His interests include international comparative education, second language acquisition, cross-cultural communication, and issues in the education of language-minority students. Dr. Ovando's most recent publications include *Bilingual and ESL Classrooms: Teaching in Multicultural Contexts*, 3rd ed., *The Politics of Multiculturalism and Bilingual Education: Students and Teachers Caught in the Cross Fire*, and *The Color of Bureaucracy: The Politics of Equity in Multicultural School Communities*.

DENISE PROUD is currently working in correctional facilities in Brisbane, Australia. She works as cultural liason manager at the Arthur Gorrie Correction Centre, which is managed by Australasian Correctional Management. She also provides programs at the state-run Brisbane Women's Correctional Centre. Denise started her career as an early childhood educator at the Cherbourg Aboriginal Settlement and has worked extensively in various early childhood and community settings.

JOHN PRYOR is a lecturer in education at the University of Sussex, UK, where he teaches graduate students from many different backgrounds and nationalities. His research interests are in assessment, equity, and pedagogy and he mainly uses ethnographic and collaborative methods. He has had a long association with Africa, especially Ghana.

HAIYAN QIANG is Professor of Comparative Education on the Faculty of Education, South China Normal University, in Guangzhou, China, and Associate Director of the Centre for Women's Studies in the same institution. Previously she served as Associate Dean of the Faculty on the Faculty of Education and Associate Director of the Centre for Women's Studies at Shaanxi Normal University. She has pursued graduate studies at the University of Massachusetts, and advanced studies and research at the Institute of Education at the University of London, and the Ontario Institute for Studies in Education at the University of Toronto. She is the editor of a series of books and textbooks on gender education in the PRChina and has published numerous articles in education journals in that country. She has been principal investigator of several large international grant and research programs.

CINTHYA M. SAAVEDRA is a bilingual third-grade teacher working on her Ph.D in Curriculum and Instruction from Texas A&M University. Her research interests include critical postmodern/Chicana feminist analysis of education, teacher accountability, and constructions of childhood. She has published with long-time friend and colleague Ellen Demas in the *Journal of Curriculum Theorizing* on the (his)torical (re)presentations of the child, a piece that critically examines the dominant historical perspectives of childhood.

VILMA SEEBERG is Associate Professor of International-Multicultural Education at Kent State University. She is an internationally known scholar in the field of contemporary Chinese Studies and Education, has authored *Literacy in China, The Rhetoric and Reality of Mass Education in Mao's China,* and articles on Chinese higher education. She also teaches courses in multicultural education and is involved in local professional development in multicultural school reform. Born in Hamburg, Germany, with a doctoral in Comparative Education from the University of Hamburg, she lives in Cleveland, Ohio, with her husband and daughter adopted from China.

LOURDES DÍAZ SOTO is Professor of Bilingual/bicultural Education at the Pennsylvania State University and is associated with the Applied Linguistics and Early Childhood Programs, and was visiting professor at Teachers College, Columbia University in 2001–2002. She has published numerous articles and chapters and her books include *Language, Culture and Power: Bilingual Families and the Struggle for Quality Education, The Politics of Early Childhood Education,* and *Making a Difference in the Lives of Bilingual/ Bicultural Children.*

BETH BLUE SWADENER is professor of Early Childhood Education and Policy Studies at Arizona State University and does research on social policy, professional development, language and culture issues, and early education in Sub-Saharan Africa. Her books include *Reconceptualizing the Early Childhood Curriculum, Children and Families "At Promise": Deconstructing the Discourse of Risk, Semiotics of Dis/ability: Interrogating Categories of Difference,* and *Does the Village Still Raise the Child?: A Collaborative Study in Changing Childrearing and Early Education in Kenya.* Beth is also active in a number of peace, social justice, and child advocacy groups.

GEETA VERMA is an assistant professor of Curriculum and Instruction at Georgia State University. She teaches introductory research courses and science methods courses for elementary and middle school educators. She has made presentations at international and national conferences and contributed a commentary focused on Indian curriculum traditions in a book titled *Curriculum Wisdom: Educational Decisions in Democratic Societies*. Her research interests include the internationalization of curriculum discourse, history and nature of science, postcolonial science curriculum development, and research on methods of science instruction.

Index

Abraham, I., 53, 58, 59, 60
Abu-lughood, L., 47
Academy: colonized existence in, x; decentering of, 4; decolonization of, 10; deconstruction of, 4; expectations of, 28; indigenous intellectuals in, 10; relationships with, 4; Western, 4, 80, 258
Adler, S.M., 4, 15, 17, 19, 107–120
Afrikaans, 204
Agassiz, L., 61
Akwesi, C., 163, 165
Akyeampong, K., 164
Alam, A., 57
Alexander, N., 201, 212$n1$
Alliances: cross-cultural, 3; decolonization and, 7; multiracial, 6
Althusser, L., 200
American Association for Advancement of Science, 62
American Educational Research Association, 80
Ampiah, J.G., 3, 17, 19, 159–175
Ansu-Kyeremeh, K., 165
Anzaldúa, G., x, 48, 50, 215, 216, 218, 219, 225, 227
Appiah, K.A., 8, 164
Apple, M.W., 198, 199, 200, 202, 204, 205, 206
Arnove, R., 181, 183
Asian-Americans: authentic voices of, 113–116; diversity among, 112; domestic violence and, 111; generational studies, 109–111; as invisible minority, 111–113; as model minority, 111; silencing of, 112
Atkinson, P., 165
Australia, 69–81, 147–158
Auto/ethnography, 16–18
Awareness: cultural, 46, 190; identity, 191

Baber, Z., 54, 55
Bailey, C., 217
Baldwin, J., 164
Basalla, G., 57, 59, 60, 64
Bauer, H., 30
Beckett, C., 15, 17, 19, 147–158
Behar, R., 48, 98
Belensky, M., x
Benchmarks for Science Literacy, 62
Bhabha, H.K., 1, 5, 9, 18, 27, 43$n1$, 43$n2$, 54, 59, 60, 67$n14$, 71, 75, 76, 163, 259
Bilingualism, 186, 219–224, 239–240
Bilken, S.K., 136
Black Atlantic, 76
Blanchard, K., 243
Bogdan, R.C., 136
Border crossing, 16
Boru, K., 141
Botswana: educational system in, 15, 87; research environment in, 87–104; use of English in, 15
Bourdieu, P., 89, 200, 201, 213$n8$

Made in the USA
San Bernardino, CA
01 March 2016